balancing flavors east&west

balancing flavors east&west

DK

Tom Kime with photographs by Lisa Linder

First published in the United States in 2005 by
DK Publishing
375 Hudson Street, New York, NY 10014
Discover more at www.dk.com

First published in Great Britain in 2005 by
Kyle Cathie Limited
122 Arlington Road, London NW1 7HP
general.enquiries@kyle-cathie.com
www.kylecathie.com

10 9 8 7 6 5 4 3 2 1

Some recipes in this book contain raw eggs, which are known to contain the potentially harmful salmonella bacterium. Do not serve dishes made with raw eggs to the very young, elderly, or those with compromised immune systems.

A CIP catalog record for this book is available from the Library of Congress.
ISBN 0-7566-2348-0

Printed in Singapore

Editor **Jennifer Wheatley** Designer and art director **Mary Evans** Photographer **Lisa Linder** Photographs on p6 (right), p102 (bottom) and p118 (right and left) **Tom Kime** Food stylist **Tom Kime** assisted by **Alice Hart** Styling **Hannah Kime** and **Nicola Phoenix** Editorial assistant **Vicki Murrell** Production **Sha Huxtable** and **Alice Holloway** Americanizer **Delora Jones** American recipe editor **Peggy Fallon**

contents

author's acknowledgments

thanks go to... **Ruth** and **Mike Edwards** at Cutting Edge Food & Wine School for helping to formulate the book in the early stages and for introducing me to Kyle Cathie. **Kyle Cathie** for all her help and advice, **Jenny Wheatley,** my editor, for all her tireless work and patience, **Sarah Epton**, **Vicki Murrell,** and the sales and publicity team at Kyle Cathie Ltd. ● **Loyd Grossman,** for commissioning me to make a film in Vietnam which set the ball rolling, and **Chantel Rutherford-Brown** for seeing the potential of the idea; **Martine Carter, Bora,** and **Michelle** at Deborah McKenna for all their hard work on my behalf. ● **Mary Evans** for all the art and wine at our layout meetings (you have made the book look amazing), and **Lisa Linder** for taking the spectacular photographs that bring my recipes to life. ● **Hannah Kime, Alice Hart**, **Nicola Phoenix,** and **Julia Kepinska** for all their hard work and for making the shoots such good fun. ● **Alfie** and **Maude Elms,** the children who photographed so beautifully. ● My mother **Helen Kime**, my sister **Hannah,** and my wife **Kylie Burgess-Kime** for their help and advice on the copy and recipes. ● **Philip Oury**, **Maria Pereira,** and **Danielle Fox-Brinner** for their literary advice at various stages of production. ● The many chefs I have worked with and been inspired by over the years; **David Burke** and **Tim Powell** of Le Pont de la Tour, **Rick Stein** for his enthusiasm and love of fish that I share so passionately, **Rose Gray, Ruth Rogers, Lucy Gray, Theo Randall,** and all the other chefs at the River Cafe for teaching me so much about food and the love of it. **Peter Doyle,** formally of Cicada in Sydney, and **David Thompson** for turning everything on its head and re-teaching me how to taste and eat (your astonishing food started my journey of balancing tastes and flavors). ● **Lady Felicity Osborne** for all of our good work at Felicitous, **Eric Treuillé, Rosie Kindersley,** and her team at Books for Cooks, **Tertia Goodwin** from Authentic Ethnic, **Alex** and **Christina Bastin** from Petit Gourmet; everyone at Leiths School of Food and Wine. Chefs **Bernie Plaisted, Sarah Rowden, Clare Kelly, Alice Hart, Celia Brooks Brown, Anna Burgess-Lumsden, Paul Young, Martin Boetz**—I couldn't do it without you. ● All my friends in the food industry and my suppliers, including **Heather Paterson** for all her support, **Norma Miller, Helen Chislet, Tim Lee, Toby Peters, Carme Farre, Ash Huntington** for his brilliant wine and great discussions, **Susan Pieterse** from FBDC, **Charlie Mash** of Mash Purveyors, Harvey Nichols' meat department, **Alan** on the Portobello Road Market, **George, Helen,** and **Steve** from Golborne Fisheries, everyone at Chalmers and Gray, Mr Christian's, The Edwardian Butchers, **Birgit Erath** from The Spice Shop, **Lindy Wiffen** at Ceramica Blue, Tawana Thai, **Lulu Grimes, Mary Cadagon, Angela Nilsen, Liz Galbraith,** and everyone at *Olive,* **Kara O 'Reilly** at *The Sunday Times Style* magazine, **Jaimin, Amandip,** and **Situal Kotecha** at The Lotus Food Company, and all of the clients who have eaten my food. ● **Gil Reddick** and **Mukesh Patel,** my partners at Food @ The Muse, and my chefs, **JJ Holland, Tom Smith,** and **Jose Porfirio**. ● All of my friends for their support and help, and understanding when I can't come out again!

To my mother Helen, for inspiring me to cook delicious food; to my father Robert and my sister Hannah, for their continuous love of food and meal times; to my wife Kylie, for all her love and support.

introduction

imagine if there was a simple rule of thumb which, when applied, could enable you to make truly delicious food, every time. What is good food? Why do some taste combinations work so well? What is the secret of knowing which ingredients will work together in a dish or meal?

It's all a question of how we taste. When the four main tastes of hot, sour, salty, and sweet are present and in balance in a dish or meal, the end result is delicious because it satisfies all the tastebuds at once. Combine this with the vibrant colors and contrasting textures of fresh seasonal ingredients, and the end result has vitality and is stimulating to all of the senses. From simple compositions such as salads, soups, and antipasti to whole meals where the wine becomes one of the taste components, food with this equilibrium will add the something extra that makes your food sublime.

A BLT has the potential to incorporate the full blend of flavor components. Have you wondered why this classic is eaten in some form around the world every day? It is because it works as a group of tastes. Bacon is salty and tomatoes are mostly sweet if they are ripe. Bread has a sweet aspect, but can be more sour if it is rye or sourdough. The mayonnaise has a sweet richness, which can be cut with a bit of sourness from vinegar or lemon juice. With lots of black pepper, English mustard, some chili in the mayonnaise, or arugula instead of lettuce, the hot or peppery aspect can be introduced.

The theory of equalizing the palate can open a great many culinary doors. Taking inspiration from the varied cuisines of Southeast Asia, the Mediterranean, Middle East, and Europe, I hope to demonstrate how balancing taste and texture will do for your cooking what the DVD and surround sound has done for home movie viewing. Balanced taste and texture create excitement and add a sophistication that was previously missing. Beginner or expert, this book will make a striking contribution to everyone who cooks.

how we taste

We have a huge capacity to savor and taste; we can differentiate between over 150 textures and flavors. The tongue has several taste recognition areas: the main four are commonly identified as sweet, sour, bitter, and salty. The Japanese also identify *umami,* which translates as "savory," and this has been called the fifth taste. These primary tastes can be recognized anywhere on the tongue, but certain areas of it are more sensitive to different sensations. Foods are chemical mixtures so we rarely experience any of the basic taste sensations in isolation. The tip of the tongue is the area most sensitive to sweetness and the tongue's front edges are the most sensitive to salt. The sensation of sour is recognized down the sides of the tongue, and the back of the mouth detects bitter tastes. Bitter crosses over the boundaries between sour and peppery hot, and is a taste that is not present in many foods though it can often bring a certain sophistication to a dish.

hot, sour, salty, sweet

Thai and Vietnamese cooking provide some of the most exciting and stimulating taste sensations I have ever encountered, and this is achieved through the deliberate arrangement of ingredients in relation to one another. This balance is called *rot chart* or "correct taste" and every meal must have two, three, or all of the taste elements of hot, sour, salty, and sweet present and in balance. An excess of any one element can stress the body: too much chili makes you sweat, too much salt dehydrates the body, too much sugar makes you feel sick.

When I first traveled to Vietnam to research the food from this amazing country (which basically meant eating about six meals a day or at any given opportunity!) I learned to make deliberate adjustments to my food by watching everybody at the street food stalls. A selection of condiments representing the four tastes is present on every street vendor's table, enabling you to fine-tune your dish to suit your palate. Some peppery-tasting leaves, a bowl of fish sauce with chopped chiles, or some other type of chili sauce and slices of chile on their own provide the heat. A saucer of lime quarters for sourness, some light soy sauce or fish sauce to give you the essential salty flavor of Southeast Asian food, and usually a small bowl of sugar as well. In total you have hot, sour, salty, and sweet. We all taste slightly differently, so this enables each person to make their individual mark on their own food while still respecting the integrity of the recipe.

bitter

I will primarily be dealing with the four flavors but bitter should be included in the balance where possible. See the lists of food in the different categories (pages 20–21) to help you identify tastes and see how they can be combined.

applying the principles to Western food

This balance of tastes also exists in many traditional Mediterranean and European recipes, though it is less consciously applied. However, Western food is frequently flat and two-dimensional as a result of addressing only a couple of the taste areas in any dish or meal. This can be rectified without necessarily using Asian ingredients like ginger, cilantro or lemongrass. For example, roast pork with cracklings and applesauce is heavenly because of the contrasting flavors and textures. In fact, the traditional Sunday roast is held in such reverence that you may ask how it can be improved upon. But if some crushed dried chili, coriander seed or fennel seed were to be added to the salt of the cracklings and the pork was served alongside some spicy red cabbage—then the four taste areas would be represented and your lunch would be a taste sensation. Hot from the chili,

The tip of the tongue is the area most sensitive to sweetness and the tongue's front edges are the most sensitive to salt. The sensation of sour is recognized down the sides of the tongue, and the back of the mouth detects bitter tastes.

sweet and sour from the applesauce and roasted meat, salt in the form of the cracklings, plus sour from the cabbage and few drops of balsamic vinegar in the gravy. We are often nearly there when creating a contrast with different flavors, yet we may be missing the one aspect that would make the dish as a whole spring to life.

how to apply the principles

In order to create the required symmetry of flavors, it is important to establish to which group different ingredients belong. This goes beyond the primary observations that a cherry is sweet and a chile is hot, to encompass much broader categories. The "sweet" in Western cooking can come from broiled peppers, shellfish, fresh garden peas, beets, young fava beans, or roast pumpkin. The "salt" could take the form of anchovies, capers, salted nuts, cured meats or goats' cheese. The "heat" could be from peppery arugula, mustard greens, extra virgin olive oil, or just black pepper. You can sour a dish with any kind of vinegar, underripe tomatoes, sorrel, lemon zest or juice, apples, and other sharp tasting fruits and vegetables.

A sauce that goes with something rich, smooth-tasting, or fatty such as duck breast or scallops needs to be piquantly acid-based; this may be from wine, vinegar or lemon, as with an anchovy and rosemary sauce (see page 33) or a salsa verde (see page 29). The acid will cut the fat, forming a harmony of the flavors. When you first taste one of these sauces, it should taste more sour in isolation than it will when combined with the rich protein of the meal. This is because the sweet richness of the meat or fish will absorb some of the acid, and lessen its intensity. The same applies to sauces for leaner fish and poultry dishes, where the richness and acid-flavor combination are in the sauce itself. With a dish of skate wing with black butter, for example, the lemon juice and capers in the sauce are essential ingredients because their sour flavors cut the fatty texture of the buttery sauce. Without this aspect the dish would not be appealing.

a simple example of a balance of flavors

As a chef, when I finish work, I often want to eat quickly and with not much effort, because I have cooked for so many other people during the day. One of my staple mid-week snacks is cheese on toast. In my version, I have goat cheese on rye or sourdough bread with cherry tomatoes and arugula. The goat cheese is sour and slightly salty. The bread has a sour yeasty taste, but becomes richer, sweeter, and nuttier when toasted. The roasted cherry tomatoes are sweet. The arugula or other mixed greens are hot and peppery. The essential ingredient is a good-quality chutney, relish, or sweet chili sauce; this combines sweetness from the fruits and sugar, sour from the vinegar, and heat from the spices or chiles.

how the preparation and combination of ingredients can alter their qualities

Various cooking processes contribute to and change the taste characteristics of an ingredient. For example, smoking and drying make ingredients such as meat and fish saltier, whereas roasting or broiling makes foods sweeter. A raw onion tastes sour but if you roast it, it caramelizes and turns sweet. Ingredients can be made less bitter by salting or removing seeds, as is commonly done with eggplants and cucumbers—so salt can actually make them taste sweeter. The use of black pepper in cooking also has a chemical reaction that makes the other ingredients sweeter.

the origin of food can alter its qualities

The geographical source of an ingredient plays a big part in how it tastes. Some fruits and vegetables, such as tomatoes and grapes, will be much riper and therefore contain more sugar if they are grown in a hotter climate. In the world of wine, sugar content translates directly into alcohol levels. That is why red wine from southern Italy, Spain, or Australia is so often full bodied and high in alcohol. Chiles are also hotter the riper they are.

perfect taste combination Baked sweet potatoes with green chile and lemon zest sauce (see recipe on page 224) is a perfect taste combination because the balance between hot, sweet, salty, and sour is achieved in the four main ingredients, namely fresh green chiles, baked sweet potato, a little salt, and some lemon zest and juice.

the importance of tasting ingredients in isolation

Tasting the individual ingredients in isolation is vital, to see how they will relate to others on the plate or within the whole meal. One batch of Romano cheese or pancetta may be saltier than another. Lemons that are organic may be slightly sweeter, and under-ripe tomatoes will not provide the same sweetness as those picked in the height of summer, so the sweet element would have to be brought into balance using another ingredient. Note also that chiles and peppercorns vary in intensity enormously. Similarly, the difference in flavor between brands of mustards or varieties of arugula leaves make them taste like two different products. You need to make adjustments to recipes according to these variables. By getting into the habit of tasting ingredients from the very beginning of preparation, you will be able to make more delicious blends, because you know the make-up of the individual pieces. As long as the four main components that your tongue can recognize are in place, this theory of tasting and eating can be as simple or as complex as you wish it to be.

the balance of individual flavors and their opposites

The main tastes that our palates recognize are like colors: each has an opposite. The counter taste to heat or bitterness is sweetness. The opposite to salty is sour. When put together they counter each other, with the effect of toning down the intensity of a taste and bringing it into a harmony. The use of a blander ingredient will also bring the flavors back into equilibrium. Foods that would be considered bland or neutral—such as rice, bread and pasta—are often sweet more than anything else. Sometimes a salty ingredient is needed to balance the other flavors in the sequence—say by adding some fried pancetta, olives, capers, or shavings of Parmesan. For example, a

perfect taste combination Pan-fried scallops and warm lentil salad with anchovy and rosemary sauce (see recipe on page 138) is hot from the peppery leaves, black pepper, and extra virgin olive oil, sweet from the scallops and lentils, salty from the seasoning and anchovies, and sour from the lemon juice and vinegar.

Caesar salad that had no Parmesan or anchovies would be cloying and sickly. Often, lemon juice is needed to highlight other ingredients. I frequently use a squeeze of lemon to accent other flavors in the same way a brightly colored pen highlights details on a page and brings them to the attention of the reader.

hot and sweet

Hot and peppery doesn't have to mean chiles—this aspect can also be provided by black pepper, horseradish, raw ginger, or spices such as cayenne pepper. Hot and peppery flavors are the perfect partner for sweet. You would not consider eating sushi without wasabi. The wasabi provides the vital heat to complement the sweetness of the sushi. Other classic hot and sweet partnerships include Indian curry with mango chutney, beets and horseradish, rare roast beef with English mustard, and steak au poivre.

Similarly, bitter and sweet flavors often go hand in hand. A bitter coffee is tempered by adding cream, milk, or sugar. For me, there is nothing better than a small café macchiato (an espresso with a spoonful of frothy hot milk) after a meal served with a glass of *vin santo* or other dessert wine and either some nut biscotti or dark chocolate. Here I am not intentionally trying to balance all the flavors; they are just the ones that are truly satisfying because my tongue naturally responds all over its surface to the bitter from the coffee and the sweet, nutty, and slightly sour characteristics of the *vin santo*. The frothy milk provides some sweetness to cut the intensity of the coffee, while the biscotti provides some sugar and a little salt.

salt and sour

Have you ever wondered why salty snacks taste so good with the sour and bitter flavors of alcohol? It is

because they are complementary tastes. Vodka and tonic with lots of fresh lime accompanied by some salted nuts, tortilla chips, or marinated olives is a combination that is more than just refreshing. The tonic water is bitter from the quinine. The alcohol registers on the palate as heat at the back of the mouth. Extra heat could be provided in the form of some chili with the tortilla chips or in the olive marinade, which also provides the salt. The lime refreshes and awakens the mouth with its sourness. Similarly, a margarita with salt around the glass works because the salt is there in every mouthful to complement the sour tequila. Tequila with salt and lime hits the spot for exactly the same reason.

The balance of the whole meal

This is not only achieved on the plate of the main course but with the side dishes that accompany it, the appetizers that precede it, and the desserts that follow—not forgetting the subtle characteristics of the wine that you have chosen. The colors and textures that you select are all very important; you don't want a meal that is all the same color or one that you could eat through a straw. You need to avoid repetition of cooking methods, types of ingredients, and colors.

The weight of the meal often lies with the main course. It can bring all the other courses into balance and make the whole meal sing, or it could be too heavy and unbalanced and make the meal collapse in a heap.

A Thai menu is a classic example of all the flavors working together in a pleasurably undulating journey throughout the whole meal. You have a number of components that arrive in a near constant stream, some simultaneously, and your choices are based on what you previously had, and what will follow. A hot-and-sour salad of green mango and shrimp may be presented alongside a crispy salad of salted pork, fish, or duck eggs. Depending on how hot the previous dish was, you might have a palate-cleansing *geng juet* soup, which is quite mild and sweet, or the classic hot-and-sour soup, *dom yam*. The main course could be a sour or hot curry with some salted components like crispy pork or dried shrimp, or alternatively something sweet and caramelized in the form of braised meat such as crispy venison, lacquered chicken, or honey-roast duck. In each dish the key flavors will be balanced but one area might predominate, such as salty fish, sour mango, hot spices, or sweet roasted vegetables or meats. This same principle must also apply to Western foods—you only want to have a few of the components in the title, but all of them there on the fork.

When it comes to desserts, choose something that fits with the balance of the whole meal. If the tastebuds have already been bombarded, a simple mango sorbet may be all that is needed. However, if you want a more dazzling finish, then the taste theory can be applied to desserts with stunning results (see pages 228–249).

perfect taste combination An appetizer of crostini with crushed broad beans (page 56) followed by harissa-spiced lamb with jewelled couscous (page 179), finished with a simple dessert such as hot chocolate puddings (page 244) with crème fraîche. Each dish is balanced and contributes to an overall equilibrium of the meal.

the principles of wine tasting

The way our tastebuds are arranged on the tongue (see page 10) is made apparent when wine tasting. To get the most out of a sip of wine, you want to distribute it all around your mouth, moving it around as many parts of your palate as possible.

An exercise you can try to see this for yourself is to compare two sips of good wine. The first, you swallow immediately (this is how most people drink wine). The second, you move around inside your mouth, working it into your cheeks and across the sensitive spots of the back of your tongue, before finally swallowing. Notice how much more intensely you taste the wine.

matching wine with spicy food

Choosing a wine to complement Asian or spicy food does not have to be complicated. By identifying which category the ingredients on the plate represent, the wine can complement and fit into the balance of tastes.

White wines that work with crisp, spicy, aromatic, and acidic dishes such as Asian salads, appetizers, fish, and shellfish must represent similar elements as well as providing a balance. A crisp or acidic wine is often served to cut the richness of fish or shellfish. Here, wines from cooler climate regions would be preferred: in the northern hemisphere, wines from Brittany or Alsace in France, Germany, northern Italy and northern Spain; in the southern hemisphere, countries such as South Africa, Chile, New Zealand, Tasmania, and cooler regions of Australia such as the Hunter Valley. White grape varieties noted for their subtle fragrance and aromatic qualities include Viognier, Riesling, Gewürztraminer, Pinot Gris, and Tokay. Served chilled, these wines ably match flavors such as lime leaves, lime zest, and herbs. Sauvignon Blanc or blends using this grape, particularly ones from the New World, can be described as having "flinty" or "mineral" qualities and go very well with Asian seafood dishes. Certain white wines, such as Sauvignon Blanc, Semillon and the Portuguese Verdelho, when they are fresh and crisp, can be described as "grassy," similar to green apples in their tartness. These wines are a good match for ginger, lemongrass, and other fragrant ingredients. A small glass of dry manzanilla sherry—which is acidic, minerally, and very slightly salty—also works well with Asian appetizers or soups, such as a Vietnamese fisherman's soup or a *dom yam* soup, with grilled chicken, caramelized shallots,and Thai basil.

Wines that spend too long aging in oak barrels can develop a strong vanilla-like taste from the tannins of the oak. Chardonnay is one variety that can suffer from the over-use of oak; this does not work well with Asian flavors. Unoaked Chardonnay from a cool climate, however, can have the tartness and crispness needed to complement other fragrant acids present in the food.

Red wines that go well with stronger, spicier Asian flavors need to have similar characteristics. Rioja and other Spanish reds made with the Tempranillo grape have a spicy nature—man enough for garlic, chili, ginger, paprika, and cayenne and other strong flavors, such as game. They are good with foods of similar flavors from cuisines that historically have not been matched with wines. The Cabernet-based Lebanese wine Château Musar has intense, spicy, fruity, sun-baked undertones that can partner the hot, sour flavors of Middle Eastern food. Pinot Noir is another wine that can have a peppery aspect. It can work well with a hot-and-sour beef salad or any medium-spiced duck or pork dish. A lighter style of Pinot Noir, slightly chilled before serving, is good with "meaty" fish such as sea bass, halibut, and monkfish. And a Cabernet Sauvignon–Merlot blend has the strength and backbone to stand up to strong, hearty, meaty flavors. The Merlot's velvety smoothness complements Asian one-pots and hot-and-sour, slow-cooked meat, and the salty, spicy caramel of lacquered duck (see page 201). Syrah, the grape that hallmarks the big intense red wines of the southern Rhône in the south of France such as Hermitage and Chateauneuf du Pape, is one to match with strong flavors or spices such as cinnamon, coriander seeds and star anise. As a rule, medium- to full-bodied wines work best with more intense flavors and slow methods of cooking. The greater the depth of flavor of the wine, the greater the contrast with strong Asian flavors: an intensely aromatic Shiraz from the Barossa valley in south Australia, for example, works surprisingly well with a spicy southern Thai curry.

Once you understand the food, you can confidently partner it with wines that have been created with similar understanding. This will take your food and the whole eating experience to a totally different level of enjoyment.

use all your senses when you cook. Taste all the time—from start to finish. The smell will tell you when it is time to add the next ingredients, because the previous ones have become aromatic, as with a Thai curry paste. See when something is cooked or not quite there yet, as with the color of bread or pastry baking in the oven. Use your hands to feel textural differences.

you must use your hands to mix ingredients so you feel the textural differences; you then know that a soft goat cheese might be quite strong because it is ripe. The sound of sesame seeds dancing in the pan or the difference in the tune of a sugar syrup when the water has evaporated both alert you to the fact that they are done.

all of your senses are needed to make something really delicious. It is very important that you exercise your tastebuds to their full potential, working them as you would your muscles in the gym. Chefs may taste one dish up to 20 times to get all the flavors working together in harmony.

by constantly using all of your senses to cook and being aware of all of the different taste sensations on your tongue, you will begin to use your intuition to make food that stimulates the brain. Your cooking will become harmonious, effortless, and more naturally fluid because everything will be in tune and working together.

taste directory

Most foods have one or two dominant tastes as shown below. Use this directory to help you to see how tastes can be combined. If you need to make a substitution in a recipe, choose a similar ingredient from the same category.

sweet **Techniques:** roasting, sautéing, frying

ROASTED VEGETABLES AND NUTS e.g. beets, sweet potatoes, butternut squash, pumpkin, carrots, potatoes, parsnips, red and yellow peppers, tomatoes, onions, garlic, chestnuts, coconut, almonds, pine nuts, peanuts.
GREEN VEGETABLES e.g. peas, fava or green beans, asparagus, green beans. Lettuce, bamboo shoots, salad greens, cucumber.
RIPE FRUITS AND THEIR JUICES e.g. mangoes, bananas, pears, nectarines, peaches, oranges, plums, figs, grapes, strawberries, and melons.
DRIED FRUIT e.g. dates, apricots, raisins, golden raisins, figs, and prunes.
Note: the riper the fruit, the sweeter it will be. The less ripe the fruit, the more sour it will be.
SEAFOOD e.g. scallops, prawns, shrimp, crayfish, clams, mussels, crab, and lobster.
FIRM WHITE-FLESHED FISH e.g. monkfish, sea bass, cod, sole, halibut, flounder and porgy (sea bream).

sour **Techniques:** pickling and preserving

CITRUS e.g. lemon juice, lemon zest, preserved lemons (the salt removes the bitterness), lime juice, lime zest, kaffir lime leaves and juice, lemongrass, pomelo, and pink and white grapefruit.
OTHER FRUITS e.g. tamarind, apples, damson plums, gooseberries, rhubarb, pineapple, sour plums, and grapes.
DRIED FRUITS e.g. cranberries and sour cherries.
UNRIPE FRUIT AND VEGETABLES e.g. green tomatoes, green olives, unripe star fruit, (green) mangoes, unripe figs.
Note: the less ripe the fruit, the more sour it will be.
HERBS e.g. tarragon, dill, cilantro, fennel, sorrel, Thai basil, mustard leaves, mizuna, and lemon verbena.
DAIRY PRODUCTS e.g. crème fraîche, sour cream, sharp goat and sheep's milk cheeses, ricotta cheese, yogurt.

salty **Techniques:** smoking, salt cure, dry cure

SALTED FISH e.g. anchovies, sardines, dried shrimp, salt cod, gravadlax, dried squid, and Asian dried fish.
SMOKED FISH e.g. smoked salmon, gravadlax, smoked tuna, cod roe, smoked mackerel, and smoked trout.
SMOKED MEATS e.g. smoked duck, smoked beef, smoked pork, and smoked venison.
CURED MEATS e.g. prosciutto, salami, coppa di parma, bacon, pancetta, bresaola, chorizo. Pork crackling.
NATURAL AND SMOKED CHEESES e.g. Romano, feta, haloumi, Parmesan, smoked cheese, hard and soft goat cheese, sheep's milk cheese such as Manchego and Spenwood.

hot and peppery

HERBS AND GREENS e.g. arugula, cilantro, watercress, peppery lettuces and herbs, mustard leaves, mizuna, savoy cabbage, cavolo nero, and Italian cima di rapa leaves.
SPICES e.g. cayenne pepper, paprika, red chili, green chili, dried chili, black pepper, white pepper, pink pepper, green pepper, harissa spice mix, coriander seeds, mustard seeds, cardamom, and cloves.
CONDIMENTS e.g. Dijon mustard, English mustard, coarse-grain mustard, horseradish, radish, wasabi, ginger, galangal, raw garlic, and extra virgin olive oil.
PEPPERY RED WINES e.g. Pinot Noir, Rioja, Tempranillo, Syrah, and Barolo.
SPIRITS e.g. whiskey.

OILY FISH e.g. fresh tuna, swordfish, and salmon.
OTHER FISH e.g. fresh tuna, trout, and wild salmon.
ROAST MEATS e.g. beef, lamb, pork, and chicken.
RARE MEATS e.g. beef carpaccio.
DAIRY AND SIMILAR PRODUCTS e.g. mascarpone, cream cheese, milk, cream, butter, full-fat cheese, coconut milk, and coconut cream.
BAKED GOODS e.g. bread, brioche, pastries, cakes, cookies.
GRAINS & OTHER STAPLES e.g. rice, pasta, faro, barley, couscous, and potatoes.
SWEETENERS e.g. honey, rice syrup, white sugar, brown sugar, soft sugar, palm sugar, raw sugar cane, agave syrup, maltose, golden syrup, corn syrup, maple syrup, and molasses.
HERBS AND SPICES e.g. basil, cinnamon, cassia, allspice, saffron, apple pie spice, and nutmeg.
DESSERT AND OTHER SWEET WINES e.g. Sauterne and other botrytised wines, Tokay, Muscat, *vin santo*, ice wines, Pinot Gris, aged Chardonnay, champagne (doux), Madeira, Marsala, port, and some sherries.

BAKED GOODS e.g. sourdough bread, rye bread, pumpernickel, and flatbreads.
VINEGARS of all kinds e.g. malt, sherry, red wine, white wine, champagne, cider, tarragon, raspberry, balsamic, aged, coconut, and rice vinegar.
PICKLES, chutneys, relishes, gherkins, pickled ginger, pickled cabbage, pickled walnuts, pickled capers, and olives.
SPICES AND SEEDS e.g. fennel seeds, caraway seeds, star anise, licorice, juniper berries, fenugreek, and dill seed.
TART-TASTING AND CRISP YOUNG WHITE WINES e.g. Sauvignon Blanc, Muscadet, unoaked Chardonnay, Pouilly Fumé, Pouilly Fuissé, champagne (sec), Pinot Gris, Riesling.
FERMENTED SPIRITS e.g. pastis, Pernod, Campari, and gin.

SALTY CONDIMENTS e.g. light and dark soy sauce, miso, Asian fish sauce, tamari, anchovy paste, yeast extract, and bouillon.
SALTED SNACKS e.g. potato chips, french fries, and other preserved and dried snacks.

bitter

BITTER LEAVES AND SALAD GREENS e.g. endive, radicchio, trevise, cicoria, savoy cabbage, cavolo nero, brussels sprouts, dandelion, chicory, romaine lettuce, frisée lettuce, oak-leaf lettuce, spinach, and leafy greens.
BERRIES e.g. black currants.
GAME BIRDS AND MEATS e.g. venison, hare, wild boar, pheasant, grouse, teal, pigeon, and wild duck.
COCOA and chocolate with at least 70% cocoa solids.
COFFEE, TEA, AND WINE WITH TANNINS PRESENT e.g. black tea, green tea, jasmine tea.
SOFT DRINKS e.g. tonic water.
ALCOHOL FROM HOPS e.g. beer, ales, stout, and Guinness.
RED WINES HIGH IN TANNIN e.g. Madiran, Valpolicella.

sauces

sauces

Sauces, relishes, salsas, marinades, dressings, and other condiments have the power to transform your food. In European cuisine, they are often considered an afterthought and for this reason are usually found at the end of cookbooks. However, I want to introduce you to them first.

Although you wouldn't necessarily eat them in isolation, sauces and other condiments are absolutely key in many classic combinations—think about cheese without a chutney or relish, hot dogs without mustard or roast beef without horseradish. It is the same with Asian food, where for example sushi is always served with soy sauce, wasabi, and pickled ginger. When creating a balance of tastes and textures, these sauces are very important and will make your food stand out, making it taste exhilarating and three-dimensional.

Fish and meat in the sweet category of ingredients—such as scallops, monkfish, and roast pork—need a salty or sour component in their accompanying sauce or dressing. This cuts the richness and acts as a counter-flavor, bringing everything into balance. Without this sour component the dish would be overly rich and cloying and harder to digest. Similarly, many salty foods—cured meats like bacon, prosciutto and serrano ham, cheeses like Parmesan or Romano, and cured or smoked fish such as gravadlax, smoked mackerel or anchovies—require some of the other taste elements of sweetness, sourness, and heat in the accompanying sauce. By providing a contrast, a more rounded set of flavors will be created. Let me illustrate with some delicious combinations.

- Salty Parmesan or prosciutto paired with a sweet fruit or vegetable like melon, figs, or asparagus, together with a sour and hot dressing of lemon, balsamic vinegar, olive oil, and black pepper works very well (see page 57). Here the heat from the pepper is subtle but still traceable, and some peppery arugula could be added with great effect.

- A classic partner for a salty cured fish such as gravadlax is a slightly sweetened smooth-tasting mustard and lemon dressing (see page 88).

- A perfect companion to an oily fish such as smoked mackerel is roast beets, which is high in earthy sugars, and this can be served alongside some hot horseradish (see page 41).

What is most exhilarating when all these taste areas are represented is that your tongue tastes each flavor separately and then as a whole. With each mouthful the flavors move around the mouth, stimulating all the tastebuds. Your tongue feels like it has been the platform for a culinary fireworks display.

There is an astounding salad of roasted shrimp and watermelon (see page 93) that has variations around Southeast Asia. It is the exciting punch of the dressing that sets it apart from any other salad, providing sourness, heat, and salt that bind the sweetness of the fruit and the shellfish. The sauce is absorbed and soaked up by the crisp watermelon, so that you savor all four areas of taste in every mouthful. Without the sauce, you do not have very much.

SWEET fennel, pears, mangoes, cooked eggplant, pineapple, cooked onions, cooked tomatoes, honey, cinnamon, dates, plums, milk SOUR lemons, sherry vinegar, red wine vinegar, cilantro, crème fraîche, tamarind SALTY anchovies, capers, roasted peanuts HOT extra virgin olive oil, black pepper, chili, garlic, paprika, ginger, horseradish

TOM KIME

preserved lemons

makes 1 small jar

These are great to have on hand and are used in several Mediterranean-style recipes in this book. They bring an intense salty and sour flavor to dishes.

2 lemons
3 heaping tablespoons sea salt
olive oil

Place the lemons in a small saucepan with a tight-fitting lid. Cover with cold water. Add the sea salt (the salt removes the bitterness from the lemon skin).

Bring the water to a boil. Reduce heat and simmer until the lemons are soft when pierced with the tip of a sharp knife. Drain and refresh under cold running water.

When cool, cut each lemon lengthwise into quarters. Use a sharp knife to cut along the skin to remove all the fruit and pith. Then slice the lemon peel quarters lengthwise into strips

If not using right away, place the strips in a jar, cover completely with olive oil, and cover with the lid. They will keep in the fridge for up to 6 weeks.

black olive and preserved lemon salsa with basil and parsley

serves 6

This is a fantastic salsa which works well with fish, shellfish, or roasted meat. It can also be used in a salad or to stuff fish such as red snapper, or a chicken or poussin.

3 tablespoons coarsely chopped pitted black olives, such as kalamata
1 x recipe preserved lemons (see above), finely chopped
juice of 1 lemon
5 tablespoons extra virgin olive oil
1/2 fennel bulb, finely chopped
1 red chile (jalapeño or serrano), seeded and finely chopped
salt and freshly ground black pepper
20 basil leaves
20 mint or flat-leaf parsley leaves

Mix the olives and the preserved lemon zest in a bowl. Stir in the lemon juice, olive oil, fennel, and chile.

Season well with freshly ground black pepper and then salt (the olives are salty, so taste before adding).

Do not add the basil and other herbs until you are ready to serve, otherwise the acid in the lemon juice will turn them black.

chef's tip

A good method of pitting olives is to place them under a sheet of parchment paper or plastic wrap, and push down on them with the bottom of a heavy pot or the fat side of a chef's knife, smashing the flesh. Remove the covering paper. The pits of the olives can now be quickly removed.

asian pear salsa

serves 6

This is a delicious fresh salsa, which is not fully pickled but has acid from the lime juice and vinegar. It can accompany meat such as roast chicken, grilled pork, or roast duck. It would also work well with some cooked shrimp or served alongside some cheeses as a pickle or relish.

2 firm but ripe pears
3 tablespoons extra virgin olive oil
juice of 1 lime
1 tablespoon red wine vinegar
1 red chile (jalapeño or serrano), seeded and finely chopped
3 scallions, thinly sliced
1 1/4-inch piece of fresh ginger, peeled and grated
salt and freshly ground black pepper

Quarter and core the pears. Cut into 1/2-inch cubes.

Mix in a bowl with all the other ingredients. Season well with salt and pepper to taste.

The heat will come from the chile and the black pepper, and the pear provides sweetness. The vinegar and the lime juice will be sour, and salt will also be present. Adjust the seasoning accordingly.

mango salsa with red chile, cilantro, and lime

serves 4–6

This is a zesty and refreshing salsa using ripe fruit, chile, and lime to make a simple, flavor-packed sauce or relish that can transform tired palates. The citrus and red chile are perfect for cutting the richness of roasted or grilled meat such as chicken breast or rare duck breast.

1 ripe mango
1 red chile (jalapeño or serrano), seeded and finely chopped
juice of 1 lime
2 scallions, trimmed and thinly sliced
salt and freshly ground black pepper
2 tablespoons coarsely chopped cilantro leaves

With a sharp knife, peel the mango, discarding the stem. Try not to remove too much of the flesh when you cut away the skin. Cut the flesh of the fruit away from the thin central pit of the mango, then cut into small cubes and place in a bowl.

Mix in the chile, lime juice, scallions, and mango pieces. Season with salt and pepper. Stir in the cilantro leaves.

This salsa can be left for up to 2 hours at room temperature to develop the flavors. However, if making it in advance, do not add the cilantro and scallions until ready to serve because their aroma and taste will be destabilized by the acid.

variation

With a sharp knife, cut the skin and all the white pith from 1 ripe pink grapefruit. Remove the fruit segments and cut into 1/2-inch pieces. Ensure that the flesh has no white pith attached because it is bitter and unpleasant. Mix in along with the mango.

salsa verde

serves 6

A fantastically fresh-tasting salsa that will transform simple meat, fish, or chicken dishes. Make it fresh each time you need it as the herbs will blacken.

1 garlic clove
2 tablespoons capers, rinsed
4 anchovy fillets
20 basil leaves
20 mint leaves
small handful of flat-leaf parsley
juice of 1/2 lemon
2 tablespoons red wine vinegar
3 tablespoons olive oil
salt and freshly ground black pepper

Place the garlic, capers, and anchovy fillets in a food processor or in a mortar and pestle. Blend or pound until smooth.

Add all the fresh herbs and puree until you have a smooth green paste. Add the lemon juice and red wine vinegar, then stir in the olive oil. Season with salt and pepper.

Check the seasoning and add more lemon juice if necessary.

salsa rosa picante

serves 6

A spicy tomato sauce to be served hot or warm with any roasted or poached meat.

1 tablespoon coriander seeds
1/2 tablespoon fennel seeds
1/2 tablespoon cumin seeds
1 small dried chili
2 garlic cloves
salt and freshly ground black pepper
1 tablespoon olive oil
1 (14 1/2-ounce) can plum tomatoes
1 cinnamon stick
1 fresh red chile (jalapeño or serrano), seeded and finely chopped
1 tablespoon red wine vinegar
juice of 1 lemon

Crush the coriander seeds, fennel seeds, cumin seeds, and dried chile to a fine powder in a mortar and pestle. Add the garlic and a pinch of salt and continue to pound until you have a smooth paste.

Heat the olive oil in a heavy pan. Fry the spice paste until fragrant and aromatic.

Add the tomatoes, cinnamon stick, chile, and salt and pepper to taste, then the red wine vinegar. (When making a tomato sauce, it is important to add the salt right away, because it will change the nature of the tomatoes by countering the acid in them.)

Cook the tomato mixture slowly over medium heat. With a wooden spoon, break down the tomatoes every time you stir them. The tomatoes start as two consistencies: the bulky fruit and the juice. You want to break them down so you have a combined consistency of a thick sauce.

Adjust the seasoning and add the lemon juice. It should be sweet, salty, slightly sour, and hot.

salsa romesco

serves 4–6

This sauce has a smoky heat from the paprika and dried chile. The sweetness comes from the roasted pepper and tomato, and sourness from vinegar or lemon juice. Serve with scallions (see below) or chicken or pork.

1 dried chile
1 large red bell pepper, seeded
3 tablespoons olive oil
2 plum tomatoes
1 teaspoon brown sugar
3 garlic cloves, 2 left whole, 1 chopped
1 thick slice of white bread, crusts removed
3 tablespoons shelled hazelnuts
3 tablespoons blanched almonds
1/2 fresh red chile (jalapeño or serrano), seeded
1/2 teaspoon sweet smoked Spanish paprika
1 tablespoon sherry vinegar or lemon juice
salt and freshly ground black pepper

Adjust the broiler rack 4 to 6 inches from heat source. Preheat the broiler.

Cover the dried chile with hot water and let it soak for 10 minutes until soft. Reserve the soaking liquid.

Brush the pepper with a little oil and place on a broiler pan. Cut the tomatoes in half, sprinkle with brown sugar, and place on the pan. Broil until the tomato is caramelized and the red pepper skin is blistered and blackened. Place the red pepper in a bowl and cover with plastic wrap. Let cool, so the trapped steam loosens the skin as it cools. Remove the skin and seeds.

Heat the olive oil in a heavy skillet. Add the 2 whole garlic cloves. Sauté until golden. Remove the garlic from the pan and set aside. Tear the bread into bite-sized pieces and cook in the garlic-infused oil until golden and crisp. Reserve the oil.

In another skillet, dry-toast the hazelnuts and almonds until pale golden.

Cut the soaked chile in half, remove the stem and seeds, and finely chop the flesh. Place in a food processor. Add the broiled red pepper and the tomatoes, and pulse the machine once or twice to incorporate. Add the toasted bread and the raw and cooked garlic. Puree until smooth. Add the fresh red chile, paprika, and sherry vinegar. Slowly add the garlic-infused olive oil in a thin, steady stream and work until a smooth paste forms. Add 2–3 tablespoons of the chile soaking liquid until the paste is not too thick but still a dip-like consistency.

Taste the sauce and check the seasoning. Add a little sherry vinegar or lemon juice if necessary.

grilled scallions with salsa romesco

4 scallions or baby leeks per person
extra virgin olive oil
salt and freshly ground black pepper
juice of 1 lemon
1 tablespoon finely chopped thyme
1 garlic clove, finely chopped
salsa romesco (see above)

Preheat a grill pan.

Toss the cleaned scallions or baby leeks with a little oil, salt, and pepper in a large bowl. Grill until nicely charred.

Return to the original bowl with some extra virgin olive oil and the lemon juice, salt, and pepper. Add the thyme and garlic.

Let the scallions cool in the marinade.

To serve, remove scallions from marinade. Serve salsa remesco on the side, or drizzled over the top of the scallions.

asian vinaigrette

serves 6

You could use fresh chile instead of dried if you like.

juice and zest of 1 orange
$^1/_2$ tablespoon fresh ginger
$^1/_2$ teaspoon crushed dried red pepper flakes
$^1/_2$ teaspoon sugar
3 tablespoons sesame oil
2 tablespoons peanut or light olive oil
1 tablespoon rice wine vinegar
1 tablespoon soy sauce
juice of 1 lime
salt and freshly ground black pepper

Combine the orange juice and zest, ginger, red pepper flakes and sugar in a small bowl.

Mix in all the other ingredients. Taste, and adjust the flavors accordingly. The dressing should be hot, sweet, salty, and sour.

sauce antiboise (warm tomato and basil dressing)

serves 6–8

When making a warm dressing, the flavors infuse and intensify like a pot of tea. You could use some chopped fried bacon or pancetta instead of anchovies or capers; all these ingredients are salty.

$^1/_2$ cup extra virgin olive oil
4 shallots, finely chopped
2 garlic cloves, crushed with a pinch of salt
small handful of flat-leaf parsley, leaves coarsely chopped and stems reserved
juice of 1 lemon
1 tablespoon red wine vinegar
1 tablespoon chopped anchovy fillets or finely chopped capers
20 basil leaves, coarsley chopped
3 tomatoes, chopped, or 20 cherry tomatoes, cut in half
salt and freshly ground black pepper

Heat the olive oil in a small saucepan. Add the shallots, garlic, and parsley stems. Continue to heat without frying the ingredients.

When the oil is hot, remove the pan from the heat and let the ingredients steep and infuse.

When the oil is warm, remove the parsley stems. Add the lemon juice and vinegar. Add the anchovies or capers. Mix in the basil and tomatoes. Taste, check the seasoning, and adjust with salt, pepper, and a little extra lemon juice if necessary.

caper and marjoram sauce

serves 6–8

This is a fantastic sauce which works well with fish, shellfish, or roasted meat. It is fabulous with the seared rare tuna on page 190.

1 tablespoon capers, rinsed
1 x recipe preserved lemons (see page 27), finely chopped
juice of 1 lemon
6 tablespoons extra virgin olive oil
1 tablespoon red wine vinegar
salt and freshly ground black pepper
2 tablespoons finely chopped marjoram, basil, or flat-leaf parsley

Coarsely chop the capers and mix with the preserved lemon. Add the lemon juice, olive oil, and vinegar.

Taste and check the seasoning. Season well with pepper and then salt (the capers are salty so taste before adding salt).

Do not add the marjoram or other herb until you are ready to serve, because the acid in the lemon juice will turn them black.

anchovy and rosemary sauce

serves 6–8

Based on a classic from London's River Cafe, this sauce may sound unlikely but it works well with many other dishes. Because of the salt and sour flavors, it marries well with anything sweet or rich such as scallops or grilled sea bass, or rare roast lamb or beef. It is also delicious with some braised broccolini or asparagus.

3 sprigs rosemary
1 (2-ounce) can flat anchovy filets, drained
juice of $^{1}/_{2}$ lemon
5 tablespoons olive oil
salt and freshly ground black pepper

Pick the rosemary leaves from the stem and chop finely. (This is going to be an uncooked sauce, so you do not want large pieces of rosemary floating around.)

Pound the anchovies to a paste in a mortar and pestle. Add the finely chopped rosemary.

Add the lemon juice, and keep pounding until the anchovies become creamy and pale. Continue to mix, adding the olive oil in a thin stream.

Taste and check the seasoning. Add a little salt, pepper, and a little extra lemon juice if necessary.

green herb sauce for crispy vegetables

serves 6–8

Serve with crunchy vegetables or grilled fish or meat.

- $1^1/_4$-inch piece of fresh ginger with peel, sliced (see page 38)
- 3 cilantro (fresh coriander) roots, rinsed well and chopped (if not available, use cilantro stems)
- 1 small red or green chile, seeded and finely chopped
- salt and freshly ground black pepper
- 30 mint leaves
- 30 cilantro leaves
- juice of 2 limes
- 1 tablespoon olive oil

Pound the unpeeled ginger in a mortar and pestle to a rough pulp, then remove the pulp from the mortar with a spoon and set aside.

Crush the cilantro roots and the chile in the mortar with a little salt (to work as an abrasive) until smooth.

Take some of the ginger pulp in your hand and squeeze all the liquid into the mortar and pestle. Repeat until all of the pulp has been wrung out. Discard the dry pulp.

Add the herbs and continue to pound until a smooth paste is formed.

Add the lime juice and oil. Season to taste if necessary. Add more ginger or chile to taste.

green chile nahm yum

serves 4–6

This dressing is fantastic for an Asian salad (see facing page) or with grilled fish or shellfish.

- $1^1/_2$-inch piece of fresh ginger or galangal, sliced
- 2 garlic cloves
- 3 small green or red chiles, seeded and finely chopped
- 3 cilantro (fresh coriander) roots, rinsed well and chopped (if not available, use cilantro stems)
- $^1/_2$ teaspoon salt
- $^1/_2$ teaspoon sugar
- juice of 1 orange
- juice of 2 limes

Put the ginger in a mortar and pestle and pound to a rough pulp, then remove the pulp with a spoon and set aside. Alternatively, puree the ginger in a food processor with a couple of spoonfuls of water.

Place the garlic, chile, and cilantro root in the mortar and pestle along with the salt and sugar, which will act as an abrasive and help break down the fibers. Pound until you have a smooth puree.

Take some of the ginger pulp in your hand and squeeze all the liquid into the mortar. Repeat until all of the pulp has been wrung out. If you used a food processor, press the ginger through a fine sieve to get the liquid. Discard the dry pulp.

Add the orange and lime juice to the mortar and pestle.

Taste the dressing and adjust the seasoning with more salt, black pepper, lime juice, or sugar if necessary. The sauce should be hot from the chile, sweet from the orange and sugar, and refreshingly acidic with a savory taste from the garlic and salt.

fresh chile jam

serves 6–8

Serve with just about anything, from scrambled eggs to grilled chicken. It keeps for ages in the fridge.

- 1/2 cup peeled and grated fresh ginger
- 12 red chiles (jalapeño or serrano), seeded and finely chopped
- 6 garlic cloves, chopped
- 6 cilantro (fresh coriander) roots, rinsed well and chopped (if not available, use cilantro stems)
- 16 tomatoes
- 1 cup sugar
- 2 tablespoons Asian fish sauce
- salt and freshly ground black pepper
- juice of 2 limes

Place the ginger, chiles, garlic, and cilantro roots in a food processor. Pulse until a rough paste has formed.

Cut 8 of the tomatoes into quarters. Working in batches, add tomatoes to the food processor, pulsing on and off until mixture is well blended.

Place the tomato and spice puree in a saucepan along with the sugar and fish sauce and cook until the puree starts to look syrupy and the liquid has reduced—about 20–25 minutes.

Cut the remaining tomatoes in half and remove the seeds. Cut the flesh into small pieces. Add the cut-up tomato to the pan, season well, and add the lime juice. Remove from the heat, let the flavors settle, and then taste and add more freshly chopped chile if you like. As the mixture cools it will condense into a syrupy paste.

Moroccan chermoula with tomato, roast peppers, mint, and cilantro

serves 6

Chermoula is a spectacular Moroccan spice and herb mixture which can be used as a sauce or marinade for anything from grilled meat and roast chicken to seafood such as squid or scallops. The red peppers provide a brilliant depth of sweetness, which works well with the spices and the sourness of the lemon.

3 red bell peppers
2 garlic cloves
1 teaspoon salt
1/2 teaspoon chile powder
1 teaspoon saffron strands
1 tablespoon crushed coriander seeds
1 teaspoon paprika
1 cup chopped tomatoes or halved cherry tomatoes
20 mint leaves, coarsely chopped
3 tablespoons coarsely chopped fresh cilantro
juice of 1 lemon
1/4 cup extra virgin olive oil

Grill the peppers on a heavy ridged grill pan, or directly over a gas flame until the skin is blackened and blistered all over. Alternatively you could cut them in half, brush with a little oil and put them under a preheated broiler for 12–15 minutes. Remove from the heat, place in a bowl, and cover with plastic wrap. Let cool, so the trapped steam loosens their skins as they cool. Remove their skins, stems, and seeds.

Using a mortar and pestle, crush the garlic cloves, then add the salt and work into a smooth paste (this dressing is eaten raw so you do not want large chunks of raw garlic).

Transfer the garlic paste to a bowl and mix in all the dry spice ingredients.

Add the tomatoes to the bowl. Finely chop the peppers and add to the mixture.

Stir in two thirds of the herbs followed by the lemon juice and olive oil. Check the seasoning. Garnish with the remaining herbs.

chef's tip

You can use this chermoula as a chunky marinade. Use just one of the peppers and, after cooking your meat or fish in the marinade, add the other two peppers and tear in some mint and cilantro leaves to give some definition.

mortar and pestle

A stone mortar and pestle is an essential—if cumbersome—tool for making sauces and pastes. As a piece of kitchen equipment it is exceptionally versatile: perfect for grinding whole roast spices to a powder, for crushing nuts and seeds such as pine nuts, pistachios, sesame seeds, or peanuts, or for pounding garlic and ginger. Anything can be thrown in and easily made into a sauce, paste, or relish. The mortar can then be quickly wiped out and used again. For me the benefits of this tool are infinite. I would almost go as far to say that I cannot cook without one.

The mortar and pestle has a truly international reputation—from the Mediterranean to the Gulf of Siam. They are used for making *rouille* in Marseilles, which is added to *soupe de poisson*, for making pesto in Genoa, and for pounding salt cod or almonds in Spain. Spices are ground in them on the southern Mediterranean coast for sauces such as harissa and chermoula, or in the Middle Eastern pastes such as hummus and almond tarator. In southern India, masala curry pastes are made with them for fish and vegetable curries. In Indonesia the fiery chili sambals are pounded to eye-watering perfection. Across Southeast Asia in households and markets, mortars and pestles are used almost continuously as cooking tools for everything from the hot-and-sour green mango salads—called *yam som tam* in Thailand—to the infamous *nam prick*—a spicy Thai relish made from shrimp paste and chiles.

There is no mechanical or electrical action that reproduces that of the mortar and pestle. The technique is to bruise and crush to break down the consistency of the ingredients. Unlike cutting or chopping, the pounding action releases the essence and the oils from the ingredients. In Southeast Asian cooking there is a technique that could never be achieved with an electric blender. Ginger pieces, including the peelings, are pounded until bruised, forming a coarse pulp, which is then scooped out with a spoon and set aside on a board. Next, a paste is made using the mortar and pestle from garlic and chopped chile with a pinch of salt and sugar to help break them down. The ginger then comes back into play: the pulp is tightly squeezed in the palm of the hand so that all the juice runs into the mortar. When it is all wrung out, you discard the crushed pulp. Fresh lime juice and orange juice are then added to create an astonishing dressing for salads or marinating fish. All the flavors are incredibly fresh and vibrant, and the whole process takes about 2 minutes.

There is a place for at least one mortar and pestle in every modern kitchen—I would urge you to buy one. I have a portable one—well, relatively speaking; it is made from a piece of black granite and weighs about 5 pounds—but I still take it on every cooking job! I also have one that is about the size of a cinder block. It cost about £25 in London's Chinatown, and then another £20 to get it home in a taxi. If you buy one from an Asian store or grocer rather than a boutique or kitchen store, they will cost about half the price. The stone ones are the best and the most robust—I always think that I am going to crack the white porcelain ones, and the noise is not very kind on the ears.

The technique for using a mortar and pestle is quite gentle and does not require great exertion of energy—you don't see anyone in an Indonesian night market breaking into a sweat over a mortar! Hold the pestle lightly with quite a loose wrist and let the weight of the stone do all the pounding. Move it freely around the bowl, bringing anything on the sides of the mortar down with each stroke. The versatility of this primitive kitchen utensil is endless, and you get a lot of simple satisfaction from using one, as well as a free aromatherapy session from the intense perfumes that are released!

horseradish and bread sauce

serves 4–6

3 slices stale white bread, crusts removed
1/3 cup milk
2 tablespoons red wine vinegar
1 garlic clove
salt and freshly ground black pepper
2 tablespoons grated hot horseradish (fresh or from a jar)
1/2 cup olive oil
juice of 1 lemon
small handful of flat-leaf parsley or arugula, coarsely chopped

Break the bread into a bowl and cover with the milk and vinegar.

Crush the garlic with a little salt to make a smooth puree.

Squeeze the milk from the bread and reserve. Place the bread in a food processor with the crushed garlic and the horseradish. Pulse to incorporate. With the motor running, add enough of the reserved milk in a thin stream to make a thick paste.

Add the olive oil in a thin stream with the motor still running (as if you were making a mayonnaise) until an emulsion forms.

Add the lemon juice and season with salt and pepper.

Remove the lid and taste the sauce. Adjust the seasoning if necessary. If the sauce is very thick, add a little splash of milk to thin it.

Do not add the basil and other herbs until you are ready to serve, otherwise the acid in the lemon juice will turn them black.

horseradish and watercress crème fraîche

serves 6

This is delicious with roast beef or steak, or with something sweet and roasted like beets (see picture on facing page and instructions for roasting beets on page 88).

2 tablespoons grated horseradish (fresh or from a jar)
1 bunch of watercress, trimmed
2 tablespoons red wine vinegar
juice of 1/2 lemon
1 teaspoon Dijon mustard
1 cup crème fraîche
salt and freshly ground black pepper

Place the horseradish and watercress in a food processor. Pulse until you have a coarse green puree. Add the red wine vinegar, lemon juice, and mustard, and pulse again.

Add the crème fraîche,salt, and pepper. Process, pulsing on and off, until you have a smooth, pale green puree. Don't over-process, because the crème fraîche may curdle.

Taste the sauce: it needs to be hot, sour, and salty at the same time, bound by the creaminess.

tamarind caramel

serves 6–8

This might sound strange but it is absolutely delicious and works with many dishes, particularly sweet roasted or braised meats like pork or beef. Add a couple of spoonfuls of the meat juices to the caramel before serving.

splash of oil
1 garlic clove, finely chopped
1 red chile (jalapeño or serrano), seeded and finely chopped
$1^1/_2$-inch piece of fresh ginger, sliced
2 tablespoons brown sugar
2 tablespoons tamarind pulp (available in Indian and Asian markets)
2 tablespoons Asian fish sauce
juice of 1 lime

Heat a small saucepan over medium heat and add the oil. Sauté the garlic, chile, and ginger until the garlic is pale golden brown.

Add the soft brown sugar and stir to dissolve. Add the tamarind pulp and the fish sauce and simmer gently for 4 minutes until the sauce becomes syrupy. Add the lime juice.

This sauce should be sweet, salty, and sour and hot at the same time. Adjust with a little more sugar, tamarind pulp, or chile if necessary.

roast caramelized quince

serves 6–8

Fantastically perfumed, this is ideal to accompany roast meat or game such as partridge or quail. Use for a tarte Tatin or other fruit dessert, or cool it and make into a salad with Stilton or goat cheese. Alternatively, when you are caramelizing the quince, add a little chopped garlic, rosemary, and fresh chile; this version is great served with serrano ham, prosciutto, or lomo embuchado (see page 169).

6 ripe quinces
$2^1/_2$ tablespoons sugar
$1^1/_2$ tablespoons butter

Preheat the oven to 425°F.

Peel and quarter the quince. Remove the core and all the woody bits that surround the core. If these bits are not removed, then they will remain tough after cooking.

Tear off a large piece of aluminum foil and fold it in half so that it is doubly as thick. Place quince in the center. Sprinkle with a little of the sugar, wrap to enclose the quince, and crimp the edges to seal.

Place on a baking sheet and bake about 40 minutes, or until soft.

Remove quince from the foil.

In a heavy nonreactive skillet, melt the butter. Add the quince, stirring to coat. Add the remaining sugar and cook, stirring occasionally, to caramelize.

Cook for 4–5 minutes until the quince are a deep red-brown color.

caramelized peanut and chile dressing

serves 6

This sauce is so good that you will probably eat quite a bit right from the bowl! Try it with some salty roast meat such as pork belly (see page 168) or a crunchy vegetable salad.

1 tablespoon olive oil
2 garlic cloves, finely chopped
1 red chile (jalapeño or serrano), seeded and finely chopped
3 cilantro (coriander) roots, rinsed well and finely chopped (if not available, use cilantro stems)
4 shallots, finely chopped
2 teaspoons sugar
2 tablespoons raw peanuts
2 tablespoons peanut or olive oil
1 tablespoon toasted sesame oil
1 tablespoon soy sauce
juice of 1 lime
20 cilantro leaves

Heat a heavy skillet over a medium-high heat. Add the olive oil and sauté the garlic, chile, and cilantro root for 1 minute.

Add the shallots and sugar and cook for 2 minutes, until the sugar starts to caramelize. Stir to prevent the sugar from sticking.

Add the peanuts and continue to cook until the peanuts are a pale golden brown and the shallots have caramelized—about another 3–4 minutes. If the sugar is beginning to scorch, then add a splash of water.

Remove the mixture from the heat and scrape into a mortar and pestle. Pound until you have a semi-smooth paste. Stir in the peanut oil, sesame oil, soy sauce, and lime juice. Add 2 tablespoons water to thin the sauce (the flavors are strong so you will not really dilute the taste).

Coarsely chop the cilantro and add to the sauce. Serve warm.

pickles and preserving

Every culture has its own traditions of pickling fruit and vegetables at the height of the season, so that they will keep for the leaner months when there is less fresh produce. This method of preserving with an acidic agent can offset the effects of another method of preserving; that of salting, curing, and drying. As sour and salt are direct opposites in terms of how we taste, they work to counter each other's negative effects, and so complement each other. By combining spices, chili, and sweet ingredients like tomatoes, onions, apples, plums, nectarines, and mangoes with an acidic component when making a chutney or relish, you can create a rich blend of several flavors. That is why the simple coupling of a relish with something salty such as ham or cheese is a perfect marriage of flavors—you do not need anything else.

northern indian smoky spiced eggplant

serves 6–8

This spectacular dish comes from my friend, Amandip Kotecha, who translated the recipe from her mother. I had it once and remembered it forever after. It is delicious as a snack or as part of a larger meal. You get a fantastic combination of tastes from the hot spices, smoky sweet eggplants, and onions. The sourness from the lemon at the end brings it all together to make a fantastic intense relish.

3 medium eggplants
3 tablespoons olive oil
1 teaspoon whole cumin seeds
4 garlic cloves, finely chopped
1 large knob of fresh ginger, peeled and grated
3 medium red onions, finely chopped
3 scallions, finely sliced
2 tomatoes, coarsely chopped
1 teaspoon ground coriander
1 teaspoon paprika
1/2 teaspoon garam masala
1/2 teaspoon medium-hot chile powder
salt and freshly ground black pepper
1/2 bunch of cilantro, chopped
juice of 1/2 lemon

Preheat a broiler to hot.

Prick the eggplants lightly with a fork. Roast them under the broiler, turning intermittently, for 15–20 minutes, until they are soft in the middle and dry on the outside. Remove from the broiler and let cool. Peel off the skin, saving any juice from inside. Coarsely chop the flesh with knife.

Heat a large, heavy saucepan over medium-high heat. Add the oil and sauté the cumin seeds until fragrant. Lower the heat, add the garlic and ginger, and cook, stirring for about 1–2 minutes until the garlic is pale golden.

Add the red onions and cook for about 5 minutes until they are pale golden at the edges. Add the scallions and tomatoes.

Add the chopped roasted eggplant and cook until the liquid is absorbed. Add the remaining dry spices and season well with salt and pepper. Cook for another 10 minutes and then add the cilantro and lemon juice to awaken all the flavors. Taste and adjust the seasoning. Serve with plain yogurt or cucumber raita and some toasted flat bread or pita bread.

roast shallot, tomato, and chile relish

serves 6–8

This roast shallot sauce pairs well with any salty meat such as pork or smoked duck.

4 tablespoons olive oil
6 shallots, coarsely chopped
$1^1/_4$-inch of fresh ginger, peeled and coarsely chopped
2 garlic cloves, coarsely chopped
1 red chile (jalapeño or serrano), seeded and finely chopped
3 tomatoes, cut in half
salt and freshly ground black pepper
$^1/_2$ teaspoon sugar or honey
juice of 1 lime

Heat a heavy saucepan over medium-high heat. Add 1 tablespoon of the oil and cook the shallots, ginger, and garlic until they start to caramelize. You want the shallot and garlic to get quite brown, and if they stick or scorch in a few places, don't worry—this will impart a deep smoky flavor, but avoid them completely burning. Alternatively, you could roast these vegetables on a baking sheet, drizzled with a little oil and cooked under a preheated broiler or in a hot oven.

When the shallots are a medium deep brown with flecks that are more blackened, push the shallots, ginger, and garlic to the side of the pan and add the red chile.

Add the tomatoes without mixing them with the other ingredients. Cook the tomatoes until they are well browned, adding a little extra oil if necessary.

Remove the shallot, ginger, chile, and garlic from the pan and place in a mortar and pestle. Add a pinch of salt, some black pepper, and the sugar. Pound the mixture until it forms a semi-smooth paste.

Remove the tomatoes from the pan and add to the mortar and pestle. Pour the lime juice into the pan and de-glaze the pan with a wooden spoon to pick up all the browned bits that stick to the bottom.

Crush the tomatoes gently to avoid splashing. Remove any large pieces of tomato skin. You are making a rustic sauce, so leave some texture. Add the juices from the pan.

Taste to check the seasoning before serving. The sauce may need a little extra chopped chile, or lime juice, and maybe some extra sugar depending upon how caramelized the shallots are, and the original sweetness of the tomatoes.

Add the remaining oil, mix together, and taste. It should taste sweet, hot, sour, and salty.

onion marmalade

makes 1 jar

This is a fantastic condiment to keep on hand. It is great with anything from grilled cheese sandwiches to sausages, or served with some grilled rare meat such as beef, and some arugula leaves as a salad. It is easy to make, and you can fine-tune and alter each batch with the addition of extra vinegar, chile, or other spices or tomatoes to make it into more of a relish.

1 tablespoon olive oil
2 garlic cloves, finely chopped
1 tablespoon chopped thyme leaves
1 red chile (jalapeño or serrano), seeded and finely chopped
4 medium onions, finely chopped
salt and freshly ground black pepper
1 tablespoon sugar
2 tablespoons red wine vinegar

Heat a heavy sauté pan over medium-high heat. Add the oil and cook the garlic, thyme, and red chile for 1 minute until fragrant. Add the chopped onions. Season with salt and pepper. Stir in the sugar.

Reduce the heat and cook slowly until the onions are barely golden. If the sugar or onions start to stick, just add a little water, stir, and continue to cook.

When golden brown, stir in the vinegar. Cook until absorbed. Taste and adjust the seasoning. Remove from the heat. Serve hot, warm, or cold.

pineapple relish

serves 4–6

Perfect as an accompaniment to curries or grilled or roasted meat.

2 tablespoons oil
1 tablespoon grated fresh ginger
2 garlic cloves
2 red chiles (jalapeño or serrano), seeded and finely chopped
2 teaspoons sugar
salt and freshly ground black pepper
1 pineapple
juice of 1 lime

Heat half the oil in a sauté pan and cook the ginger and garlic for 2–3 minutes or until golden brown.

Remove the ginger and garlic and place in a mortar. Add the chile, sugar, and 1/2 teaspoon salt, and use the pestle to grind to fine paste. Slice off and discard both ends of the pineapple. Cut off the skin and cut the pineapple lengthwise into quarters. Cut off and discard the tough center core; then cut each quarter pineapple into 1/2-inch thick slices.

Heat the remaining oil and, working in batches, cook the pineapple slices, turning once, until golden, 2–4 minutes total.

Remove from the heat, coarsely chop the pineapple, and place in a bowl. Stir in the chile mixture and lime juice. Check the seasoning and adjust accordingly. It should be hot, sweet, salty, and sour. The relish will keep for up to three days, covered, in the fridge.

sweet and sour roasted orange relish with honey, saffron, and cinnamon

serves 6–8

The sourness and spice in this sauce make a perfect foil for rich roast goose, duck, or pork.

2 tablespoons olive oil
1 onion, finely chopped
2 garlic cloves, finely chopped
1 red chile (jalapeño or serrano), seeded and finely chopped
2 cinnamon sticks
2 tablespoons honey
1/2 teaspoon saffron threads
1/4 cup sherry vinegar
juice of 1 orange
juice of 1 lime
5 oranges, peeled and cut into segments
salt and freshly ground black pepper
2 tablespoons skinned, dry-roasted almonds, coarsely chopped
1/2 bunch of mint or cilantro leaves, chopped

Preheat the oven to 400°F.

Heat the oil in a heavy ovenproof pan and cook the onion until light golden brown.

Push onions to the sides of the pan and add the garlic, chile, and cinnamon to the center of the pan. Cook until fragrant, then mix in with the onions.

Add the honey to the pan and let it caramelize for 1–2 minutes.

Mix the saffron with 1/2 cup hot water and add to the pan along with the vinegar, orange juice, and lime juice.

Stir in the orange segments and season with plenty of salt and pepper.

Place the pan in the oven for 4–5 minutes to cook.

Carefully remove the pan from the oven and mix in the chopped nuts and half of the chopped herbs. Use the remaining herbs for garnish. Serve the orange relish hot or warm alongside the meat.

date and tamarind relish

makes 6–8 jars

The dried fruits make this strong, aromatic relish deliciously rich and complex. There is lots of spice, and you could add more chile if you want. The use of tamarind and vinegar means this relish will be predominately hot, sour, and sweet. This is great alongside curries or roasted meats and it transforms cheese and ham.

4 ounces fresh ginger, grated
4 red chiles (jalapeño or serrano), seeded and finely chopped
1 pound raisins
1 tablespoon coriander seeds
1 tablespoon cumin seeds
1 teaspoon ground cinnamon
1 teaspoon ground nutmeg
1 teaspoon ground cloves
1 pound pitted dates, coarsely chopped
1 pound dried figs, coarsely chopped
8 ounces onions, finely chopped
8 ounces tomatoes, chopped
4 garlic cloves, finely chopped
4 cardamom pods
1 cup packed brown sugar
1 package (8 ounces) tamarind pulp
2 cups malt or cider vinegar
sea salt and freshly ground black pepper

Place the ginger and chile in a food processor along with the raisins, and pulse until you have a thick dark paste.

In a small, dry pan over medium-high heat, toast the coriander seeds, cumin seeds, cardamom pods, and powdered spices until fragrant and aromatic.

Remove from the pan and, using a mortar and pestle or a spice grinder, grind until smooth. Pass through a fine mesh strainer to get rid of any coarse woody pieces.

Place all the remaining ingredients and the ground roasted spices in a large, heavy saucepan with 1 cup water. Cook on low heat for 1–2 hours to make a thick, dark relish. Stir frequently to prevent the sugar from burning. Taste and season well with salt and pepper to create a great blend of flavors.

spicy plum chutney

makes 6–8 jars

I owe much of my love of food and cooking to my mother, Helen Kime, who makes fresh bread every day and always makes her own jams, chutneys, and marmalade. My childhood was full of the great smells of her cooking, particularly her chutney. I cannot better her recipe so this is a variation of one of her best chutneys.

- $3^1/2$ pounds black and red plums
- 1 pound damsons (if not available, then use other plums)
- 8 ounces tomatoes, coarsely chopped
- 1 pound tart cooking apples, peeled, cored and chopped
- 1 pound onions, chopped
- 3 garlic cloves, chopped
- 4 ounces fresh ginger, grated
- 3 red chiles, seeded and finely chopped
- 1 pound seedless raisins
- 2 teaspoons ground cloves
- 2 teaspoons ground allspice
- 2 teaspoons ground cinnamon
- $2^1/2$ cups packed brown sugar
- 2 cups malt or cider vinegar
- 1 tablespoon tamarind pulp
- 2 bay leaves
- salt and freshly ground black pepper

Preheat the oven to 400°F.

Place the plums and damsons (if available) in a high-sided roasting pan in the oven. Bake about 20 minutes to soften.

Working in batches, place the tomatoes, apples, onions, garlic, ginger, chiles, and raisins in a food processor. Pulse until a thick paste forms.

Heat a heavy pan over low heat and add the blended mixture.

Take the plums from the oven and remove all the pits. They may be too hot to handle so you could use a clean pair of heavy rubber gloves, which will insulate your hands against the heat. Work methodically from one end of the tray to the other to ensure that you don't miss any pits.

Add all the plum flesh and juice to the pan along with the dried spices, sugar, vinegar, tamarind pulp, and bay leaves. Season with salt and pepper.

Cook slowly over low heat for at least 2 hours until all the vinegar is absorbed and it is thick and dark. Stir regularly to avoid sticking.

Spoon into warm sterilized jars and cover with lids while still hot to create a vacuum. Store for a couple of months before using to develop the flavors.

light **bites**

light bites

There is no better way to begin a meal or evening out than with delicious bite-sized appetizers. The social ritual of cocktails and light bites marks the end of the working day and takes place in bars and cafés around the world.

The Italians call these light bites *aperitivi,* literally "openers," a term which encompasses not only the food but also the drinks and relaxed conversation that accompany it. The Spanish version is a vast array of tapas that you order at the bar along with your drink, while in the countries of the Middle East, mezze is the cement that binds society together. In Asia you find sushi and sashimi and regional streetfood. This food is not supposed to be a whole meal but rather something that awakens the palate and keeps the proverbial wolf from the door, until you have decided what to eat for dinner. It does not have to be elaborate; a bowl of salted and chili-roasted almonds, a few olives, some warm focaccia bread, or some grilled toast rubbed with garlic and sprinkled with salt and extra virgin olive oil are all good places to start.

There is vast scope for creativity in the balancing of flavors in a single bite. In Italy there are hundreds of ideas for crostini or bruschetta toppings, or for ingredients that work well with olives or anchovies. Often, the drinks form an important part of the whole taste equation, as well as being perfect taste combinations in themselves. There is a spectacular Florentine *aperitivo* drink called a Negroni which has equal measures of Campari, red vermouth, and gin, with a twist of orange and angostura bitters. Bitter, sweet, and sour flavors work together alongside the heat of the alcohol, forming a complex, multi-layered yet seamless blend. All that is needed is a simple accompaniment with a salt and sweet content, such as Romano cheese, some focaccia bread with salt and oil, or a more elaborate one of marinated figs wrapped in prosciutto (see page 57), or crostini with anchovies or black olive paste.

Throughout the world, there are numerous marinades and sauces to go with grilled shrimp or skewers of chicken; in the length and breadth of Southeast Asia there are variations of fillings for crispy spring rolls or the uncooked Vietnamese summer rolls that are refreshing, light, and tasty (see page 62).

Asian cuisine, which holds that flavors should be balanced together in one mouthful, lends itself very well to bite-sized combinations of food. There is no clearer way to describe this effect than with the Thai appetizer called *miang khom* (see page 60), a salad of shrimp with fresh ginger, lime, chile, and a sour caramel. This dish perfectly encapsulates the principle of a balance of tastes and textures in one mouthful and your tongue is taken on a spectacular rollercoaster ride as you clearly experience the four different taste sensations one after the other before they combine to bring your mouth alive. First the sour lime juice, followed by the rich salty-sweet caramel of the sauce whose smooth texture coats the tongue and protects the tastebuds from chile burn. Next you taste the fresh spiciness of the raw chopped ginger, before experiencing the crunch and flavor of the crushed toasted peanuts and coconut. All of these flavors happen almost simultaneously, followed by the slight bitterness of the lime zest, which is different from the fresh sourness of the lime flesh and juice experienced at the beginning of the mouthful. The salty tang of the shrimp paste, *gapi* (found in Asian stores), is enhanced by the other flavors, and the final sensation is the heat from the chile. *Miang khom* is the perfect canapé or appetizer because it revitalizes the palate, preparing it for the rest of the meal. All the flavors are complete in just one amazing mouthful.

SWEET **figs, fava beans, asparagus, sweet potatoes, cucumber, fish, tiger shrimp, roasted coconut, rice vermicelli, heavy cream, palm sugar** SOUR **lemon juice and zest, lemongrass, rice wine vinegar, balsamic vinegar, lime juice** SALTY **Romano, Parmesan, fish sauce, soy sauce** HOT **garlic, galangal, wasabi, arugula, chiles, cilantro, ginger**

crostini with crushed fava beans and manchego

serves 4

Crostini are made from sliced and toasted Italian bread and are usually served with simple toppings as an appetizer. If you have any leftover fava bean mixture, just toast some more ciabatta and keep going!

- 1 garlic clove
- 20 mint leaves, finely chopped
- handful of basil, finely chopped
- 1 pound small raw fava beans, shelled
- juice of 1 lemon
- 2 tablespoons extra virgin olive oil
- salt and freshly ground black pepper
- 4 ounces Manchego cheese, plus extra for garnishing
- 8 thin slices of ciabatta bread
- 1 garlic clove, for rubbing the crostini

In a large mortar and pestle, crush the garlic with a pinch of salt until smooth. Add the mint, basil, and fava beans and crush to form a rough paste. Add the lemon juice and olive oil and season with salt and pepper.

Take the Manchego in one hand, and with a small pointed knife flick out little nuggets or chunks of the cheese (you could grate it, but this method gives more texture). Combine with the bean mixture.

Grill or toast the ciabatta. Cut into small pieces if preferred. Rub one side of the crostini with the garlic clove.

To serve, mound the fava bean mixture onto the crostini. Garnish with some shaved Manchego.

variation

Mix 1 tablespoon crème fraîche with 2 tablespoons olive oil, and some coarsely chopped arugula and mint or basil leaves. Season with salt and pepper. Stir in 2 sliced mozzarella balls. Mound onto garlic-rubbed crostini and serve.

marinated figs with thyme, mint, and mozzarella

serves 4

The sour marinade works beautifully with the sweetness of the figs and the richness of the mozzarella. You can use crumbly goat cheese instead of mozzarella if you prefer, and slices of prosciutto, which you can tear over the figs.

8 ripe figs
1/4 cup balsamic vinegar
2 tablespoons extra virgin olive oil
juice and zest of 1 lemon
salt and freshly ground black pepper
1 tablespoon chopped thyme
20 mint leaves, roughly chopped
20 arugula leaves, torn up
3 (3-inch) balls of buffalo mozzarella, sliced

Trim the figs, then cut each one lengthwise into four slices.

To make the marinade, mix together the balsamic vinegar, olive oil, lemon juice, and salt and pepper.

Arrange the figs in the center of a shallow dish so they overlap. Scatter the thyme and lemon zest over the figs, pour the marinade over them, then let stand for 30 minutes.

When ready to serve, mix half the mint and arugula with the mozzarella in a bowl, and season with salt and pepper.

Arrange the mozzarella mixture around the figs, scatter the remaining mint and arugula over the top, and drizzle with a little extra olive oil.

chef's tips

For a pre-dinner canapé, you could cut the figs into quarters, marinate them, and wrap each piece in a slice of prosciutto.

Place the mozzarella and marinated figs on a piece of crusty bread and broil until the cheese has melted and the toast is crisp, then scatter with arugula. As an alternative, serve as bruschetta.

asparagus and parmesan tart

serves 6–8

This tart is perfect for a summer picnic. It looks amazing because the asparagus is pureed and then cooked, just once, in the oven and so the color of the filling is bright green. Shortly after it is baked, eat warm or cold, as the tart will lose its fabulous color within a couple of hours.

300g Shortcrust Pastry
1 bunch asparagus
2 eggs
4 ounces Parmesan, grated
$1\frac{1}{4}$ cups heavy whipping cream
salt and freshly ground black pepper
1–2 egg yolks (optional)

Roll out the dough to a $\frac{1}{4}$-inch thickness on a lightly floured surface and use it to line a 12-inch metal tart pan with a removable bottom or eight 4-inch tartlet molds. Let rest in the fridge for 30 minutes.

Preheat the oven to 350°F.

Line the pan with parchment paper or foil and fill with dried beans. Bake for 10–12 minutes until pale golden brown and crisp all over.

Meanwhile, prepare the filling: cut the top 3 inches from the asparagus and set it aside.

Cut the remaining asparagus stems into small chunks, discarding the tough root ends. Place the chunks in a food processor. Pulse until a smooth green pulp has formed.

Add the eggs to the food processor and process to blend. Add the Parmesan and cream and season with salt and lots of black pepper. Pulse the mixture until it is smooth and pale green. Do not overwork.

When the edges of the pie shell are golden brown, remove the paper and beans and check that there are no cracks or holes in the crust. If there are any, beat some egg yolk and paint it into the cracks with a pastry brush. Return to the oven for 2 minutes to set the egg and plug the cracks.

Pour the creamy asparagus mixture into the pie shell. Arrange the asparagus tips on top, pointing them outwards in a clock pattern. Place gently in the oven.

Bake for 20–25 minutes until set. To check that it is set, tap the edge of the pan. If it wobbles, it needs more time.

When done, remove from the oven and let cool on a wire rack for 20 minutes or until the tart has cooled enough to hold together, before removing from the pan.

miang khom (salad of shrimp with ginger, lime, and chile)

serves 4

This has all the characteristics of authentic Thai cuisine. It is absolutely delicious and quite complex, so it works well as a bite-sized taste explosion. Shredded coconut and gapi shrimp paste are available in Asian food stores.

1/2 pound raw tiger shrimp, peeled and deveined
salt and freshly ground black pepper
1 lime, peeled and cut into small pieces
2 red chiles (jalepeño or serrano), seeded and finely chopped
1 1/4-inch piece of fresh ginger, peeled and finely chopped
4 small shallots, finely chopped
2 tablespoons raw peanuts, dry-roasted until golden brown, then coarsely ground in a mortar and pestle
2 tablespoons toasted shredded coconut
1 stalk of lemongrass, tough outer leaves removed, finely sliced
8 betel leaves (baby spinach or Bibb lettuce leaves will do)

for the miang sauce
1 tablespoon grated galangal or fresh ginger
1 teaspoon shrimp paste
2 tablespoons toasted coconut
3 tablespoons Asian fish sauce
2 tablespoons palm or brown sugar
juice of 1 lime

Preheat the oven to 400°F. Put the shrimp on a baking sheet, season with salt and pepper, and bake for about 5 minutes. Set aside.

To make the sauce, place the grated galangal or ginger, and shrimp paste in a hot pan and dry-fry until aromatic and golden.

Transfer the mixture to a mortar and pestle, add the toasted coconut, and pound until smooth. Return to the pan with the fish sauce, palm sugar, and 6 tablespoons water. Simmer for 10 minutes to reduce the sauce by half.

Strain the sauce and let it cool. Add the lime juice. The sauce should be sweet, sour, and salty: the heat will come from the fresh chile.

Chop up the shrimp if they are large. Mix together with all the other main ingredients and toss them in 1/2 cup of the sauce.

Arrange the betel leaves on 4 serving plates and spoon the shrimp mixture on top. Alternatively, fold the heart-shaped betel leaves in half along their spine, and then fold across at the widest part of the "heart." By overlapping the two sides of the base and gently placing a teaspoon of mixture in the leaf you can make it stable enough to stand up as shown in the picture opposite.

vietnamese summer rolls

serves 6–8

These very refreshing rolls are usually eaten raw. They can be made with any filling or deep-fried, if preferred. To make canapés, just make the rolls smaller.

4 ounces fine rice vermicelli noodles (thin rice noodles)
10 raw tiger shrimp, peeled and deveined
salt and freshly ground black pepper
juice of 1 lime
2 tablespoons Asian fish sauce
2 tablespoons soy sauce
2 scallions, thinly sliced
1/2 English cucumber, grated
3/4-inch piece of fresh ginger, peeled and grated
10 mint leaves, chopped
10 cilantro leaves, chopped

2–3 rice paper wrappers per person

Preheat the oven to 400°F.

Place the vermicelli in a heatproof bowl and cover with boiling water. Leave until white and soft – about 5 minutes. Drain and refresh in cold water. Use scissors to cut into smaller pieces, about an inch long.

To cook the shrimp, place on a baking sheet, season with salt and pepper, and bake for about 5 minutes. Slice thinly and add to the vermicelli along with the lime juice, fish sauce, soy sauce, scallions, cucumber, ginger, mint, and cilantro. Season with salt and pepper. Toss gently to mix.

Soak the rice paper wrappers in warm water (about 5 at a time). After 30–60 seconds the wrappers will soften, resembling wet cloth.

Place a clean, damp, lint-free towel on a work surface. Lay 4 or 5 soaked wrappers on the towel.

Place 1 tablespoon of mixture in the center of each wrapper, about an inch from the bottom edge, leaving a border of 1 to 2 inches on either side of the mixture. Fold each side of the wrapper into the center. Fold the bottom edge over the top of the covered mixture like an envelope. Pressing firmly, roll into a cigar shape.

Place on a tray covered with another damp clean towel.

Repeat the process until all the mixture has been used. Serve raw or, alternatively, deep-fry until golden brown. Serve with an Asian-style dipping sauce (see facing page).

fishcakes on stalks of lemongrass

serves 4

The lemongrass perfumes the whole fishcake, and you have to taste it to appreciate just how delectable this is. These are great as an appetizer or as part of a larger meal. For variation, use pork or chicken instead of fish.

for the fishcakes

20 mint leaves, finely chopped
30 cilantro leaves, finely chopped
salt and freshly ground black pepper
1 red chile (jalepeño or serrano), seeded and thinly chopped
3 scallions, thinly sliced
1-inch piece peeled and grated fresh ginger
1 pound firm, white-fleshed boneless, skinless fish, such as cod, pollock, snapper, hake or sea bream

vegetable oil, for deep-frying
6 stalks of lemongrass, cut in half lengthwise (leave the hard heart on the stems so the strands of the grass stay together)

for the dipping sauce

2 tablespoons Asian fish sauce
2 tablespoons lime juice
1 scallion, thinly sliced
1/2 red chile (jalepeño or serrano), seeded and finely chopped
1 teaspoon sugar
a few cilantro leaves

Place all the aromatic ingredients for the fishcakes in a food processor or a mortar and pestle until a paste forms. Mix together with the fish.

Before deep-frying the fishcakes, you need to check the seasoning. Heat a little oil in a frying pan, take a small nugget of the mixture, flatten it between your fingers, and cook it quickly in the pan. Taste and adjust the seasoning accordingly.

Fill a pan or wok about one-third full with oil and heat to 365°F.

Rub a little cold vegetable oil on your hands so the fish mixture will not stick to them. Work a ball the size of a small egg in your hands and form it into a cylinder. Press a stalk of lemongrass through the center and press the fish mixture firmly around the stalk. Repeat with the remaining mixture, one fishcake per stalk. Arrange on a lightly oiled baking sheet or plate so they do not stick to each other.

To test the oil for deep-frying, drop a little of the mixture into the hot oil. It should sizzle and give off bubbles right away. If it does not, wait until the oil is hotter.

Deep-fry a few of the fishcakes until golden brown. Work in small batches, otherwise the pan will be overloaded and will not maintain the proper temperature. Drain on paper towels to soak up excess oil before serving.

Mix all the dipping ingredients together in a small bowl and serve alongside the fishcake skewers.

rolled sushi

serves 4–6

Hoso-maki are thin rolls with one ingredient inside. Futo-maki are thick rolls with several ingredients inside such as crab and avocado or tuna and scallions to add different flavors, colors, and textures. You can make completely vegetarian sushi, filled with raw or blanched vegetables and fresh herb leaves.

hoso-maki (thin rolls)

1–2 tablespoons unseasoned rice vinegar
4–5 nori (seaweed) sheets
1 x recipe sushi rice (see page 66)
wasabi
1 tuna fillet (5–6 ounces) skinned and cut into pencil-thin lengths (salmon, crab meat, or avocado could also be used)
small handful of toasted sesame seeds

for serving
dark soy sauce
wasabi
pickled ginger

Mix the vinegar with 1 cup water in a bowl and set aside.

Fold a sheet of nori in half against the grain. Pinch along the folded edge and break it neatly in two equal pieces.

Lay a sushi mat on your counter. If you do not have one, improvise with a triple-thick square of plastic wrap. Place a sheet of nori on the mat, at the edge, with the shiny side facing down.

Dip your hands in the vinegared water to prevent the rice from sticking to them. Take a handful of rice and form into a log shape. Place the rice in the center of the nori, using your fingertips to spread it out evenly. Dab a little wasabi down the center of the rice, then lay down a strip of tuna.

Take the edge of the mat nearest to you. Lift up and roll away from you, applying even pressure. Roll until you are at the far edge and there is a thin strip of nori that is still exposed.

Gently shape the roll with your fingers to make it even. Lift the edge of the mat and push the roll slightly forward, so the uncovered strip of nori seals it. The moisture from the rice will work as an adhesive.

Store in a cool place (but not in the fridge or it will become soggy) while you assemble the remaining rolls.

When ready to serve, cut the rolls into even-sized pieces. Dip the ends of some of the pieces in the sesame seeds. Serve with a little bowl of soy sauce, a dab of wasabi, and some pickled ginger for each person.

to make futo-maki (thick rolls)

Use the same principles as for hoso-maki but with a whole sheet of nori, more rice, and a combination of fillings.

to make temaki-sushi (hand-rolled sushi)

Cut a small rectangle of nori. Place a tablespoon of rice in the top left-hand corner. Hold the nori and rice in your left hand and lay the fillings on top. Dab with wasabi. Roll into a cone shape, keeping a tight even pressure on the roll with your fingertips. Seal as before.

wasabi is green Japanese horseradish, available in tubes or in powdered form like English mustard. Wasabi should not be used solely to prove one's bravery; it is very pungent! It merely enhances the flavor of the sushi.

gari is pickled ginger, usually served on the corner of the sushi plate. It should be eaten a slice at a time to cleanse the palate, and to aid digestion.

nori is Japanese seaweed that is dry-toasted and sold in sheets. It is used for wrapping the sushi.

sushi rice

Japanese short-grain rice is used for sushi. The quality of the sushi depends upon the rice.

10 ounces (about 1 1/2 cups) Japanese short-grain rice
1/4 cup unseasoned rice vinegar
2 tablespoons sugar
1/2 teaspoon salt

Place the rice in a fine sieve and submerge in a large bowl of water; rinse, and then discard the milky water. Keep rinsing and changing the water until it runs clear. Drain the rice and leave it in the sieve for 30 minutes.

Put the rice and 1 1/2 cups water in a heavy pan. Cover with a lid. Bring to a boil over medium heat. Avoid the temptation to lift the lid; listen to the sound of the water instead.

When the water starts to boil, turn up the heat and cook for 5 minutes. Reduce the heat to low, and simmer for another 10 minutes. Remove the pan from the heat and let it stand, covered, for 10 minutes.

Heat the vinegar in a saucepan, and dissolve the sugar and salt in it. Do not let it boil. Remove from the heat and set aside to cool.

Transfer the rice to a bowl. Gently add a little of the vinegar mixture by drizzling it over the back of a wooden spatula.

Spread the rice out in the bowl, slowly incorporate a little more of the vinegar mixture, using a slicing action with the spatula. This coats the grains of rice and separates them.

The rice will begin to look glossy. Let it cool to room temperature before using.

preparing fish

When buying fresh fish, check the following:
The eyes – should be clear, bright, and plump, not dull and sunken
The gills – should be clean, bright, and bloody, not brown, gray, or bruised
The body – should be firm to the touch, not flaccid and sagging or spongy
The smell – should be clean and fresh like the sea, not unpleasant

Make full use of the person at your fish counter. If the specific fish you want is not available, don't be afraid to try an alternative. Instead of cod, try pollock or hake, which also break into large, firm flakes. Ocean perch, gilthead bream, and the bream family make good substitutes for snapper as they can also be cooked whole on the bone. Monkfish (angler fish) can be used in a similar way to large, deep-water meaty fish such as halibut and sole. Sea bass has rich sweet meat which is highly protected by hidden spikes and thorny spines on its back. Other, equally tasty, fish with similar protection include John Dory, hake surf bass and striped bass.

Fish that are good for sushi include tuna, salmon, mackerel, John Dory, sea bass, red snapper, sea bream (porgy), halibut, and sole.

curing fish

Curing fish with something acidic, like lemon, lime, or orange juice, wine or alcohol, is very different from salting it (see page 87). The latter firms the texture while curing tenderizes it with a marinade of subtle flavors that effectively "cooks" the flesh. Oysters, for example, are traditionally served with a little lemon or shallot vinegar and, after a while, are pickled in these juices. This method of pickling with vinegars and citrus fruits is especially popular in tropical countries as it eases the digestion of rich and fatty foods during the long, hot summers.

In South America, seviche is a fabulously simple start to any meal and incorporates cilantro leaves, lime juice, and fresh green chile. These three key regional ingredients plus salt and scallions are used to cure strips of firm, white-fleshed fish or shellfish, such as shrimp, crayfish, and lobster. My variation on this recipe (see page 71) includes the segments and juice of a pink grapefruit to add a depth of flavor.

Also included in this chapter is a recipe for a spectacular Thai dish called *sang wa* (see facing page) which is like a royal Thai version of seviche. It can be served as an entrée or small salad. Thin strips of salmon are cured in a mixture of orange zest and orange and lime juice with salt, sugar, chopped red chile, and crushed garlic. Shreds of ginger, lemongrass, and lime leaves are also added, and the result is an intensely aromatic and refreshing balance of tastes. It takes about 10 minutes to prepare all the ingredients and about 4 minutes to cure the fish. This dish works well with a crisp, dry champagne or a perfumed white wine such as a chilled Viognier or Tokay Pinot Gris and is therefore a great party entrée.

Delicate fresh fish and shellfish suffer in the heat, and so tropical regions like Southeast Asia generally preserve them by salting. Fishermen salt their catch and then spread it out in the hot sun to dry. From Singapore to northern Vietnam you find different varieties of dried fish, shrimp, prawns, and squid graded by quality, size, and color, brightening rows and rows of colorful market stalls.

Dried fish has hundreds of different uses. In Thailand, dried prawns and shrimp are used in scores of dishes with many regional variations across Southeast Asia. They can also be snacked on, just like a bag of nuts or chips. In Vietnam, pork and dried squid is a popular combination in soups and stews. The dried squid is grilled to give it a strong smoky taste, almost like bacon. It is also eaten as a high-protein snack rather like beef jerky or biltong. In Japan, dried bonito fish flakes are a cooking staple. They can be used as a base for stock (dashi) or sprinkled over dishes as a garnish.

sang wa of salmon on grilled sweet potato

serves 8

I learned this recipe when I worked with David Thompson at Darley Street Thai in Sydney. He had a huge influence on the way I cook, introducing me to the idea of balancing tastes.

2 sweet potatoes, peeled and sliced
1 tablespoon vegetable oil
salt and freshly ground black pepper

for the marinade

1 garlic clove
1 red chile (jalepeño or serrano), seeded
1/2 teaspoon each salt and sugar
3 tablespoons orange juice
3 tablespoons lime juice
1 stalk of lemongrass
3 lime leaves
1 pound skinless salmon fillet
1 1/4-inch peeled ginger, grated
2 scallions, finely sliced
1/2 red chile (jalepeño or serrano), finely chopped
3 sticks wild ginger, peeled and grated
20 cilantro leaves, finely shredded

Place the sweet potato in a bowl with the oil and some salt and pepper. Toss gently to coat. Grill on a hot grill pan or in a skillet for 1–2 minutes on each side.

To make the marinade, pound the garlic, chile, and salt and sugar in a mortar and pestle until a smooth paste is formed. Add the orange juice and lime juice.

Remove the outer leaves of the lemongrass, and finely slice the center. De-stem the lime leaves, roll tightly together, and slice into thin strips.

Slice the salmon finely.

Ten minutes before serving, pour the marinade over the salmon. Season with salt and pepper. Mix in all the remaining ingredients except the fresh cilantro leaves.

Just before serving, arrange the grilled sweet potato on a serving dish. Mound some seviche on top of each slice and scatter some cilantro over the top.

seviche of salmon with avocado, green chile, and pink grapefruit

serves 4–6

1 pound salmon fillet
2 pink grapefruits
3 limes
2 tablespoons olive oil
2 ripe avocados, thinly sliced
salt and freshly ground black pepper
2 green chiles, seeded and finely chopped
3 scallions, finely chopped
2 handfuls of arugula (optional)
small handful of cilantro leaves, roughly chopped

Remove all skin, bones, and any gray flesh from the underside of the salmon. Remove any brown colored flesh from the rest of the salmon. (It does not look good and can taste bitter.) Cut into thin slices.

Holding the grapefruit over a bowl to catch the juice, cut down on both sides of the membranes to release the grapefruit segments. (Be sure the fruit has no white pith attached, as it is bitter and unpleasant.) Squeeze the membranes over a bowl to release as much juice as possible.

Segment two of the limes in the same way as the grapefruit. Mix their juice with that of the third lime and add to the grapefruit juice with the olive oil and set aside.

Mix the avocado with the grapefruit and lime segments. Season well with salt and pepper.

Season the salmon with salt and pepper and place in a bowl. Pour in the juice mixture and add the chiles and scallions.

Coat both sides of the salmon with the marinade before leaving it to soak for about 5 minutes, or until it starts to go pale and the texture softens.

When the salmon has turned pale, add the avocado and citrus fruit segments to the bowl, along with the arugula and cilantro. Toss gently to mix so you do not break up the avocado or salmon. Check the seasoning. Serve with toasted pita bread or ciabatta.

vietnamese crispy pork spring rolls

serves 4

Vietnamese spring rolls are delicate in size—about 1 1/4 inches wide and 2 1/2 to 3 1/2 inches long. You can make different fillings with other kinds of meat or vegetables.

for the filling

2 1/2 ounces dried shiitake mushrooms
4 ounces fine rice vermicelli noodles (thin rice noodles)
8 ounces ground pork
4 scallions, finely chopped
1 small onion, finely chopped
2 eggs
2 tablespoons Asian fish sauce
1/2 teaspoon salt
20 mint leaves, plus extra for serving
20 cilantro leaves, plus extra for wrapping
freshly ground black pepper

rice paper wrappers (allow 4 per person)
vegetable oil, for deep frying

for the dipping sauce

2 tablespoons Asian fish sauce
2 tablespoons rice wine vinegar
1 red chile (jalepeño or serrano), seeded and finely chopped
1 teaspoon sugar

Soak the mushrooms in boiling water for 10 minutes. Drain, finely chop, and place in a bowl.

Place the vermicelli in a bowl and cover with boiling water. Let sit until white and soft—about 5 minutes. Drain, remove two thirds of the noodles, and chop into 1/2-inch lengths. Combine these with the unchopped noodles and mushrooms.

Add all the remaining filling ingredients and toss gently to mix.

Soak a rice paper wrapper in warm water for 30–60 seconds to soften. Lay it on a clean, damp, lint-free towel. Repeat with two other wrappers; you can work on three wrappers at a time.

Place 1 tablespoon of filling on the wrapper, an inch from the edge nearest to you. Fold in the two sides and roll away from you, tightly, like a cigar.

Repeat with the other two wrappers on the towel. The dampness of the wrappers will be enough to seal them closed. If they have dried too much then splash a little water on the dry patches. Place your rolls on a lightly oiled plate.

Place a wok or high-sided, heavy pot over medium heat for 2 minutes. Fill one third of the pot with vegetable oil (when cool, oil can be strained and used again for deep-frying) and heat to 365°F.

To test if the oil is hot enough for deep-frying, carefully add one spring roll. It should sizzle and give off bubbles right away. If it does not, remove and try again in a few minutes.

When the oil is hot, reduce the heat to medium–low and maintain a constant temperature.

Fry the spring rolls in small batches so that the oil remains hot. Carefully move them around and turn them over in the oil so they become golden brown all over—about 5 minutes.

Place the rolls on paper towels to absorb any excess oil. Let the oil reheat for a minute before cooking the next batch.

Mix together the ingredients for the dipping sauce. Put the sauce in the center of the table with the extra mint and cilantro leaves. To eat, take a hot spring roll, wrap a couple of leaves around it, and dip into the sauce.

bun cha (marinated spicy pork)

serves 4 – 6

These grilled strips of pork with garlic, chile and ginger are cooked at *bun cha* stalls in Hanoi, northern Vietnam. They are cooked over very hot coals and fanned so the fat from the pork drips and sizzles onto the coals, creating aromatic smoke. First you smell the smoke and then you find the *bun cha* stall!

1 pound pork tenderloin
2 garlic cloves
1 1/2 ounces fresh ginger, peeled
1 red chile (jalepeño or serrano), seeded
salt and freshly ground black pepper
2 limes (1 juiced; 1 cut into wedges)

Cut the pork into thin strips.

Finely chop the garlic, ginger, and chile (this can be done in a food processor).

Marinate the pork with salt and pepper, lime juice, and the finely chopped spice paste. Marinate for at least 20 minutes or up to 4 hours in the fridge.

Preheat an outdoor grill, grill pan, or broiler pan until smoking hot. Quickly grill the pork strips, turning once, until done. Serve with lime wedges.

chef's tip

This is simple but absolutely fantastic as a snack or part of a large meal. You could thread the pork on bamboo skewers. Try using chicken, beef, or fish cut in the same way.

salads

salads can be anything that you want to make them. Bright colors combine with contrasting textures and tastes—crunchy, crispy, caramelized, peppery, spiced, slow-roasted, warm, shaved, crumbly—and the possibilities are endless for both quick snacks and elaborate entertaining.

For me, a salad is so much more than a few iceberg lettuce leaves with some sliced cucumber and tomato and so I use the term "salad" here in its broadest sense, preferring not to rule anything out. Anything can be included, from leftover cuts of meat and cold or warmed vegetables from Sunday dinner, to prime fillets of fish and meaty lobster tails or beef sirloin. Salads are an especially good showcase for seasonal fruit and vegetables, which I often combine with cheese or seafood to get the balance between sweet and salty, as in spiced pear and goat cheese salad (page 81) or roasted shrimp and watermelon salad with green chile and roasted peanuts (page 93).

Color and texture are important components of every salad as food is always more appealing when it stimulates the eye as well as the stomach. Vary and contrast ingredients such as crunchy raw vegetables, roasted nuts, crispy fried pancetta, and the melting softness of ricotta or goat cheese. Use the vibrant colors of roasted beets, butternut squash, fresh green peas, red and yellow peppers, and pomegranate seeds—and don't be afraid to experiment.

Taste each ingredient in isolation as you go along. The saltiness of different batches of bacon and cheese can vary and the fruit may be riper than the last time you used it. If the arugula is not very peppery, then add a little extra black pepper or some freshly chopped red chile. A combination of arugula and good quality olive oil that is grassy and peppery can also really make the flavors jump. Equally, adding Parmesan or another hard, slightly salty cheese like Spenwood or Manchego will provide the saltiness necessary to bring out all the nascent flavors. Different methods of cooking also dramatically affect flavors of ingredients. Slow cooking generally makes fruit and vegetables sweeter, as you break down the natural sugars to caramelize onions, cabbage, and beets. Similarly, a tomato sauce that is cooked very slowly will be much sweeter and richer than if it was done in a rush.

In most salads, the identity of each individual ingredient is clear and simple and therefore it is important that the quality is the very best. There is no point trying to make a Tuscan summer salad, in which the tomatoes should evoke the juicy ripeness of the Mediterranean sun, with orange-white winter specimens that are sour and hard. Seasonality is the key because there will be no need for you to mask the flaws; the ingredients can speak for themselves.

Take a tomato and mozzarella salad as an example. This dish is made in restaurants all over the world, but those that place emphasis on the provenance and quality of each ingredient will get far superior results—fresh buffalo mozzarella; sweet, sun-ripened organic tomatoes; a top-quality extra virgin olive oil; balsamic vinegar that has been aged for at least five years, and black pepper freshly ground in a stone mortar and pestle. The black pepper and olive oil provide the heat, the tomatoes and mozzarella are sweet with a hint of acidity, and the balsamic vinegar is slightly sour with a deep underlying sweetness. Sea salt provides a raw crunch and the salad is perfect with a piece of toasted sourdough bruschetta rubbed with garlic. With a few quality ingredients you have the perfect combination of flavors and textures—and the taste is truly unforgettable.

SWEET **honey, pears, orange juice, red peppers, butternut squash, basil, beets, squid, watermelon, pine nuts**
SOUR **goat cheese, crème fraîche, gooseberries, pomelo, grapefruit** SALTY **Manchego cheese, soy sauce, chorizo**
HOT **chile, extra virgin olive oil, black pepper, watercress** BITTER **Belgian endive, baby spinach, radicchio, Treviso**

A TASTE OF EGYPT
A TASTE OF EGYPT

grilled mushroom salad with shaved parmesan

serves 4–6

8 large wild mushrooms
4 tablespoons olive oil
salt and freshly ground black pepper
2 sprigs of thyme, leaves finely chopped
2 garlic cloves, finely chopped
1 tablespoon balsamic vinegar
juice and zest of 1 lemon
handful of mixed peppery leaves, such as arugula, watercress, baby chard, mustard leaves
20 basil leaves
20 mint leaves
2 ounces Parmesan, shaved

Preheat the oven to 400°F and preheat a grill pan or skillet.

Remove and discard the stems but keep the mushrooms whole. Put them in a bowl. Pour in 2 tablespoons olive oil and season with salt and pepper. Mix together.

Grill the mushrooms in the preheated pan for 3 minutes on each side. Transfer to a roasting pan, add the thyme and garlic, and roast in the oven for 5 minutes.

When cooked, coarsely chop the mushrooms and transfer to a bowl. Pour in the remaining olive oil, the balsamic vinegar, and the lemon juice and zest.

Coarsely chop the mixed leaves, basil, and mint. Shave the Parmesan into slivers with a vegetable peeler. Toss gently to mix, and check the seasoning.

salad of roast butternut squash and goat cheese

serves 4–6

2 small butternut squash
oil, salt, and pepper, for cooking
1/2 cup blanched slivered almonds
5 ounces crumbly goat cheese, broken into small pieces
20 mint leaves, roughly chopped
20 basil leaves, roughly chopped
handful of mixed peppery leaves, such as mustard leaves, arugula, watercress, and chicory, torn up
4 scallions, finely chopped

for the dressing

zest and juice of 1 lemon
2 tablespoons balsamic vinegar
3 tablespoons extra virgin olive oil

Preheat the oven to 400°F.

Peel the butternut squash and remove all the seeds. Cut the flesh into roughly equal-sized 1 1/2 x 3/4-inch pieces. Spread out on a baking sheet and mix with a little oil, salt, and pepper. Roast in the oven until caramelized and golden—about 45 minutes. Let cool.

Dry-roast the almonds on a baking sheet in the oven for 3–4 minutes, until golden brown.

Mix the ingredients for the dressing.

Gently toss together the squash and goat cheese without breaking them up. Mix in the herbs and almonds, saving some for the garnish. Add the mixed leaves and scallions, pour in the dressing, and gently toss together.

When ready to serve, garnish the salad with the remaining chopped herbs and roasted almonds.

yam som tam (hot and sour green mango salad)

serves 6

This is a deliciously fresh salad that has variations all over Southeast Asia. It also makes a great accompaniment to pork and many other dishes. You see vendors pounding the ingredients for this taste sensation in street stalls, in markets, and on beaches from Hanoi to Singapore. I had this version at the night market in Trang in southern Thailand. The tiny old lady who offered me a seat at her stall held one of the most popular stalls in the market, and I watched a line of hungry shoppers wait expectantly for their salads.

2 unripe (green) mangoes (or 1 unripe mango and 1 unripe papaya)
2 tablespoons raw, skinless peanuts
2 small fresh red or green chiles, or to taste
2 garlic cloves
6 cherry tomatoes (the less ripe, the better), quartered
2 shallots, thinly sliced
pinch of salt
1/2 teaspoon sugar
1 1/4-inch piece of palm sugar (see chef's tip)
2 tablespoons small dried shrimp (optional)
juice of 2 limes
1 tablespoon Asian fish sauce
20 cilantro leaves

Peel the mango, and papaya if using, and discard the skin. With the peeler, continue to peel the flesh into thin strips. Continue to work all the way down to the pit. Stack the slices into piles of about 5 or 6 pieces. With a sharp knife, cut the stacks crosswise into thin matchsticks, and arrange in a serving dish.

Preheat the oven to 350°F. Place the peanuts in a roasting pan and bake for about 3–4 minutes until pale golden. Don't let them get too dark or they will taste bitter.

Place the whole chiles, garlic, tomatoes, shallots, salt, and sugars in a mortar and pestle. Pound until you have a smooth paste. Add the dried shrimp, if using, and continue to pound. Add the lime juice, fish sauce, and roasted peanuts. Pound until broken up, so you will get bits of nuts in every mouthful. Tear in the cilantro leaves.

Check the seasoning. It should be hot from the chile and sour from the lime juice and the unripe fruit. The fish sauce provides the salt while the sweetness from the palm sugar removes some of the power of the chile. Adjust the flavorings to suit your palate.

Pour the dressing over the mango and serve.

chef's tips

Palm sugar is made from the sap of the coconut palm and tastes like nutty fudge. It can come soft (in tubs) or hard (in logs), dark or light. If unavailable, use soft brown sugar.

Adjust the chile content to suit your taste. To make the salad less hot you could cut the chiles in half and remove the seeds with the point of a knife. To make the salad more substantial, you could add some fresh cooked shrimp at the end.

spiced pear and goat cheese salad

serves 6 as a starter

This salad is simple to assemble and is fantastically effective at the start of a special meal. The complex and three-dimensional nature comes from all the flavors that are put together in balance. You can experiment with other possibilities by adding strips of bacon. The pears can be served warm or cold, but not so hot that they melt the cheese.

for the spiced pears

4–5 firm but ripe pears, peeled, cored, and quartered
splash of olive oil
salt and freshly ground black pepper
1 teaspoon ground cinnamon
1/2 teaspoon coarsely ground coriander seeds
1/2 teaspoon apple pie spice
juice of 1 orange
2 tablespoons red wine vinegar

3 tablespoons extra virgin olive oil
juice of 1 lemon
1 bunch arugula and/or watercress leaves
2 ounces Parmesan, shaved
11 ounces goat cheese, crumbled
30 flat parsley leaves, coarsely chopped
2/3 cup pine nuts, toasted until pale golden-brown

Preheat a grill pan or skillet and preheat the oven to 400°F.

Mix the pears in a bowl with the oil, salt, pepper, and dried spices.

When the grill is hot, grill the pears for 1 1/2 minutes on each side until they are beginning to caramelize. Remove from the pan and place in a small roasting pan. Pour the orange juice and red wine vinegar over them, and roast in the oven for 8 minutes. Transfer the pears to a large bowl and let cool.

Mix the extra virgin olive oil and lemon juice into the pear juices in the roasting pan to make a dressing. Season to taste (remember the cheese is salty).

Mix the leaves with the pears. Add the slivers of Parmesan, along with some of the crumbled goat cheese and the parsley. Pour in the dressing and toss gently to mix.

Serve on a large plate and scatter the toasted pine nuts, remaining goat cheese, and Parmesan over the top.

artichoke and salted lemon salad with honey, thyme, and roasted almonds

serves 4

This fantastic salad (see picture on page 83) is a variation of a staple from London's River Cafe and is one of my favorites. It is commonly made in Sicily and Sardinia and uses honey to counter the sharp flavor of salted lemons. The nuts give a much-needed crunch to the other textures. Serve with cured meats, smoked or cured fish, or a fresh goat cheese (all of which have saltiness to them). For this recipe you can use raw artichokes and cook them fresh or, to save time, you can use pre-cooked artichokes from a can.

8 medium artichokes
1 cup (4 ounces) blanched slivered almonds or pine nuts
large handful of arugula
8–12 slices bresaola or gravadlax (see page 87)

for the dressing

1 tablespoon finely chopped thyme leaves
juice of 1 lemon
2 tablespoons honey
1 tablespoon red wine vinegar
1/4 cup peppery extra virgin olive oil
1 x recipe preserved lemons (see page 27), rind finely chopped
salt and freshly ground black pepper

If using fresh artichokes, bring a large pot of salted water to a boil and cook until soft when pierced with the tip of a sharp knife. When cool enough to handle, remove the tough outer leaves and cut the top off the artichokes. Cut in half and remove the inner choke with a small spoon. If using canned artichoke hearts or bottoms, wash off all the liquid they were packed in. Cut into quarters, depending upon the size.

Toast the nuts in a hot oven or dry skillet until they are golden brown in color. Set aside.

Mix all the dressing ingredients together.

Stir the artichokes in the dressing. Taste and check the seasoning. If it is too salty, add some more fresh lemon juice. This part of the dish will benefit from being made up to 3 hours in advance to blend flavors.

When ready to serve, tear the arugula and bresaola into the salad and add the roasted nuts.

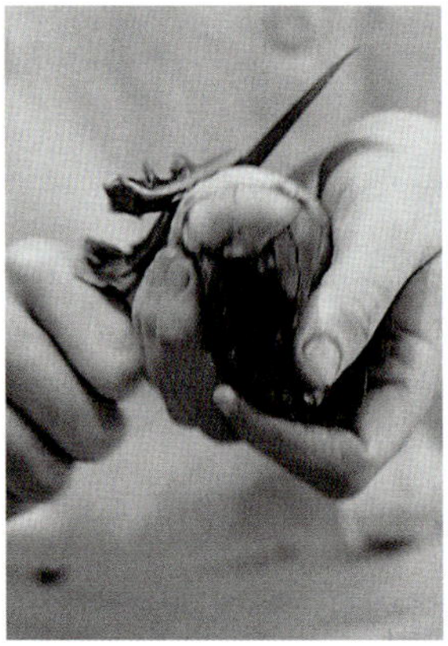
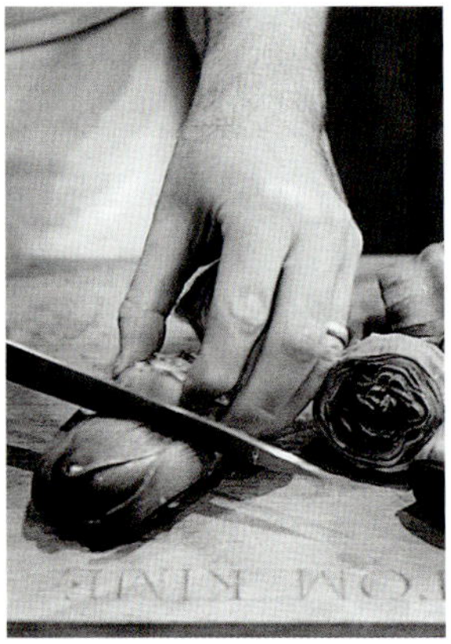
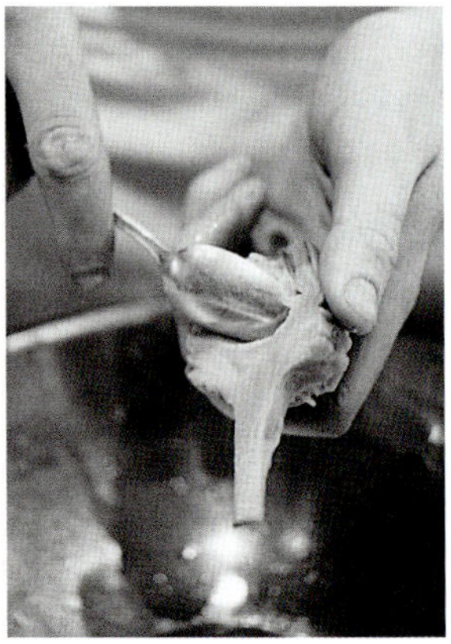

peppery leaf salad with almonds, pomegranates, and goat cheese

serves 4

If some sweet ripe figs are available, they can also be torn into this salad.

for the dressing

juice and zest of 1 lemon
3 tablespoons balsamic vinegar
3 tablespoons olive oil
salt and freshly ground black pepper

1/2 cup (2 ounces) blanched slivered almonds, pine nuts, or a combination of chestnuts and other nuts
4 Savoy cabbage leaves, from the mid-color range
10–12 ounces mixed bitter, peppery leaves (such as sorrel, watercress, arugula, baby spinach, mustard leaves, young Treviso, radicchio, or Belgian endive)
2 pomegranates (or 1 cup pomegranate seeds)
7 ounces crumbly goat cheese, broken into small pieces
2 ounces Parmesan, shaved
15–20 mint leaves, coarsely chopped
small handful of basil, coarsely chopped

Mix the ingredients for the dressing and season to taste (not too much salt because the two cheeses have a high salt content).

Toast the almonds in a hot oven or dry skillet until golden brown. If using chestnuts, peel by scoring them and blanching in boiling water; then roast until golden brown.

Remove and discard the center stem from the cabbage leaves. Roll up the leaves, cut crosswise into thin strips, finely shred, and put in a large serving bowl along with the salad leaves.

Seed the pomegranate, discarding the skin and white connecting pith.

Mix the goat cheese into the salad and scatter the pomegranate seeds and roasted nuts on top. Finish with the Parmesan shavings, mint, and basil.

gravadlax

Gravadlax is a Scandinavian preparation of salmon and is another example of how fish can be cured and subtly flavored at the same time. It is usually made with oily fish like fresh sea trout, salmon, or herring, though it can also be made successfully with firm, white-fleshed fish such as sea bass or grouper, sea bream (porgy), or snapper. Like many traditional recipes that have been made for generations across large geographical regions, there are many variations. Fennel seeds, juniper berries, and other wild herbs are often used, or just lots of fresh dill. You can also puree two raw beets into the salt mixture, which dyes parts of the fish a vibrant color and makes a great party dish. In my recipe I use a combination of fennel seeds and star anise to impart an intense anise flavor. This works well with the fresh chopped dill, which is pressed into the flesh when it is ready to serve. I also use a bit of lemon, to help with the cure.

The fish is salted for 6–12 hours, depending upon the thickness of the fillet. The salt must be coarse and granular like kosher salt, since if it is too fine the liquid will dissolve the crystals and the fish will absorb too much salt too quickly. Making gravadlax requires a little forward planning, but it is not complicated and never fails to impress!

salting mix to cure one side of salmon or two sides of sea bass

6 juniper berries
6 whole star anise
2 tablespoons fennel seeds
1 teaspoon whole black peppercorns
1 pound coarse kosher or sea salt
2 tablespoons granulated sugar
1/2 lemon, cut into chunks

to finish

freshly ground black pepper
zest of 1 lemon
handful of freshly chopped dill

- The side of salmon should first be cleaned, scaled, and all pinbones removed (ask the fishmonger to do this for you).
- Place the juniper berries, star anise, fennel seeds, and peppercorns in a food processor with 1 tablespoon of the coarse salt. Pulse the mixture to break up the spices.
- Add the rest of the salt, sugar, and lemon. Process, pulsing the machine on and off, for about 1 minute, until the lemon is broken up and you have a well mixed, coarse-textured mixture.
- Cut the fish into 2–3 pieces, roughly the same size and thickness. It is important that all the fish salts at the same time so, if your fish fillet is particularly thick, cut the pieces in half horizontally to make thinner slices. (Smaller pieces are preferable because you can use a piece as and when you need it, and keep the rest in the freezer.)
- Scatter a layer of the salt and spice mixture at least 1/2-inch thick into a high-sided container (plastic is fine) that can fit into the fridge.
- Place the pieces of fish side by side on the salt. Scatter another 1/2-inch layer of the salt mixture over the fish and repeat the layering until all the salt is used up and the fish is covered.
- Cover with plastic wrap and place in the fridge for 8–12 hours depending upon the thickness.The fish will become quite hard, tough, and pale in color. (The longer you leave it, the longer you have to soak it afterwards.)
- Rinse off the excess salt under cold water. If you are not going to use all the fish immediately then pat dry, wrap in plastic wrap, and keep in the fridge or freezer until needed.
- If using the fish immediately, soak the fish in cold water for 10 minutes, then change the water. Repeat the process for an hour, changing the water every 10–15 minutes. Pat dry with paper towels.
- Season the fish with freshly ground black pepper. Scatter the lemon zest over it and press the dill into the flesh.
- Place the fish on a clean work surface. With a thin, sharp knife cut slices horizontally, as thinly as possible. Use a gentle sawing action to let the sharpness of the blade do the work.
- Lay the fish slices on double layers of plastic wrap so that they are not touching.
- Press the slices of fish with a rolling pin or the bottom of a saucepan to make them the same even thickness. Remove from the plastic wrap; they are now ready to use.

Gravadlax should be served with a combination of sweet, sour, and hot accompaniments. It is delicious with the sweet flavors of beets or asparagus, and a hot, peppery horseradish sauce. Try it with a peppery, bitter watercress and arugula salad or a horseradish and watercress crème fraîche (see page 41). Its flavors also marry well with the artichoke and salted lemon salad with honey, thyme, and roasted almonds on page 84. Gravadlax and other kinds of cured or salted fish are often served with a slightly sweetened mustard and dill dressing, which could be accompanied by some pickled cucumber. You could use it for canapés with small blinis or arranged on potato pancakes with a herb crème fraîche.

salad of fennel and cured gravadlax with roast beets

serves 6

I often serve this as an appetizer on Christmas Eve or for lunch on Boxing Day, as a break from turkey. It is great as a simple hors d'oeuvre served with blinis or toasted rye bread with mustard sauce.

6 medium beets
1 tablespoon olive oil
salt and freshly ground black pepper
1 sprig of thyme
2 garlic cloves
1 fennel bulb, trimmed and thinly sliced
20 mint leaves, torn
7 ounces mixed leaves, e.g. arugula, watercress, Belgian endive, mizuna, mustard leaves, sorrel, spinach
3 thin slices of gravadlax per person (see page 87)

for the dressing

2 tablespoons Dijon mustard
1 teaspoon sugar
juice of 1/2 lemon
1 tablespoon red wine vinegar
5 tablespoons olive oil
1 tablespoon yogurt or crème fraîche
1 tablespoon chopped dill
salt and freshly ground black pepper

Preheat the oven to 400°F.

Scrub the beets. Place in a small roasting pan with the olive oil, salt and pepper, thyme, and garlic. Mix together. Add 1/4 cup water to the pan and seal with aluminum foil, making sure it is airtight.

Roast in the oven for 40 minutes. Check with the tip of a sharp knife to see if the beets are tender. Return to the oven if they need more time. Let cool and cut into quarters.

To make the dressing, whisk together the Dijon mustard, sugar, lemon juice, and red wine vinegar in a bowl. Slowly whisk in the olive oil until emulsified. Mix in the yogurt or crème fraîche and the dill. Season to taste (the dressing should have the consistency of sour cream and should be slightly sweet and sour, as well as hot from the mustard).

To assemble the salad, mix the fennel, mint, and mixed leaves. Arrange on serving plates and scatter the beets on top, but do not mix, because the beets will dye everything pink.

Lay the slices of gravadlax over the beets. Drizzle the leaves and salmon with the mustard dressing.

moroccan grilled squid salad with chermoula

serves 6

The Moroccan chermoula provides a freshness and intensity which perfectly complements the chargrilled squid. You could add some arugula or mustard leaves to the salad if you like.

1 red bell pepper
2 1/4 pounds baby squid, cleaned and cut to lay flat
small handful of mint leaves, chopped
small handful of cilantro leaves, chopped
1 x recipe Moroccan chermoula (see page 37)
salt and freshly ground black pepper

Grill the pepper in a heavy ridged grill pan, or directly over a gas flame until the skin is blackened and blistered all over. Place in a bowl and seal with plastic wrap to make it airtight. The steam from the pepper will soften the skin and make it easier to peel.

Heat a grill pan until smoking hot. Working in batches, grill the squid until it turns white and starts to curl.

Peel and seed the pepper and cut into strips. Combine with the squid, mint, and cilantro in a serving dish. Dress with the chermoula, season with salt and pepper if needed, and serve.

lime and crab salad with cucumber and mint

serves 4–6

Fresh, crisp, and delicious. The chile, black pepper, and raw ginger provide the heat, and the crab (or shrimp, lobster, or crayfish) and cucumber add the sweet component. The dressing is salty and sour from the Asian fish sauce, soy sauce, lime juice, and vinegar, and the fresh mint and cilantro provide a refreshing bite to the salad.

1 pound white crabmeat
1 cucumber
4 scallions, thinly sliced
2 shallots, cut into wafer-thin slices
salt and freshly ground black pepper
2 tablespoons mint leaves
2 tablespoons cilantro leaves

for the dressing
juice of 2 limes
1 tablespoon soy sauce
2 tablespoons Asian fish sauce
1 teaspoon vinegar
1 red chile (jalapeño or serrano), seeded and finely chopped
1 1/2-inch piece of fresh ginger, peeled and cut into thin matchsticks

Pick through the crabmeat, removing any shell or cartilidge. Even when buying crabmeat from a fishmonger, check it over for any pieces that may have been overlooked. Try to keep the crabmeat in as large pieces as possible.

To make the dressing, combine the lime juice, soy sauce, Asian fish sauce, and vinegar. Add the chile and ginger. Seed the cucumber and cut into thin matchsticks.

Combine the crabmeat, cucumber, scallions, and shallots in a large bowl. Toss gently to mix Season well with a little salt and lots of pepper (not too much salt as the Asian fish sauce and soy sauce are both salty). Add the dressing.

Just before serving, tear the mint and cilantro leaves into the bowl and toss gently to mix. Add these only when you are ready to serve, otherwise the acid in the dressing will cook the leaves and make them turn black.

Taste the salad and adjust the seasoning. Serve either as a plated appetizer or as part of a multi-course meal.

spice-crusted tuna sashimi

serves 6

This dish could also be called tuna carpaccio, as the center of the fish should be very rare. The sashimi could be served with any other Asian-style dressing or alternatively, the caper and marjoram sauce on page 33.

2 tablespoons coriander seeds
1 tablespoon fennel seeds
1 tablespoon cumin seeds
1 pound fresh tuna
salt and freshly ground black pepper
mixed salad greens, containing peppery leaves and mixed herbs (optional)

for the dressing

3/4-inch piece of fresh ginger, peeled and grated
juice of 2 limes
2 scallions, chopped
10 mint leaves, chopped
20 cilantro leaves, chopped
1/4 cup soy sauce

In a mortar and pestle, coarsely crush the coriander, fennel and cumin seeds. They do not have to be a fine powder.

Preheat a griddle or heavy-bottomed skillet.

Season the tuna with salt and pepper. Roll it in the crushed spices to coat completely. Cook on the hot griddle for 2 minutes on each side. If the tuna piece is thin and narrow, then cook only for 1 minute on each side.

Remove from the grill and leave to cool. Wrap tightly in plastic wrap and place in the freezer for at least 1 hour or up to 3 hours. This firms up the flesh and enables you to cut very thin slices.

Mix all the ingredients for the dressing. Cut the tuna into thin slices with a very sharp knife.

Arrange the tuna slices on a plate, with a small mixed leaf salad if desired. Pour the dressing over the top and serve.

roasted shrimp and watermelon salad with green chile and roasted peanuts

serves 4

There are variations of this salad all across Southeast Asia. David Thompson taught me the subtleties of making this salad when I worked with him at at Darley Street Thai in Sydney.

12–16 raw tiger shrimp, shells on
olive oil, soy sauce and lime juice, for drizzling
salt and freshly ground black pepper
1 medium-sized watermelon (or pomelo, see page 102)
handful of raw peanuts
15 mint leaves
20 cilantro leaves

for the dressing

1 inch piece of fresh ginger, peeled
1 green or red chile, seeded and finely chopped
2 small garlic cloves
3 cilantro (coriander) roots, rinsed well (if not available, use the cilantro stems)
1 teaspoon sea salt
1 teaspoon sugar
zest of 2 limes and juice of 4 limes
juice of 2 oranges
salt and freshly ground black pepper

for garnishing

2 stalks of lemongrass, trimmed and coarsely chopped
4 kaffir or other lime leaves, spine removed and thinly sliced
1 1/4 inch piece of fresh ginger, peeled and grated
3 scallions, thinly sliced
3 shallots, peeled and thinly sliced

Preheat the oven to 400°F.

Put the shrimp in a roasting pan. Sprinkle some olive oil, soy sauce, and lime juice, over them and season with salt and pepper. Roast in the oven for about 6 minutes until pink and just beginning to curl.

Peel the watermelon with a sharp knife. Cut into wedges and remove the seeds with a teaspoon. Cut into irregular chunks about 1 1/4 inches long and place in a large bowl. If using pomelo, peel, break up the segments, and add to the bowl.

When the shrimp have cooled, remove and discard their heads and shells and place on a board. With a sharp knife, slice in half lengthwise through the back of the shrimp. With the tip of the knife, remove the black intestinal tract. Add the shrimp to the bowl with the watermelon.

Gently roast the peanuts for 3–4 minutes in a dry frying pan or hot oven until golden. Prepare all the other garnish ingredients.

For the dressing, in a mortar and pestle, pound the ginger into a rough pulp. Use your hands to squeeze out the juice into the mortar, but discard the fibers. Add the chile, garlic, cilantro roots, salt, and sugar and pound to a smooth puree. Mix in the lime juice and orange juice. Season with salt and pepper.

Pour the dressing over the watermelon and shrimp and let it marinate for 10 minutes before serving. (Watermelon is sweeter than pomelo, so taste the dressing to ensure it is piquant enough to balance the sweetness of whichever fruit you use.)

Coarsely crush some of the roasted peanuts and add to the salad. Tear the mint and cilantro into the bowl and mix together. Sprinkle with the garnish ingredients and serve.

smoking mix

Hot smoking with an aromatic smoking mix is an excellent way of imparting flavor to meat and fish. The best types of fish to use are ones that are slightly oily such as salmon, trout, mackerel, and tuna. Firm, white-fleshed fish such as hake, sea bream (porgy), ocean perch, grouper, or bass work best smoked whole, otherwise they tend to break up too much. Chicken, wild duck, or other game birds are also delicious cooked in this way (see page 196). Chicken should be browned in a pan first to add color and additional flavor, otherwise it can look a bit pale and unappetizing.

You can alter the aromatics to suit your taste. Shrimp could be smoked with mostly lemongrass and lime leaves, whereas meat and game work better with cinnamon, star anise, and other hard spices. Jasmine tea gives a delicious scent to the ingredient smoking, perfuming it to the core.

A wok is a good utensil for hot smoking. It is important to lay down a double layer of tin foil in the bottom before the smoking mix goes in, otherwise the sugar will catch. If you are feeding a multitude, a domed lid barbecue with a number of layers is ideal for smoking lots of trout, a whole salmon, or a few whole chickens.

When the cooking is complete you can discard the smoking mix. The meat or fish can be eaten hot or cooled down and then broken into pieces, which can then be used in another dish such as a curry, salad, or soup.

aromatic smoked trout

serves 4

This is a simple way of transforming the flavor of delicate fish. Other fish can be used, but oily ones such as mackerel, snapper, and salmon are best. The fish can be smoked a few days in advance, and can be used in salads, curries, soups, or noodle dishes.

2 whole rainbow trout

for the marinade

2 tablespoons raw sugar such as Demerara or Turbinado
2 tablespoons soy sauce
1 tablespoon Asian fish sauce
juice of 1 lime
freshly ground black pepper

for the smoking mix

1 cup Jasmine rice
$^{1}/_{2}$ cup Jasmine tea leaves
2 stalks of lemongrass, tough outer leaves removed, trimmed and coarsely chopped
$1^{1}/_{4}$ inch piece of fresh ginger, peeled and coarsely chopped
3 tablespoons brown sugar
4 ounces unsweetened dried, shredded coconut
4 star anise
2 small dried chiles
1 tablespoon fennel seeds
1 cinnamon stick

Clean the trout; you can remove the head, but keep the fish in one piece.

Mix all the ingredients for the marinade in a large shallow bowl, add the trout and marinate for 10 minutes.

Line a large wok with a double thickness of aluminum foil.

Mix together all the smoking ingredients and place in the center of the wok. Set up a rack in the wok and place the fish on it. Put the wok lid on top (if you do not have a lid, make a dome-shaped one out of some foil).

Wrap some foil around any gaps between the pan and the lid. You need a tight seal, so that all the smoke remains inside the wok.

Start the heat on high, and turn down to medium after 5 minutes. The trout will take 40–60 minutes to cook in this way, depending upon the heat. Turn the fish once during the cooking process.

Remove the trout from the wok and once it is cool, remove the skin, fins, and tail. Fillet the fish with a knife and fork, removing all the bones. Try to keep the fish in large pieces, as it will break up when mixed into a salad or a curry.

salad of aromatic smoked trout with red peppers, roasted rice, and thai basil

serves 4

Roasted rice has a perfumed nutty taste which is quite distinctive. You could substitute sesame seeds for a similar effect. This salad was often on the menu at Darley Street Thai in Sydney.

3 red bell peppers
1/2 cup Jasmine rice (or sesame seeds)
1/4 cup thinly sliced fried shallots
3 scallions, finely sliced
1 1/2 green chiles, seeded and finely chopped
3 stalks of lemongrass, tough outer leaves removed, trimmed and coarsely chopped
zest of 2 limes
zest of 1 orange
1 1/4-inch piece of fresh ginger, peeled and grated (peelings reserved for dressing)
2 smoked rainbow trout (see page 95)
20 Thai basil leaves
20 mint leaves

for the dressing

1 garlic clove
1/2 green chile, seeded
1 teaspoon salt
1 teaspoon sugar
peelings from the ginger used in the salad
20 cilantro leaves
juice of 2 limes
juice of 1 orange

Preheat the oven to 350°F.

Grill the peppers in a heavy ridged grill pan, or directly over a gas flame until the skin is blackened and blistered all over. Place in a bowl and seal with plastic wrap to make it airtight. The steam from the peppers will soften the skins and make them easier to peel.

Pour the rice onto a baking sheet and roast in the oven for about 10–12 minutes until golden brown. Let cool.

Place the shallots, scallions, chiles, lemongrass, lime and orange zest, and ginger in a large bowl with the trout fillets.

Peel the skins of the peppers (use a little water to help remove all the black pieces of skin). Split them in half and scrape out all the seeds. Tear the flesh into strips and add to the bowl.

In a mortar and pestle or spice grinder, grind the roasted rice so it is broken up but not a powder.

To make the dressing, place the garlic, chile, salt, sugar, and ginger peelings in a food processor and puree. Add the cilantro, lime juice, and orange juice. Work to a smooth paste.

Add half the roasted rice to the bowl. Tear the Thai basil and mint and add most of it to the salad.

Garnish with the remaining torn herbs and roasted rice. The salad should be sweet and hot with a salty and sour sauce.

tataki of beef or venison

serves 4–6

Nanami togarashi is a classic Japanese 7-spice mixture available in any Asian store. It contains dried chile, orange peel, black and white sesame seeds, Japanese pepper, ginger, and seaweed. If not available then use sesame seeds, orange zest, and dried chile. You could serve this dish with some mixed peppery leaves such as mustard leaf, mizuna, and arugula, with perhaps some cucumber and torn mint as well.

1 pound venison or beef loin
2 teaspoons olive oil
salt and freshly ground black pepper
1 1/2 teaspoons nanami togarashi (Japanese 7-spice mixture)

for the dressing

1/2 cup grapeseed or olive oil
2 tablespoons white wine vinegar
2 tablespoons honey
1 tablespoon Japanese soy sauce
salt and freshly ground black pepper

for garnishing

2 tablespoons sesame seeds
1 red chile (jalapeño or serrano), seeded and finely chopped
3 scallions, thinly sliced
1 1/4-inch piece of fresh ginger, cut into thin matchsticks
handful of cilantro, picked off the stem

Trim the meat of any fat or sinew. Rub with the olive oil and season with salt and pepper. Roll the meat in the togarashi.

Heat a heavy frying pan and sear the meat for 2 minutes on each side until nicely browned on the outside.

Remove from the pan and let cool slightly. Wrap in plastic wrap and place in the freezer for 30 minutes. This will firm the texture and make it much easier to cut into thin slices.

Mix all the ingredients for the dressing.

Gently toast the sesame seeds in a dry frying pan until golden brown.

Remove the meat from the freezer and unwrap. With a very sharp knife, slice crosswise into thin slices.

Arrange the slices on a large serving platter and drizzle with the dressing. Scatter the chile, scallions, ginger, sesame seeds, and cilantro over the top.

salad of chorizo, mushrooms, and roast sweet potato

serves 4

This salad can be served warm or cold. A goat cheese could be used instead of chorizo for a vegetarian version. The sweetness of the potatoes counters the heat of the chile, so you get the flavor and perfume of the chile without too much heat, which could be overwhelming. The perfumed heat of the sauce is mellowed by the caramelized sweetness of the sweet potato, and with the saltiness of the chorizo all the different flavor groups work together.

2 medium sweet potatoes
2 tablespoons olive oil
salt and freshly ground black pepper
12 ounces oyster mushrooms or flat field mushrooms
juice of 1/2 lemon
8 ounces chorizo for cooking, cut into 3/4-inch chunks
handful of flat-leaf parsley
handful of arugula
2 scallions, finely chopped

for the dressing

2 green chiles, seeded and finely chopped
zest and juice of 1 lemon
1/2 teaspoon sugar
salt and freshly ground black pepper
3 tablespoons extra virgin olive oil

Preheat the oven to 400°F.

Peel the sweet potatoes if you prefer. Wash and cut in half lengthwise then cut into 1 1/4-inch chunks.

Mix in a bowl with 1 tablespoon of the olive oil and a good pinch of salt and pepper.

Roast in the oven for about 25 minutes until soft and caramelized. Move them around the pan while cooking, so they brown on all sides.

Tear the oyster mushrooms into equal-sized pieces. Cut the wild mushrooms (if using) into thin, equal-sized slices.

Heat the remaining tablespoon of olive oil in a heavy skillet. When the pan is smoking hot, add the mushrooms and cook quickly over a high heat for about 5–7 minutes, stirring frequently. You want the mushrooms to brown and caramelize, not sweat in their own watery liquid. Add the lemon juice and season with salt and pepper. Transfer to a large mixing bowl.

Add the chorizo to the used mushroom skillet. (No extra oil is needed because the sausage contains fat). Fry until golden brown and cooked through, about 5–7 minutes. Add the chorizo and its oil to the mushrooms.

Coarsely chop the parsley and arugula. Add two thirds to the bowl along with the scallions.

Mix all the ingredients for the dressing.

Add the cooked sweet potatoes to the mixing bowl. Pour the dressing over them, toss gently to mix, and serve. Garnish with the remaining chopped herbs.

chef's tip

Chorizo for cooking is different to the hard, cured chorizo. It looks more like a bulk sausage than salami. If you can't find it, use bulk sausage and add some chopped chile to the salad to provide the heat.

CHORIZO
ROSARIO PICANTE
HUESOS DE
JAMON

the pomelo

The pomelo is a fantastic citrus fruit with a unique character. It resembles a large grapefruit and tastes like a cross between that and an orange. The bitter skin is a pale yellow-green and the flesh can be yellow or pale rose pink. Its segments are encased in pith about an inch thick and are individually surrounded by a thick membrane and therefore it is quite labor intensive to prepare, but it is well worth the trouble. However, the final yield of the fruit can be disappointingly small and so I tend to buy two to be on the safe side.

Grown throughout Southeast Asia, pomelos are used in a similar way to green, unripe mango and papaya, and have a delicious sweet and sour quality that brings a three-dimensional depth to any dish. The texture works very well, because it is firmer than other citrus fruits, has less juice, and does not reduce to a pulp. It is very refreshing without being overly juicy. As an ingredient, it is a great accompaniment to many savory flavors, from roast duck or pork to shrimp, squid, and other seafood. The fruit also marries perfectly with other Asian ingredients such as chile, ginger, lime, lemongrass, and refreshing herbs like cilantro and mint.

On a recent trip to southern Thailand and Singapore that coincided with the build-up to Chinese New Year, I noticed the fruit and vegetable markets were piled high with pomelos. They were tied with red and gold ribbons and sold as gifts alongside small clementine trees, which have the same significance as a Christmas wreath or Christmas tree in the West.

to peel the fruit

- Score the outside of the thick skin with a sharp knife. Pull away segments of skin and then break the fruit open, as you would an orange.

- Pull away the thick, white pith and also the leathery membrane that surrounds each segment. It is important to remove all of this as it is bitter and not good to eat.

- Using a small knife where necessary, score along the thin side of each segment to open the pocket, exposing the fruit inside.

- When preparing each segment, make sure you remove all the connecting pieces of membrane from the curved thicker side, and all the seeds.

Pomelos are available from many supermarkets and Asian grocers. If they are unavailable, you can substitute fresh pink grapefruit segments, or a combination of grapefruit and Asian pear to get the right balance of sweet and sour.

crisp spice-rubbed pork and pomelo salad

serves 6

You can use beef rump instead of pork belly; it can be roasted in the same way. Any leftover meat can be saved and eaten with the roast shallot, tomato, and chile relish (see page 46).

1 pork belly
salt and freshly ground black pepper

for the spice rub

1 tablespoon coriander seeds
2 star anise
1 teaspoon cloves
1 teaspoon fennel seeds
1 cinnamon stick
1/2 teaspoon ground nutmeg

for the salad

2 pomelos (see facing page)
handful of peanuts or cashews
3 scallions, thinly sliced
2 shallots, thinly sliced
1 red chile (jalapeño or serrano), seeded and finely chopped
1 tablespoon soy sauce
1 1/4-inch piece of fresh ginger, peeled and grated
zest and juice of 1 orange
zest and juice of 2 limes
20 cilantro leaves

Preheat the oven to 400°F.

Place the pork on a board. Trim off the skin (your butcher can do this) and cut in half. Place your hand flat on the meat and gently cut each piece in half horizontally.

Grind the spice rub ingredients in a mortar and pestle. Sift them to get rid of any husks and woody bits.

Rub the spice mixture into the pork on all sides. Season well with salt and pepper.

Heat a heavy skillet over medium-high heat. Add a splash of oil to get things started. Add the pork belly—you will have to cook it in batches, but you should be able to get two slices in the pan. Cook over a medium-high heat for 5–6 minutes on each side until a deep golden brown. While it is cooking, carefully pour off any excess fat. You do not want it to boil in its own grease.

Remove the pork from the pan and place on a wire rack fitted into a baking sheet.

Bake for 30 minutes in the oven until it is predominantly crispy with a lot of the fat rendered away (but not hard and dry).

While the pork is roasting, prepare the pomelo by removing all of the white pith and tough membrane, and extracting all the flesh.

Dry-roast the nuts in a roasting pan in the oven until golden brown. Crush coarsely in a mortar and pestle.

Gently toss all the salad ingredients (except for the peanuts and cilantro) together in a large bowl.

When the pork has cooled to warm, slice thinly, saving all the crispy bits and juices on the board for the salad. Check the seasoning: it should be hot and spicy. The pork meat itself will be sweet and rich.

Mix the pork into the salad, then add the reserved cilantro and roasted nuts.

soups

soups

The word soup means different things around the world with variations from region to region. Some are thick enough in which to stand up a spoon, like an Italian ribolita. Others are as thin as water and delicately flavored like a consommé, or have a powerful kick like a spicy Thai soup (see page 117).

In the West, soup is served as an individual course, often at the beginning of a meal, or between courses to cleanse the palate. In Southeast Asia, the soup comes alongside other dishes and is served whenever it is ready. A mouthful can be taken now and again or poured into the eating bowl to moisten the rice and ensure that not one of the precious grains is wasted. In Thailand and Vietnam the soup you have depends upon what dish preceded it and what dish will follow. There are mild, almost bland, soups such as *geng juet* which work well with a hot and salty salad. An invigorating *dom yam* on the other hand, with its combination of striking heat from the chiles and mouth-puckering sourness from the limes and tamarind, could accompany a milder curry or seafood dish.

Sometimes a soup can cover a couple of courses. Traditionally, a *bouillabaisse* from the south of France would provide both appetizer and main course. To start, you would have the broth, and then the main course would consist of the poached whole fish served on a central platter with the boiled potatoes, some of which had been used to thicken the soup. In Asia, fish head soup is served in a similar way: a thin, highly perfumed and aromatic broth to start and then the meat from the fish heads, especially the highly prized cheeks of the fish, which are accompanied by rice or noodles which can also be used to soak up the last of the broth.

The identity of a region and its cultural integrity are often proudly displayed in the soups that are served. A common thread that binds soups from all countries is that they are designed to be filling and nutritious, and that they are frequently made from leftovers or produce that is sun-spoiled or over-ripe. It is important to remember, though, that they are not a trash can for kitchen scraps. When making a stock or broth (see facing page), it must be clean and clear in appearance and sweet tasting, not cloudy and bitter. In Italy it is said that your risotto is only as good as the stock that you make. If your stock is cooked-down garbage, then it is difficult to improve on that.

Soups can be thickened and made much more substantial by many different means. An Italian tomato and bread soup such as *papa pomodoro* is made from the juiciest, ripest tomatoes that may have been sun-spoiled or split, and are therefore not good enough for the market, and the bread that is used is always stale bread from yesterday. In fact, the more stale the bread, the more juice it will soak up. Nothing is wasted. In Spain and Italy soups are often thickened with bread, or rice, or small wheat-based pasta shapes such as in a minestrone soup. In many areas of Spain and southern France and Italy, soups can be thickened and made to go a lot further by adding grains such as bulgur, faro, cracked wheat, and barley.

Common across Southeast Asia are soups made with the addition of rice noodles or egg noodles, dumplings, wontons, or small patties made from meat or fish, such as a wonton soup or a spicy Thai soup with curried fishcakes and shrimp (see page 117). In many cases in the Far East you can have exactly the same dish of meat, noodles, and vegetables served with or without the broth. Soups like the Vietnamese *pho* (see page 118) become a meal in themselves; the combination of noodles, meat, and broth makes a hearty dish.

SWEET **stock, coconut cream, mussels, snapper, cod, prawns, celery, cannellini beans, cinnamon, cherry tomatoes** SOUR **scallions, white wine, lime leaves, goat cheese, sour cream, tamarind** SALTY **fish sauce, bacon, sea salt** HOT **arugula, watercress, white peppercorns, horseradish, coriander seeds, cumin seeds, red curry paste**

fish stock

makes 2 quarts

Save the fish bones from any fish recipe where stock is required and use them as follows.

fish bones, cleaned
2 bay leaves
10 peppercorns
2 celery stalks, coarsely chopped
1 leek, coarsely chopped
1 red onion, coarsely chopped
small handful of parsley stalks
sprig of thyme
8 cups cold water

Put the bones in a pot with the other ingredients. Cover with the water and bring to a boil. Turn down the heat, simmer for 20 minutes, and skim regularly with a ladle. The stock should be sweet and clear, not cloudy and bitter.

When the stock has been strained, it can be kept in the freezer.

For chicken broth, use raw chicken bones or cooked from a leftover roast chicken and simmer for 2 hours.
For vegetable broth, omit the bones and add more celery and another onion. Simmer for 20 minutes.

creamy butternut squash soup with coconut cream, ginger, and cilantro

serves 4

$2^1/4$ pounds butternut squash, peeled, seeded, and cut into $^3/4$-inch cubes
3 tablespoons olive oil
salt and freshly ground black pepper
$^1/2$ bunch of fresh cilantro, leaves picked and stems reserved
2 garlic cloves, finely chopped
$1^1/2$-inch piece of fresh ginger, peeled and grated
1 red chile (jalapeño or serrano), seeded and finely chopped
1 onion, finely chopped
2 celery ribs, finely chopped
$2^1/4$ cups homemade vegetable or chicken broth (see page 107)
1 (14-ounce) can coconut milk
juice of 1 lime
Chili powder or chopped herbs, for garnishing

Preheat the oven to 400°F.

Mix the butternut squash with 2 tablespoons of the oil, salt, and pepper and spread out in a roasting pan. Roast for 15–20 minutes until soft and caramelized.

Finely chop 5 cilantro stalks and mix with the garlic, ginger, and chile.

Heat a heavy pot over medium heat. Add the remaining oil and fry the garlic mixture for 2 minutes until fragrant. Add the onion and celery, turn down the heat, and cook gently for 10 minutes. Season well with salt and pepper. Add the broth and the coconut cream. Bring to a boil then turn down to a simmer. Cook gently for 10 minutes.

Set up a food processor. Remove the soft and caramelized butternut squash from the oven and blend until you have a semi-smooth paste.

With a slotted spoon, transfer half the cooked onion and celery from the pan to the blender and puree until smooth. Return the puree to the pan and bring back to a boil.

Roughly chop the cilantro leaves and add to the soup along with the lime juice, stirring to mix.

Taste the soup and judge the balance of hot, sweet, salt, and sour. It should be hot from the chile, black pepper, and ginger, sweet from the roast squash, and coconut cream, and there should be a hint of sourness from the lime juice and saltiness from the seasoning.

Serve garnished with a sprinkling of chili powder or chopped herbs.

chef's tip

Cilantro stems hold a lot of flavor and are an important base in many Asian dishes.

southern thai soup of baby vegetables with ginger and lime

serves 4 – 6

10 white peppercorns
1/2 teaspoon salt
4 cilantro (fresh coriander) roots, rinsed (if not available, use cilantro stems)
3 shallots, peeled and coarsely chopped
1 tablespoon olive oil
4 garlic cloves, finely chopped
1 red chile (jalapeño or serrano), seeded and finely chopped
1 1/2-inch piece of fresh ginger, peeled and finely grated
8 cups vegetable or chicken broth (see page 107), heated
1 pound selection of baby vegetables such as baby corn, green beans, asparagus, snow peas, spinach, Chinese cabbage, bok choy
juice of 2 limes
1 tablespoon soy sauce, or to taste
small handful of cilantro, coarsely chopped
3 kaffir or other lime leaves, central rib removed, finely shredded
3 scallions, thinly sliced

In a mortar and pestle, place the peppercorns, salt, and cilantro roots and pound to a paste. Add the shallots and continue to work until smooth.

Heat a heavy pot over medium heat. Add the oil and cook the garlic for 1 minute until it starts to turn pale golden. Add the shallot paste and cook, stirring, for about 2 minutes, until fragrant.

Add the red chile and half the ginger. Cook for another minute to blend all the flavors. Add the simmering broth and mix together. Simmer for 5 minutes.

Add the hardest vegetables to the broth (such as the beans, baby corn, and stems of bok choy) and cook for 2 minutes. Then add the softer vegetables, such as the asparagus and cook for another minute. If you are including leaves, such as Chinese cabbage or spinach, add them about a minute before the end, so all the vegetables of different textures will be ready at the same time.

Turn off the heat and stir in the lime juice and soy sauce. Scatter with the cilantro, lime leaves, scallions, and remaining ginger. Check the seasoning before serving because the soup may need a little more lime juice or light soy sauce to taste. The heat will come from the white pepper and the chile, and the vegetables and rich broth will provide a sweet background for the other flavors.

roast chestnut and mushroom soup with horseradish and arugula cream

serves 6

You can use a mixture of different varieties of mushrooms in this recipe; wild mushrooms mixed with cultivated mushrooms will add depth of flavor.

for the horseradish and arugula cream

1 1/4-inch piece of fresh horseradish, peeled and finely grated
juice of 1 lemon
1 bunch of arugula, coarsely chopped
5 ounces mascarpone cheese
1 tablespoon sour cream
salt and freshly ground black pepper

for the soup

2 1/4 pounds cremini mushrooms, skinned
5 ounces chestnuts, boiled and peeled (vacuum-packed are fine)
8 sprigs of thyme
2 garlic cloves, crushed or finely chopped
1 red chile (jalapeño or serrano), seeded and finely chopped
8 small shallots, finely chopped
1/4 cup olive oil
salt and freshly ground black pepper
8 cups vegetable or chicken broth (see page 107)
2 tablespoons sour cream

Preheat the oven to 425°F.

To make the horseradish cream, combine the horseradish with the lemon juice and arugula and then mix in the mascarpone and sour cream, seasoning to taste. If making in advance, chill in the fridge until ready to use.

Combine the mushrooms, chestnuts, thyme, garlic, chile, and shallots in a large roasting pan. Drizzle with olive oil and season with salt and pepper. Toss to mix until well combined and roast for 12 minutes.

Transfer the mixture to a soup pot, add the broth, bring to a boil, then reduce heat and simmer for 10 minutes.

Blend the mixture in batches in a food processor until coarse puree is formed. (Small flecks of mushroom and chestnuts should be visible.)

Return the mixture to the pot along with the sour cream and cook over low heat, stirring, until heated through.

Serve in individual bowls with a spoonful of horseradish and arugula cream on top.

roasted fennel and leek soup with arugula and watercress

serves 4

2 fennel bulbs, cut into thin wedges
3 tablespoons olive oil
salt and freshly ground black pepper
1 onion, finely chopped
2 leeks, finely chopped, dark green tops discarded
4 cups vegetable or chicken broth (see page 107)
large handful of arugula leaves
large handful of watercress leaves
2 ounces soft cheese (such as mascarpone or goat cheese)
juice of 1/2 lemon
1/2 cup heavy whipping cream

Preheat the oven to 400°F.

Mix the fennel wedges with 2 tablespoons of the olive oil, and season with salt and pepper. Spread out on a baking sheet and roast in the oven for 20–25 minutes, or until golden brown and caramelized at the edges.

Meanwhile, heat the remaining olive oil in a pot over medium heat. Add the onion and leeks and cook for 10 minutes, stirring to avoid sticking. Season with salt and pepper.

Add the broth, bring to a boil, and then reduce heat to low and simmer for 10 minutes.

Set up a food processor and carefully blend the arugula leaves and watercress until you have a coarse paste. Add the soft cheese and lemon juice and continue to blend until you have a smooth, bright green puree. If you are using goat cheese, the paste can be left with more texture.

Scrape the puree into a bowl and set aside. You do not need to wash the food processor since you are going to use it again.

When the fennel is golden brown and soft, remove from the oven and place in the food processor. With a slotted spoon, transfer half the cooked onion and leek from the pot, without too much liquid.

Puree these vegetables into a paste. Add the cream, blend until smooth, and then return the creamed vegetables to the pot. Add half of the the arugula, watercress, and soft cheese puree and stir into the soup until incorporated.

Check the seasoning; the arugula and watercress will be peppery and the cheeses may be quite salty, so taste carefully before adjusting. Spoon a teaspoon of the remaining paste onto the top of each bowl of soup.

Serve this soup hot, warm, or chilled with some crusty fresh bread.

hot and sour fisherman's soup

serves 4

This very refreshing and delicious soup balances all the taste elements—the sour comes from the tamarind, tomatoes, and lime juice, and the sweet from the caramelized flavors of the wok, particularly the squid and the orange juice. The tomatoes should not be completely ripe because you want their sourness. You can also use chicken or any combination of fish and shellfish for variety.

1 tablespoon olive oil
2 garlic cloves, finely chopped
1 medium onion, thinly sliced
5 small shallots, thinly sliced
2 stalks lemongrass, tough outer leaves removed, thinly sliced
1 red chile (jalapeño or serrano), seeded and coarsely chopped
8–10 ounces squid bodies and tentacles, cleaned and cut into 1 1/2-inch pieces
salt and freshly ground black pepper
4 sprigs cilantro (fresh coriander), roots and stems rinsed and finely chopped, leaves set aside
6 tomatoes, coarsely chopped
1 pound firm-fleshed white fish, such as snapper, bass, cod or hake, cut into bite-size chunks
8 cups prepared fish or chicken stock (seepage 107), strained and heated
2 tablespoons tamarind paste dissolved in 5 tablespoons hot water
2 tablespoons orange juice
2 tablespoons Asian fish sauce
4 ounces bean sprouts
juice of 1 lime

Heat the oil in a wok, add the garlic, onion, shallots, and half of the lemongrass. Cook quickly over medium-high heat for 3–4 minutes to caramelize.

Add the red chile. Pat the squid dry, season with salt and pepper, and stir-fry for 2 minutes before adding the cilantro roots, stalks, and tomatoes.

Keep the wok over a medium heat and cook, stirring and tossing, for 2–3 minutes—you want the spices to release their oils and become aromatic and the squid and tomatoes to combine with the smoky flavors from the wok.

Add the pieces of fish, cover with the hot stock and gently simmer for 10 minutes. Stir in the tamarind liquid, orange juice, and fish sauce.

To garnish, add the bean sprouts, cilantro leaves, and lime juice.

spicy italian mussel soup

serves 4

This soup from southern Italy is a robust and delicious start to any meal. The mussels and slow-cooked tomatoes provide the sweetness, the spices provide the heat, and these need to be balanced with salt and sour so check the seasoning before serving. Crab or shrimp work as well as mussels.

2 teaspoons coriander seeds
2 teaspoons fennel seeds
1 teaspoon cumin seeds
3 garlic cloves
2 small, dried Thai chiles
sea salt and freshly ground black pepper
1/3 cup olive oil
1 cinnamon stick
1 fresh red chile (jalapeño or serrano), seeded and finely chopped
2 (14 1/2-ounce) cans tomatoes
3 1/2 pounds mussels, cleaned (discard any that are open)
2/3 cup dry white wine
handful of flat-leaf parsley
1/2 baguette, thinly sliced
splash of olive oil
1 garlic clove, peeled

In a mortar and pestle, crush the coriander, fennel, and cumin seeds, and then add the garlic and dried chilies working with a pinch of salt until it is smooth.

Heat 2 tablespoons of oil in a heavy saucepan and cook the spice mixture and whole cinnamon stick over medium-high heat until it is fragrant. Add the fresh chile.

Add the canned tomatoes and cook slowly over low heat until they have broken down to a sauce-like consistency—this should take about 30 minutes.

In a separate pot, heat the remaining oil. When hot, add the mussels, white wine, and 1/2 cup water. Cover with a lid and cook over high heat until the mussels have opened. Discard any that remain closed.

Remove from the heat. Pour off the liquid and strain through a fine sieve lined with a clean paper towel to remove any grit. Add the strained liquid to the pot of tomatoes and reduce by simmering for 5–10 minutes.

Toast the bread under a medium-hot broiler for 5 minutes (or in a toaster) to make crisp crostini. Rub with a little oil and garlic.

Remove all the mussels from their shells except a few for garnishing. Check the seasoning of the soup and add the flat-leaf parsley. Add the mussels and heat through before serving.

chef's tip

It is best to season the mussel liquid after it has reduced and the flavors have concentrated.

spicy thai soup with curried fishcakes and shrimp

serves 4–6

Instead of shrimp, you could also use the same quantity of squid pieces or 10 ounces of firm white fish pieces, or even a combination of all three.

for the fishcakes

1 pound firm white fish, such as snapper, sea bream (porgy), cod, or hake
1 tablespoon red curry paste
3 lime leaves, finely chopped
2 scallions, finely chopped
juice of 1 lime
1 tablespoon Asian fish sauce
salt and freshly ground black pepper
handful of fresh cilantro or Thai basil
oil for frying

for the soup

2 tablespoons olive oil
2 garlic cloves, finely chopped
1 medium onion, thinly sliced
5 small shallots, thinly sliced
5 slices galangal or fresh ginger
2 stalks lemongrass, thinly sliced
2 red chiles (jalapeño or serrano), seeded and coarsely chopped
4 sprigs cilantro, roots and stems finely chopped, leaves reserved
6 tomatoes, coarsely chopped
8 cups fish or chicken stock (see page 107)
2 tablespoons tamarind paste
2 tablespoons orange juice
salt and freshly ground black pepper
2 tablespoons Asian fish sauce
8–10 large peeled shrimp, deveined
2 lime leaves, finely shredded
handful of Thai basil
juice of 1 lime

Place all the ingredients for the fishcakes in a food processor and puree until smooth, scraping down the sides of the bowl once or twice with a spatula.

Lightly oil your hands and roll the fish mixture into small balls, no bigger than a golf ball. Fry in hot oil until golden brown on the outside. Alternatively, simply poach them in the soup for 3–4 minutes before you are ready to serve.

To make the soup, heat 1 tablespoon of the oil in a wok. Add the garlic, onion, shallots, galangal, and half the lemongrass (make sure to remove the tough outer leaves first), and cook quickly over medium-high heat for 3–4 minutes to caramelize.

Add the red chile, cilantro roots and stems, and tomatoes. Keep the wok over medium heat and cook, stirring and tossing, for 2–3 minutes—you want the spices to release their oils and become aromatic and the tomatoes to soak up the smoky flavors from the wok.

Cover with the hot stock, bring to a boil, and gently simmer for 10 minutes. Dissolve the tamarind paste in 5 tablespoons hot water and add to the stock along with the orange juice and fish sauce. Taste and adjust the seasoning if necessary.

Cut the shrimp in half and add to the soup, along with the fishcakes, being careful that the latter do not break up. Gently simmer for 3–4 minutes before turning the heat off and letting the residual heat of the soup finish cooking the fish—this is to prevent it from becoming overcooked and tough.

To garnish the finished soup, add the cilantro leaves, lime leaves, Thai basil, and lime juice. Add more fresh red chile to suit your palate.

pho – Vietnamese noodle soup

This is a fantastic dish that has a cult following across Vietnam and consequently in every ex-pat community. It is traditionally eaten for breakfast but it is so delicious and popular that it is available at any time of the day and night. *Pho* is pronounced "fir," which stems from the French *pot au feu*, meaning "pot on the fire." It combines an intense stock made from beef or chicken bones with ginger, cinnamon and star anise and is left on a continuous simmer, gently perfuming the whole of the surrounding area and tempting every passer-by. If a smell were to have a three-dimensional form then it would be *pho*. The scent is so tangible that you can practically eat the steam.

Much of the street food in Vietnam is carried in bamboo baskets that are suspended over the vendor's shoulder by a wooden yoke. These baskets hold fruit and vegetables or a small charcoal stove for brewing tea or heating soup. This really is fast food as you can hail a vendor and order noodles wherever you are, day or night. They even provide seating. When traveling around Vietnam you cannot help but stop at the *pho* stalls. You sense immediately that there is some treasure to be found there because all the tiny plastic stools are occupied and the sidewalk is packed with contented customers. Their heads are bowed into their bowls like work horses, not to be distracted from their nosebags, and there is little talk, just a lot of slurping. The air is thick with the perfume of ginger, cinnamon and star anise. You can see why it is the fuel of Vietnam—you cannot start the day without it. It wakes you up and grounds you, excites your palate and is the ultimate comfort food from the very first mouthful. *Pho* originates from north Vietnam but apparently the best to be had is from Ben Tanh market in Ho Chi Min City in the south. My guidebook gave a lengthy description of the experience, which I thought was a little over the top. It explained that when you are handed the bowl, you drink the broth first, because it is so delicious and you cannot wait. Then you hand up your bowl to be served another ladle of broth, before settling down to enjoy the noodles and pieces of beef. I was not going to be told how to enjoy my soup, and yet when tasting the broth I automatically drained it! I held up the bowl like Oliver Twist, pleading for another hearty refill. One bowl and you are hooked.

I can say about four words in Vietnamese and so I knew that asking for a recipe would be quite a challenge. Therefore, over countless bowls of *pho bo* (beef noodle soup) and *pho ca* (chicken noodle soup) at different stalls throughout Vietnam, I wrote copious notes on how it was made and how it tasted, making my tongue, tastebuds, and sense of smell decipher its secrets. The finished soup is rich tasting and sumptuous. The chicken and slow-cooked vegetables provide sweetness, salt comes from the soy and fish sauce, the spices provide a winter warmth, and the lime juice is essential to cut the richness of the soup. A table salad is served on the side for diners to tailor the soup to their individual palate. Cilantro, mint, and Thai basil, peppery leaves such as arugula or watercress; lengths of scallion, chopped red chile, and lime wedges are all supplied. You tear a few of each type of leaf into the bowl because by breaking them you release their distinct zesty perfumes and oils. When the taste is to your liking, you stir from the bottom to combine the flavors.

pho ca (vietnamese chicken noodle soup with ginger, cinnamon, and star anise)

serves 4

This is a deliciously rich and healthy soup, great as a winter warmer, and practically a whole meal in itself. If you substitute more aromatics, such as ginger, spices, and a few extra vegetables, for the chicken bones, *pho* also makes a very popular vegetarian dish. **See the feature on page 118.**

for the stock

1 pound chicken bones (you could use the leftovers from a Sunday dinner)
3 star anise
1 stick cinnamon
2 tablespoons coriander seeds
1 tablespoon cumin seeds
1 teaspoon coarse salt
1 1/2 ounces fresh ginger peelings (use the trimmings for the stock and save the flesh for the garnish)
1 head of garlic (unpeeled)
1/2 red chile (jalapeño or serrano), seeded
2 tablespoons oil
2 carrots, coarsely chopped
2 celery ribs, coarsely chopped
5 shallots, unpeeled and coarsely chopped
4 sprigs cilantro (stems and roots, leaves reserved)
8 cups chicken broth (see page 107)
2 tablespoons Asian fish sauce
squeeze of lime juice
freshly ground black pepper

For the stock, roast the chicken bones in a hot oven for about 20 minutes, until golden brown.

Place the whole dried spices and salt in a mortar and pestle and crush to release their oils—there is no need to pound until smooth as they will be strained out of the final soup. Add the ginger peelings, garlic, and chile, and continue to pound.

Heat the oil in a heavy soup pot. Add the spices from the mortar and pestle and cook for 3–4 minutes until aromatic.

Add the chopped vegetables and cilantro stalks and roots. Continue to cook over high heat for about 6–8 minutes until caramelized and the flavors have blended. Turn the heat down a little if the vegetables are sticking. Add the browned chicken bones, cover with the chicken broth, and simmer for 1–2 hours.

for the chicken

splash of olive oil
3 free-range chicken breasts, skin on
salt and freshly ground black pepper
1 teaspoon ground cinnamon
1 teaspoon ground nutmeg
1 teaspoon ground coriander

to finish

6 ounces dried wide rice noodles, soaked in warm water for 10 minutes until soft and pliable
1 red chile (jalapeño or serrano), seeded and finely chopped
3 stalks lemongrass, tough outer leaves removed, thinly sliced
4 scallions, finely chopped
3 shallots, thinly sliced
$1^1/2$ ounces fresh ginger, peeled and grated
4 teaspoons lime juice
4 teaspoons Asian fish sauce

for serving

2 limes, quartered
20 Thai basil leaves
20 mint leaves
20 cilantro leaves
large handful of mixed peppery leaves such as arugula, watercress, and mustard leaves

For the chicken, heat the oil in a hot grill pan. Season the chicken breasts with salt and pepper and the ground spices, and cook in the pan for about 8–10 minutes until golden brown.

When you are ready to serve the soup, strain the stock and skim the excess fat from the surface. Taste and adjust the seasoning, add the fish sauce, a good squeeze of lime juice, and lots of black pepper.

Drain the noodles and slice the chicken thinly, saving all the juices. Blanch the noodles in the hot stock. They only take about a minute to cook so make sure you do this right at the end when everything else is ready.

In each serving bowl, place a little chile and a pinch of lemongrass, scallion, shallot, and ginger, and a teaspoon each of lime juice and fish sauce. Fill each bowl one-third full with the cooked rice noodles and arrange some sliced chicken on top. Ladle the hot stock over the bowl and serve. Put the remaining garnish ingredients and lime quarters on the table.

Mix all the herbs and salad leaves in a bowl and place at the center of the table. Invite your guests to take a few of each type of leaf from the table salad and tear them into the bowl. When your bowl is complete, stir from the bottom to combine all the flavors and enjoy the rich smells and zesty combination of all the ingredients.

spicy sausage and bean soup with roast tomatoes

serves 4

Use fresh chorizo or a spicy Polish or Italian sausage for this soup. If unavailable, use fresh bulk sausage and add a little crushed dried chile. Serve with fresh bread or toast rubbed with a little garlic and drizzled with good olive oil.

20 cherry tomatoes
3 tablespoons olive oil
salt and freshly ground black pepper
6–8 ounces fresh spicy sausage, cut into 3/4-inch cubes
1 onion, finely chopped
1 (15-ounce) can cannellini beans or white beans, rinsed
3 cups chicken or vegetable broth (see page 107)
1 tablespoon balsamic vinegar
20 flat-leaf parsley or basil leaves

Preheat the oven to 350°F.

Mix the cherry tomatoes with 2 tablespoons of the oil in a roasting pan and season with salt and pepper. Bake for 15 minutes.

Meanwhile, heat the remaining oil in a large pot over medium heat. Add the spicy sausage and fry for 3–4 minutes. When golden brown, add the onion, reduce the heat to low, and cook, stirring occasionally, for 8 minutes until soft.

Stir the beans into the pot. Season well with salt and pepper and cook for 2 minutes.

Add the broth and bring to a boil, then reduce heat to a simmer and cook for 10 minutes.

Remove the roasted tomatoes from the oven and add the balsamic vinegar. Transfer the tomatoes and all the juices from the pan to the simmering soup pot. Add half the parsley or basil to the soup.

With a slotted spoon, remove half the bean and tomato mixture from the pot and add to a food processor. Carefully blend to a smooth puree. Return it to the pot—this will thicken the soup without having to add extra starch. You only puree half to keep the variety of color and texture.

Stir in the remaining chopped herbs. Check the seasoning. If you have used a cured sausage, it may be quite salty so it is important to taste first. This soup can take a lot of black pepper and you could add a little extra balsamic vinegar if you like.

roast sweet potato soup with rosemary and bacon

serves 4

You can serve the soup hot or warm, with some pieces of toast rubbed with a little garlic.

3 sweet potatoes, peeled and cut into $^3/_4$-inch cubes
3 tablespoons olive oil
salt and freshly ground black pepper
6 bacon slices, cut into $^1/_2$-inch pieces
2 garlic cloves, finely chopped
1 tablespoon fresh rosemary, finely chopped
1 onion, finely chopped
4 cups homemade vegetable or chicken broth (see page 107)
juice of $^1/_2$ lemon

Preheat the oven to 400°F.

Mix the sweet potatoes with 2 tablespoons of the oil, and the salt and pepper and spread it out on a baking sheet. Roast for 15 minutes or until golden brown and soft.

Meanwhile, heat the remaining oil in a large pot over medium heat. Add the bacon and cook, stirring occasionally, for 5 minutes or until golden brown and crispy. Add the garlic and rosemary and cook for 1 minute.

Add the onion, reduce the heat to low, and cook for about 10 minutes, until it is soft. Stir while cooking to avoid sticking. Add the broth, cover with a lid, and turn up the heat to bring to a boil.

Remove the sweet potatoes from the oven and add to the stock. Remove the lid and simmer for another 5 minutes.

With a slotted spoon, remove two thirds of the onion and sweet potato mixture without too much liquid, and add to a food processor. Carefully blend to a smooth puree. Return to the pot, leaving the remaining mixture unblended to keep some contrasting texture.

Squeeze the lemon juice into the soup and check the seasoning, being careful not to over-salt as the bacon flavor is quite strong.

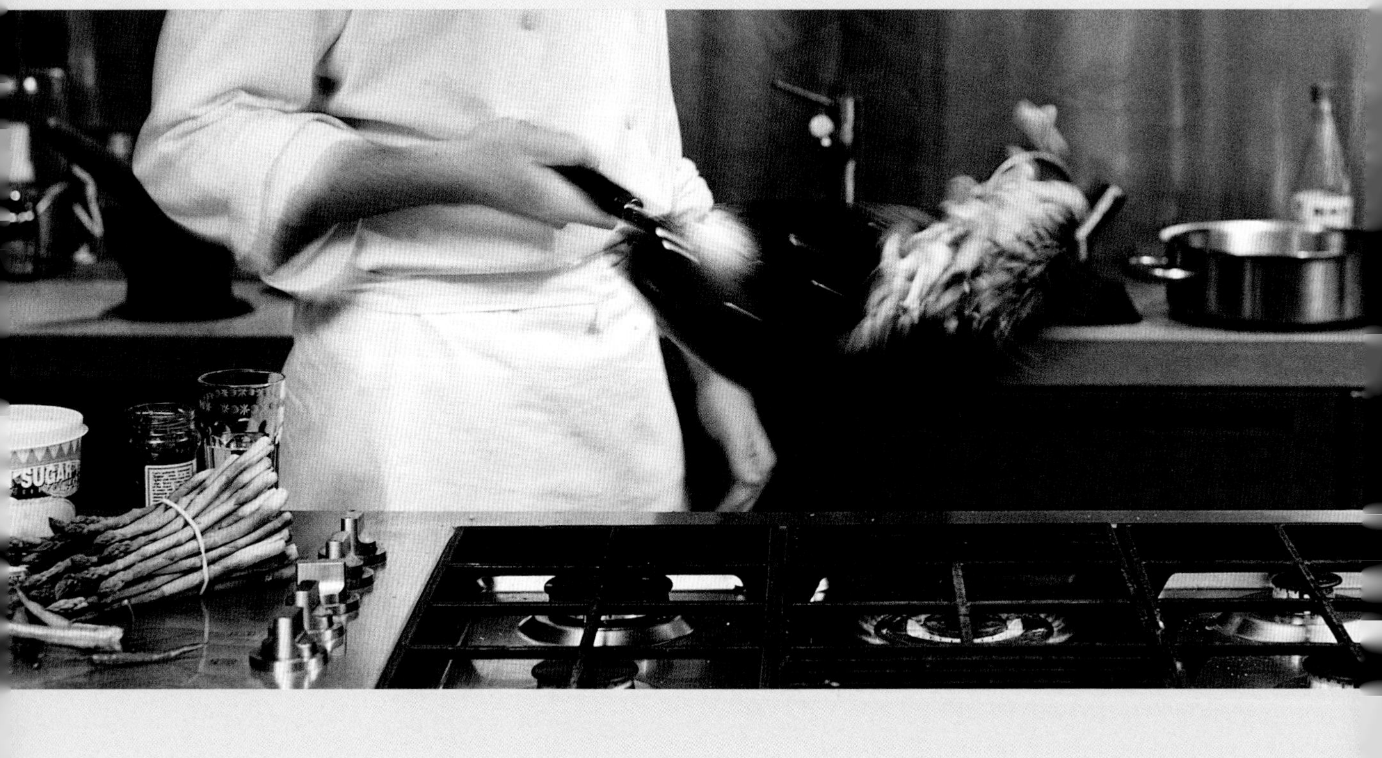
SUGAR

quick dishes

quick dishes

In our increasingly busy schedules there is always a need for simple yet satisfying dishes. Quick prep time should not mean any less flavor; in fact it should almost mean more.

Many Asian dishes take little time to cook and have a real punch of flavors, making them a great quick fix. The same is true of quite a few pasta dishes and sauces. Fried garlic, chile, and olive oil or a carbonara sauce with raw eggs, Parmesan, and fried pancetta illustrate this to mouth-watering effect; both sauces can be made while the pasta is cooking.

In order to make tasty quick dishes and to gain confidence in the process it helps to have a good stock of staple ingredients on hand for use at short notice. Anchovies, olives, and capers can add an intense flavor to quick dishes. Cured meats such as bacon, pancetta, prosciutto, salami, and chorizo work in the same way. Another important staple is a selection of mixed nuts such as almonds, pine nuts, sesame seeds, and raw skinless peanuts, which can be dry-roasted and added at the end of cooking to bring a sweet flavor and contrasting texture. Strong aromatic ingredients such as garlic, ginger, and chile are very versatile and it is always useful to have a few lemons and limes on hand to adjust the seasoning at the end, highlighting or tempering flavor groups. Dried fruits such as apricots, figs, cranberries, and sour cherries add substance and sophistication to what might otherwise be a bland or thin-tasting dish. For Asian dishes, fish sauce and soy sauce when combined with something sour like tamarind or lime juice will intensify the other flavors that are present.

The use of fresh herbs such as basil, mint, flat-leaf parsley, cilantro, and marjoram among others can add much to a quick dish. I also use a lot of peppery arugula as a herb. The color, vibrancy, and refreshing flavors will transform the simplest of other ingredients. Dried herbs and some spices benefit from slow cooking to unlock their intense oils and perfumes, whereas fresh soft herbs just need to be torn or coarsely chopped and you can smell the difference that they will make to the finished dish while the leaves are still in your hand. When buying herbs, try to buy big fresh bunches as opposed to a few leaves that cost a fortune. Most ethnic shops or markets—be they Greek, Lebanese, Thai, or Moroccan—sell big bunches that are much better quality and value for money than those bought from a supermarket.

A really good-quality olive oil is an essential staple that can transform a simple salad or pasta dish. For this you will need a cold-pressed extra virgin olive oil, which has a particularly intense flavor. However, it is important not to overheat an extra virgin olive oil because you will deaden the flavor potential. Have some decent quality oil for cooking, roasting, and general use and then a more specific one for making cold dressings and sauces and for finishing dishes. Olive oils vary enormously from region to region, so taste a few and come up with one that you like, as you would with wine. Some are fresh and citrus-like, and some have a slight saltiness to them, particularly if they have been grown in hot coastal areas. I like the northern Tuscan style of extra virgin olive oil because when the olives are harvested there are still a percentage of unripe green olives that are pressed alongside the riper ones. This gives a strong peppery, grassy taste to the oil.

Many of the sauces, pastes, and relishes in the first chapter can completely transform a quick dish, bringing the flavors into balance and creating structure and detail. Because complex techniques and slow-cooking methods are not being employed, the flavors have got to speak for themselves. Therefore, tasting and balancing the end result is essential.

SWEET **carrots, snow peas, baby corn, black figs, tagliatelle, sea bream (porgy), barley, French lentils, scallops** SOUR **lime juice, red wine vinegar, Thai coconut vinegar, dry white wine** SALTY **oyster sauce, anchovies, capers, soy sauce** HOT **sambal sauce, dried chiles, garlic, coriander seeds, cumin seeds** BITTER **greens, spinach**

hot and sticky vegetable stir-fry with honey and ginger

serves 4–6

for the sauce

2 garlic cloves, crushed
2 tablespoons honey
1 tablespoon grated fresh ginger
1 tablespoon sweet chile sauce
1 teaspoon sambal sauce (Indonesian hot chile sauce)
1 tablespoon brown sugar
juice of 1 lime

2 carrots
1 sweet potato
handful of oyster mushrooms
15–20 snow peas
6 asparagus spears
1 tablespoon oil
salt and freshly ground black pepper
small handful of cilantro, chopped

Mix the ingredients for the sauce in a bowl.

Peel the carrot and the sweet potato. Cut them into equal-sized sticks. Tear the oyster mushrooms into equal-sized strips. Trim the snow peas, and cut the asparagus into pieces the same size as the snow peas.

Heat a wok and add the oil. Working in batches if necessary, stir-fry the carrots and sweet potato for 2 minutes. Add the asparagus and the oyster mushrooms and cook for 2 minutes over a high heat. Add the snow peas and the sauce and cook just until the sauce comes to a boil.

Season to taste, and add the chopped cilantro.

using a wok

The use of a wok aids the speed of creating flavorsome dishes because of its shape. It transfers heat around the pan so that ingredients around the sides cook just as quickly as those on the bottom. Vegetables, meat, shellfish, noodles, and rice can be simply and quickly tossed through the wok over a high heat, giving them an intense smoky flavor. This technique of cooking is commonly used across the whole Southeast Asian region and in many households the wok might be the only cooking apparatus. For a special family meal in Thailand or Vietnam, numerous courses and dishes could arrive from the one charcoal brazier in very quick succession, all of them different—from stir-fries, egg-fried rice, and noodle dishes, to braised meats, curries, and relishes.

When using a wok you have to be quite ambidextrous. A sort of flattened ladle is often used to move things around the curved sides of the pan, and it can be dipped into cracked pepper, salt, soy sauce, lime juice, dried chili or other condiments when needed. The other hand grips the handle, and with a tossing motion similar to that used when making crêpes, flips the contents of the pan back onto itself. In busy restaurants in Vietnam, special wok stalls are created where the surrounding area of the stove is permanently cooled by flowing water running to a central drain. The running water also gets rid of the build-up of scraps that have caught on the bottom of the wok or cannot be used. The pace is often so furious that the lever that drops the flames from high to low gets controlled by the knee, so that the chef seems to be working like an octopus, using all limbs to achieve a mighty tasty result.

Often some intensely flavored ingredients such as cilantro (fresh coriander) roots, garlic, ginger, crushed white peppercorns, and chile are fried first to flavor the pan, then scooped out so that they do not stick and burn, and are then added back later. Hard ingredients are added to the hot wok next, while more delicate or subtle ingredients can be quickly tossed in towards the end. At any point a splash of water, broth, or other liquid could be added to the hot wok, instantly creating some steam to help speed up the cooking process or to quickly absorb some extra flavor.

A method that works well is cooking ingredients of varying textures in different batches and then combining them and adjusting the seasoning at the end. This means that each ingredient gets the full benefit of the hot, quick, and smoky wok. If everything is dumped in at the same time, the bulk of the raw ingredients drops the temperature of the wok and everything will steam and boil in its own watery juices, resulting in insipid, watery, soggy food which has taken too long to cook through. This is the complete opposite from the effect that you are trying to create.

stir-fry of mixed mushrooms, snow peas, and spinach with ginger and sesame oil

serves 4–6

handful of oyster mushrooms
handful of shiitake mushrooms
30 snow peas
2 handfuls of spinach leaves
1 ounce enoki mushrooms
2 tablespoons oil
2 tablespoons sesame seeds, toasted (optional)
salt and freshly ground black pepper

for the paste

2 garlic cloves
$1^1/_4$-inch piece of fresh ginger, peeled and grated
1 red chile (jalapeño or serrano), seeded and finely chopped

for the sauce

1 tablespoon soy sauce
1 tablespoon oyster sauce
1 teaspoon sesame oil
juice of $^1/_2$ lemon

Tear or cut the oyster and shiitake mushrooms into equal-sized pieces or slices. Cut off the thick base from the enoki mushrooms. Trim the snow peas, and rinse the spinach.

Grind the ingredients for the paste in a mortar and pestle. Prepare the sauce by mixing the ingredients together.

Heat a wok and add the oil. Stir-fry the paste for 30 seconds or until it is fragrant.

Add all the mushrooms, except the enoki. Stir-fry over a high heat for 2 minutes, until they start to brown. Add the snow peas and cook for 1 minute.

Stir in the sauce. Add the spinach leaves and stir-fry for 30 seconds, then add the enoki mushrooms and sesame seeds, if using. Season to taste and serve.

chinese-inspired lemony vegetable stir-fry

serves 4–6

***Shiso* or perilla leaves are used throughout China, Japan, Vietnam, and Korea. They have a pungent, minty, anise-like aroma and flavor and can be bought in little cartons. If unavailable, substitute fresh mint. Asian celery is more delicate looking than the Western types. Its flavor is much more concentrated, so it is more suitable as a flavoring than as a vegetable to be eaten raw. If you can't find it, use more of all the other ingredients.**

bunch of baby bok choy
bunch of baby choy sum (Chinese sprouting cabbage)
2 bunches of Chinese broccoli
1 head of broccoli florets
10 ears of baby corn
4 ribs Asian celery
2 tablespoons oil
salt and freshly ground black pepper

for the paste

2 stalks of lemongrass, coarse leaves removed, finely chopped
2 garlic cloves, crushed
zest and juice of 1 lemon
4 scallions, finely chopped
2 tablespoons sweet chile sauce

to finish

1 tablespoon mirin (Japanese cooking wine)
1 tablespoon Asian sesame oil
1 tablespoon soy sauce
small handful of perilla leaves
1/2 bunch of cilantro, leaves removed and chopped
handful of bean sprouts

Mix the ingredients for the paste together.

Cut the bok choy, choy sum, and Chinese broccoli into equal-sized pieces, about the size of the baby corn. Cut the baby corn in half lengthwise. Cut the broccoli into florets, and the Asian celery into strips (save any leaves and keep to one side).

Heat some oil in a wok. Stir-fry the bok choy, choy sum, Chinese broccoli, and broccoli over a high heat for 2 minutes.

Add the baby corn and Asian celery and cook for another minute. Add the paste and cook until the vegetables are tender.

Add the mirin and half the sesame oil to the vegetables, followed by the soy sauce, perilla leaves, cilantro, and bean sprouts.

Check the seasoning and serve garnished with the celery leaves and the remaining sesame oil.

creamy fig pasta with rosemary and lemon

serves 4–6

This is absolutely delicious and works well with ripe black figs. It is not too sweet when combined with all the other components.

- $1\frac{1}{2}$ tablespoons butter
- 2 garlic cloves, finely chopped
- 1 tablespoon finely chopped rosemary
- 1 red chile (jalapeño or serrano), seeded and finely chopped
- 12 ripe black figs
- zest and juice of 1 lemon
- salt and freshly ground black pepper
- 1 pound tagliatelle or fettucine
- 2 ounces gorgonzola cheese, preferably dolcelatte
- $\frac{1}{2}$ cup heavy whipping cream
- $\frac{1}{2}$ cup freshly grated Parmesan

Bring a large pot of salted water to a boil.

In a heavy skillet, heat the butter and cook the garlic, rosemary, and chile for 1 minute. Trim the figs, cut into quarters, and place flesh-side down in the pan. Cook for a couple of minutes, then turn them over and continue cooking until they lose their shape.

Add the lemon zest and season with salt and freshly ground black pepper.

When the water is boiling, add the pasta and cook for about 5 to 8 minutes or until al dente.

Add the cheese to the figs and let it melt. Add the cream and simmer gently to reduce. Stir in half the lemon juice and half of the grated Parmesan.

Taste the cream sauce; it will be sweet and rich, hot, sour, and salty. The lemon will cut the richness so that it is not too cloying. The blue cheese gives a depth to the flavor. Adjust the seasoning accordingly.

Drain the pasta and mix in the pasta sauce. Season with lots of black pepper and the remaining lemon juice and grated Parmesan.

baked sea bream with tamarind, green chile, and wild ginger

serves 4

This style of cooking whole fish is common across Thailand and Southeast Asia and is often served with other quick Asian-style dishes.

4 garlic cloves
2 long green chiles, seeded and finely chopped
2 cilantro (fresh coriander) roots, rinsed and finely chopped (if not available, use cilantro stems)
1 teaspoon salt
2 tablespoons oil
2 tablespoons tamarind pulp
2 tablespoons Asian fish sauce
1 tablespoon white sugar
2 whole sea bream (porgy) or other firm white-fleshed fish, such as ocean perch or snapper
salt and freshly ground black pepper
3 scallions, cut into thin stips
4 stems of wild ginger or a 1 1/2-inch piece of ginger, peeled and shredded
handful of cilantro leaves

Preheat the oven to 400°F.

In a mortar and pestle, pound the garlic, chiles and cilantro roots with the salt until a smooth paste forms.

Heat a little oil in a small skillet and cook this paste for 2–3 minutes until fragrant.

Add the tamarind pulp, fish sauce, white sugar, and 1/2 cup of water and simmer for 5 minutes. Taste the sauce. It should be hot, sweet, salty, and sour: adjust the seasoning if necessary.

Score the fish on both sides with three deep parallel cuts down to the bone. Pat dry. Season well with salt and pepper.

Heat some oil in a heavy ovenproof skillet over a medium-high heat. Place the fish in the pan. Cook until the skin is a deep golden brown and then turn over. While the fish is browning, it is important that you do not move it or you will break the crust.

When the fish is sealed on both sides, scatter half the scallions and half the shredded ginger over the fish and transfer to the oven.

Bake the fish in the oven for about 5–10 minutes, depending upon its size. When ready, place the fish on a plate and pour the sauce over it. It should be hot, sweet, salty, and sour.

When ready to serve, scatter the remaining scallions, ginger, and cilantro over the top.

marinated fish with ginger, lemongrass, and lime zest

serves 4

This recipe would also work with shellfish or shrimp, chicken breasts, or pork tenderloin.

6–7 ounces per person firm white fish fillets such as hake, snapper, sea bream (porgy), flounder, halibut, or cod

for the marinade

1 garlic clove
1 red chile (jalapeño or serrano), seeded and finely chopped
3 cilantro (fresh coriander) roots, rinsed and finely chopped
pinch of salt
$1\frac{1}{4}$-inch piece of fresh ginger, peeled and grated
3 stalks of lemongrass, tough outer leaves removed, thinly sliced
zest and juice of 2 limes
2 tablespoons soy sauce
2 tablespoons of Asian fish sauce
juice of 1 orange
4 scallions, thinly sliced
salt and freshly ground black pepper
30 cilantro leaves, for garnishing

Preheat the oven to 400°F.

In a mortar and pestle, pound the garlic, chiles, and cilantro roots with the salt until you have a smooth paste.

Mix with all the other marinade ingredients except the third of the scallions and all the cilantro leaves set aside for the garnish.

Season the fish with salt and pepper and place in an ovenproof dish. Pour the marinade over it, making sure it goes under the fish, as well as on top. Tightly cover the dish with tin foil, making sure all the edges are sealed. Place in the center of the oven and bake for 12 minutes.

When cooked, remove the tin foil and garnish with the chopped cilantro and the remaining scallions.

chef's tip

If you want to use a whole fish, scale it and clean the cavity (your fish market can do this for you). Remove the gills and any other blood. On each side of the fish, make two or three incisions in the flesh cutting right down to the bone. This will enable all the juices and flavors to penetrate the fish. Let cook about 4 minutes longer than fillets.

baked clams with barley and preserved lemon

serves 4

- 1/2 cup barley, soaked in cold water for 20 minutes
- 1 tablespoon olive oil
- 1 medium onion, finely chopped
- 1 dried chile, finely chopped and crushed to a paste with 2 garlic cloves and a little salt
- 2 imported bay leaves
- 1 preserved lemon (see page 27), finely chopped
- 1 cup of dry sherry or dry white wine
- 4 1/2 pounds cleaned clams or mussels
- salt and freshly ground black pepper
- 1/2 bunch of flat-leaf parsley, chopped

Preheat the oven to 425°F.

Drain the barley and place in a small saucepan. Cover with cold water, bring to a boil, and simmer for 15 minutes over medium heat until plump and tender, yet still firm.

Heat the oil in a heavy ovenproof pan, add the onion, and cook for 3–5 minutes until soft but not browned. Push the onion to one side of the pan and cook the chile and garlic paste until golden, then stir it back into the onion mixture. Add the bay leaves.

Drain the barley, then add to the other pan along with the preserved lemon. Increase the heat, add the sherry, and let it reduce for 1 minute. Add the shellfish and stir over a high heat. Season to taste.

Bake in the oven for about 4–5 minutes until all the shellfish have opened. Discard any that have not opened. Scatter the parsley over the top. Taste the broth and adjust the seasoning.

Spoon into large soup bowls and serve with lots of crusty bread to soak up all the sweet juices.

shrimp with tamarind, roast chile, and lime leaves

serves 4

An easy and tasty dish that takes less time than phoning for take-out food! Serve with rice noodles or plain rice.

for the chile paste

- 4 dried long red chiles (soaked in hot water for 1 hour)
- 2 shallots, quartered
- 2 garlic cloves, cut in half
- 1 teaspoon shrimp paste
- 1 teaspoon palm or brown sugar
- 2 stalks of lemongrass, coarse outer leaves removed, thinly sliced

- 2 tablespoons oil
- 2 1/4 pounds shrimp, peeled and deveined
- 3 tablespoons tamarind paste
- 5 kaffir or other lime leaves
- 5–7 fl. ounces coconut milk
- lime wedges, for serving

First make the paste. Seed and finely chop the chiles and combine with the other ingredients in a mortar and pestle or food processor.

Heat 1 tablespoon of oil in a wok, add the paste, and stir over a low-medium heat for 5 minutes or until fragrant. Transfer to a bowl.

Wipe the wok clean and place over medium-high heat. Add 1 tablespoon oil, add the shrimp, and stir-fry for 2 minutes, until only half cooked. Add half the chile paste and stir-fry for 1 minute.

Add the tamarind paste and cook quickly to reduce, then add 3 of the lime leaves and the coconut cream. Cook until the sauce is hot.

Serve at once. Shred the remaining lime leaves and scatter them over the top. Serve the lime wedges on the side.

pan-fried scallops and warm lentil salad with anchovy and rosemary sauce

serves 4

- 1/2 cup French lentils, picked over and rinsed
- 14 sage leaves
- 2 garlic cloves, unpeeled
- 3 tablespoons extra virgin olive oil
- juice of 1 lemon
- salt and freshly ground black pepper
- selection of herbs, such as basil, dill, parsley, mint, and arugula, chopped
- 3 tablespoons olive oil
- 12 sea scallops, trimmed
- 4 salted anchovy fillets, rinsed and drained
- 2 tablespoons capers, rinsed and drained
- 2 tablespoons herb vinegar or red wine vinegar
- selection of mixed leaves such as arugula, dandelion, mizuna, mustard leaves, sorrel, and other bitter and peppery leaves
- 1 x recipe anchovy and rosemary sauce (see page 33)

Follow the instructions for making the anchovy and rosemary sauce.

Put the lentils into a saucepan, cover with cold water, and bring to a boil. Reduce the heat to low. While they are cooking, place a couple of the sage leaves and garlic cloves in the water to flavor the lentils. Cook gently for about 12 minutes until tender yet firm to the bite. Drain all but 1–2 tablespoons of the cooking liquid (don't overcook, as, once drained, the lentils will continue to cook from their own heat). Season with the olive oil, half the lemon juice, salt, and pepper. Set aside to cool.

When the lentils are cool, add the mixed herbs and set aside.

Add 2 tablespoons of the oil to a skillet and cook the sage for 1 minute until crispy. Set the pan aside but do not drain.

Pat the scallops dry. Season with salt and pepper.

Reheat the sage-infused oil until very hot, add the scallops, and cook for 1 minute. Turn over and cook on the other side for another minute. Add the anchovies; they will melt into the pan. Remove scallops from pan.

Add the capers and herb vinegar to the pan. Cook, stirring up any browned bits that cling to the bottom of the pan. Remove from the heat and add the remaining lemon juice and 1 tablespoon olive oil to make the dressing.

Arrange the salad leaves in a serving dish and scatter the warm lentils over them. Place the scallops on top, then drizzle the herb vinegar dressing. Scatter the crispy sage leaves on top and dress with the anchovy and rosemary sauce.

quail with garlic and peppercorns

serves 4

I learned this fantastic recipe from David Thompson. This mixture of spices is one of the most ancient in Thai cuisine. Long before chiles arrived with the Portuguese, who had discovered them in South America in the 16th century, white pepper was used to provide the heat in food. For this dish you could substitute partridge, pheasant, chicken, guinea fowl, beef, pork, or venison for the quail.

4 quail, cleaned and quartered
2 tablespoons soy sauce
1 teaspoon sugar
freshly ground black pepper
vegetable oil, for shallow frying

for the garlic mix

3 cilantro (fresh coriander) roots, rinsed and chopped (if not available, use cilantro stems)
pinch of salt
20 white peppercorns
2 slices of fresh ginger
1 head of garlic, unpeeled

for the chile and vinegar sauce

3 red chiles (jalapeño or serrano), seeded and finely chopped
2 garlic cloves
1 cilantro (fresh coriander) root, rinsed and chopped (if not available, use cilantro stems)
2 teaspoons salt
2 teaspoons sugar
2 tablespoons Thai coconut vinegar
20 cilantro leaves

Place the quail in a bowl and add the soy sauce, sugar, and black pepper. Toss to coat.

To make the garlic mix: in a mortar and pestle or food processor, crush the cilantro roots, salt, and peppercorns. Add the ginger and garlic and continue to pound to a rough paste.

Add the garlic mixture to the quail, turning to coat, and let marinate, covered and at room temerature, for 30 minutes.

Heat the oil in the wok. When hot, working in batches if necessary, add the quail and garlic mixture. Cook for about 3–4 minutes each side until golden brown all over. Remove the meat and let it rest for a few minutes.

For the chile and vinegar sauce, crush the chiles, garlic, and cilantro root with the salt and sugar until smooth. Add the vinegar. Taste: the sauce should be sour, salty, and sweet. If it is too acidic then dilute it with a little water; this will also make it easier to pour.

Serve the cooked meat with the sauce splashed over the top of it, or on the side as a dipping sauce. Garnish with the cilantro leaves.

chef's tips

The meat could be broiled or roasted quickly as opposed to stir-frying, although if roasting, it is best to brown the meat quickly on the stovetop before transferring to the oven. You could also make skewers with this recipe: cut the meat into cubes, marinate as above, and broil until golden brown and crispy. Thread onto bamboo skewers and serve with the chile and vinegar sauce.

lemon chicken with rosemary and mascarpone

serves 6

This warm and substantial salad is great at any time. It looks extremely inviting when it is assembled with all the different colors and textures.

1 butternut squash, peeled and cut into chunks
3 sweet potatoes, peeled and cut into chunks
5 tablepoons olive oil
salt and freshly ground black pepper
8 ounces mascarpone cheese
zest and juice of 1 lemon
1 tablespoon chopped rosemary
6 boneless chicken breasts, skin on
2 garlic cloves, cut in half and sliced lengthwise
1 red chile (jalapeño or serrano), seeded and finely chopped
10 ounces fresh spinach leaves
2 tablespoons coarsely chopped flat-leaf parsley
1 tablespoon coarsely chopped mint

Preheat oven to 400ºF.

In a large bowl, combine squash and sweet potato with 2 tablespoons of the oil, and some salt and pepper. Toss to mix. Divide mixture between 2 large baking sheets, spreading into an even layer on each. Roast for about 30 minutes until tender and golden brown with caramelized edges.

Mix the mascarpone with the lemon zest and rosemary. Season well. Peel back the skin of the chicken and place a spoonful of the mixture under each breast. Fold back the skin. Save a little of the mixture. This can be done in advance and chilled until needed.

Heat a heavy skillet. Add 1 tablespoon of oil and cook the chicken over medium-low heat, skin-side down, until golden brown. Then transfer the chicken, skin-side up, to a roasting pan and roast in the oven for 10–12 minutes or until white throughout, but still juicy.

Remove the chicken from the oven. Put a small spoonful of the mixture onto each breast and let it melt. Squeeze half the lemon juice over them and let cool.

Heat 1 tablespoon of the oil in a large, heavy skillet or wok. Cook the garlic and the chile until pale golden. Add the spinach. Cover with a lid and cook until the leaves are wilted—about 2 minutes. Season and add a squeeze of lemon juice and the remaining oil.

Slice the chicken diagonally, saving all the juices. In a large serving bowl, mix the chicken with the spinach, roasted vegetables, and any cooking juices. Top with the chopped herbs.

lemon-poached chicken with lots of roasted garlic

serves 4

This dish is from rural France. Don't be put off by the quantity of garlic—when roasted, it becomes very sweet, and loses its pungency. A great way to eat—just roll up your sleeves and dig in!

2 tablespoons olive oil
chicken thighs, drumsticks, and chicken breasts, skin on, (enough for 4 people)
20 garlic cloves, unpeeled
1/2 cup dry white wine
zest of 2 lemons, juice of 1 lemon
sprig of thyme
2 imported bay leaves
sea salt and freshly ground black pepper
2 cups chicken broth, preferably homemade (see page 107)
1 French baguette
20 flat-leaf parsley leaves

Heat a large, heavy skillet over medium-high heat. Add the olive oil. When the oil is hot, add the chicken pieces, skin-side down, to cover the bottom of the pan. If the chicken won't fit in one layer, you will have to cook it in two batches. Cook for about 4 minutes on each side until golden brown.

Add the garlic cloves. Drain off any excess oil. Add the wine to the chicken and cook for 2 minutes until slightly reduced.

Add the lemon zest and juice, thyme, and bay leaves. Season well with salt and pepper. Add the broth. Cover the pan and reduce the heat to low. Simmer gently for 20 minutes.

Insert a small sharp knife into the chicken flesh, just by the bone. If the juice runs clear then the meat is done. If the juice is still pink, cook longer.

Check the seasoning and adjust accordingly with salt and pepper. Transfer to a warm serving dish. Chop the parsley coarsely and scatter it over the top.

Cut the French bread into slices and toast them.

For each serving, spoon chicken, garlic, and sauce into a shallow bowl. Serve toast slices alongside the chicken. Let each person squeeze the soft garlic out of its papery skin onto the pieces of toast, which can then be used to soak up the sauce.

chef's tip

This dish can be made with a whole chicken in much the same way, but you will need more wine and broth, and will have to cook the meat longer.

grilled pork with caramelized pink grapefruit

serves 4–6

This is a hearty winter warmer that could be made into a lighter springtime salad by serving with fresh herbs and raw baby spinach or asparagus. The caramelized spices work very well with the honey from the marinade and the sweet and sour flavors of the pink grapefruit. Serve with crushed potatoes (see page 225) and spinach braised with garlic and lemon juice.

2 pork tenderloins, well trimmed
1 tablespoon coriander seeds
1 tablespoon cumin seeds
1 garlic clove
2 grapefruits, 1 of them zested
salt and freshly ground black pepper
zest of 1 lemon
2 tablespoons honey

In a mortar and pestle crush the coriander and cumin seeds until fine. Add the garlic and crush with the spices.

With a sharp knife, remove the skin and pith from the grapefruit. Holding the grapefruit over a bowl to catch the juice, cut down on both sides of the membrane to release the grapefruit segments. Be sure the fruit has no white pith attached, as it is bitter and unpleasant. Squeeze the membranes over a bowl to release as much juice as possible.

Place the pork in a shallow bowl and season with salt, pepper, and the crushed spice mixture. Add the lemon and grapefruit zest and half of the grapefruit juice and let it marinate for about 1 hour.

Preheat a grill pan over hight heat, and preheat the oven to 400°F.

Remove the meat from the marinade and place on the grill pan. Discard the marinade. Sear the pork for 2 minutes on each side until golden brown and charred.

Mix the grapefruit segments with the honey and the remaining grapefruit juice.

Transfer the meat to an ovenproof dish and pour the grapefruit-honey mixture over it. Scatter the grapefruit segments around the pork. Roast in the oven, basting regularly to keep the meat moist.

The tenderloin is a thin piece of meat and so it will not take long to cook. After 20 minutes, check to see if it is done by inserting a skewer—if the juices run clear then the meat is done, but if still pink, continue to roast.

To serve, slice the meat into medallions and serve with the sauce and roasted grapefruit segments.

asian grilled pork with honey, soy, and ginger

serves 6

This is a delicious and easy way to marinate meat before roasting. It works for any cut of meat up to 4½ pounds; for larger quantities just increase the quantities of the marinade. Duck breast or chicken would work well, and you can also cut cubes of butternut squash or sweet potato and roast them in the mixture.

for the marinade

3 tablespoons soy sauce
1 tablespoon honey
juice of 1 lime
zest and juice of 1 orange
1 red chile (jalapeño or serrano), seeded and finely chopped
1½-inch piece of fresh ginger, peeled and grated

1 tablespoon oil
1 x 1–2¼-pound pork tenderloin, well trimmed
salt and freshly ground black pepper

Preheat the oven to 400°F.

In a large bowl, mix together the ingredients for the marinade. Remove half of the marinade to a small bowl and reserve.

Place meat in the large bowl with the marinade, turning to coat. Let sit covered, 1–2 hours at room temperature, or refrigerate up to 4 hours.

Heat the oil in a shallow, ovenproof skillet on high heat. Season the marinated meat with salt and pepper and place in the hot pan. Sear the meat for 2 minutes on each side until golden brown and charred.

Pour the remaining marinade over the pork and place the pan in the oven.

While cooking, baste the meat with its juices and the marinade to prevent it from drying out. After 20 minutes, check to see if it is done by inserting a skewer—if the juices run clear then the meat is done, but if still pink, continue to roast. Then remove from the oven and let it rest.

This method will result in the meat gently cooking through to completion, and remaining tender without drying out or overcooking.

The meat could be served hot, warm, or cold in a salad.

chef's tip

By starting the meat off on the stovetop, the pan and meat will already be hot when they go into the oven, so the cooking process will have started and will take less time overall. Another advantage is that if the meat is in small pieces, it will be nicely browned and crisp on the outside. Without this initial stage in the cooking the meat may be cooked through, but will not have had enough time to brown in the oven.

one-pot
dishes

one-pot dishes

There are many advantages to cooking an entire meal in a single pot. This traditional rural technique suits a casual occasion and is often an uncomplicated way to cook. The food may be slow-cooked and even prepared in advance. Both of these factors free the cook from any last-minute preparations.

Every culinary region in the world has its own methods and specialties of one-pot cooking. Many of them stem from the land, from peasant and home-style cooking. One-pot cooking techniques vary enormously, and include stewing, braising, pot-roasting, and slow cooking. A hearty soup or broth can be made into a one-pot meal by adding meat, vegetables, and noodles. The one-pot meal can even extend to dishes that are baked or roasted in the oven with everything in one pan, such as lamb boulangère, a recipe from rural France which originated centuries back when the bakery oven was often the only oven in the village. Similar communal methods of cooking were employed in villages in Italy and Spain, and across the Middle East, with dishes being cooked while the congregation or village was at prayer in the church or mosque. In Italy, meat, fish, and vegetables were baked *al forno* in the central wood-fired oven. Such ovens are not just for pizzas!

There are several ingredients that really benefit from one-pot cooking. In Southeast Asian and Middle Eastern cooking, tamarind is a powerful ingredient. It is a brown seedpod containing a sour pulp, which is rich in vitamins, especially vitamin C. It is used in soups, stews, and curries and is one of the essential sour elements used in Thailand and Vietnam to balance hot, sweet, and salty. Tamarind's intense, green-apple sourness has a sweet aftertaste when eaten raw, but once it is cooked it imparts a subtle and complex but distinctive flavor. It is often the essential characteristic that you can't quite put your finger on.

Other sour ingredients used in casseroles include quince, sour cherries, and semi-dried fruits like cranberries and apricots or sour plums. Green tomatoes can be used in one-pot dishes and slow-cooking methods to great effect. Preserved and salted lemons (see page 27) give a similar result to that of using tamarind. Their intensity makes the food more full-bodied.

The unique saltiness provided by Asian fish sauce and light soy sauce in Asia, and by cured salted meats and fish in Europe, such as pancetta, bacon, or anchovies, can draw out the individual characteristics of the other cooking ingredients. These salty additions help the rest of the dish to blend, and they also mean that much less sea salt is needed to season the food. Asian fish sauce, which is quite a noxious liquid when tasted in isolation, loses its fishiness when it is cooked and blended, and instead becomes a more savory element, adding a vital base note to the dish, and enhancing the flavors of the surrounding ingredients.

In Italian cooking, sauces are often started by cooking anchovies with garlic and chopped herbs or some dried chiles, to create an invigorating foundation from which to build the rest of the sauce. Slow-cooked lamb, beef, veal, and pork can all benefit from the addition of anchovies at the beginning of the cooking process. The anchovies will be the secret ingredient in the sauce that your guests will not be able to quite identify, but will make the dish exceptionally tasty.

In this section there are recipes for curries, stews, tagines, and other slow-cooked meat dishes, as well as hearty soups and rice dishes which can all be meals in themselves, with little else needed to accompany them. When a meal is created in one pot, the ingredients really get a chance to impart their characteristics to each other, creating a subtle layering of flavors. To achieve this effect successfully, it is absolutely essential to taste the food at each stage of the cooking so that the flavors contrast and complement each other.

SWEET **baguette, baby corn, new potatoes, leeks, cod, monkfish (angler fish), chickpeas, pork, cinnamon, lamb, dried apricots** SOUR **pineapple, lemon juice, lime juice** SALTY **gruyère cheese, bean curd, prosciutto, pancetta, shrimp paste** HOT **harissa, cayenne pepper, coriander seeds, turmeric** BITTER **hen pheasants, Treviso, savoy cabbage**

Pimentón de la Vera
Denominacion de Origen
"LA DALIA"
JOSE Mª HERNANDEZ,S.L.
POLG. IND. EL POCITO, PARC. A/8
10400.- JARAIZ DE LA VERA.- (CACERES)

thai curries

Several factors contribute to the intensity of the Thai curry, the first being the ingredients that are used, the second how it is cooked. The paste goes through numerous changes, and so you must taste it at the different stages, even if it is not that delicious at the beginning. Once you understand how the different ingredients work together and then change in the cooking process, you can adjust the flavors at the end to make something memorable and delicious.

Cilantro (coriander) roots and stems are often used in the base of Thai curry pastes. Here's a simple analogy: a bunch of cilantro with its roots is like a tree. The tree gets its nutrients from the roots in the soil. If you translate nutrients into flavor then the roots are the most intensely flavored, and therefore the best bit. Try to buy larger bunches of cilantro with the roots on; if unavailable, chop all the stems of the bunch into the paste.

Other intense aromatic ingredients—garlic, chile, lemongrass, whole lime leaves, ginger—are used in abundance to flavor the paste. They are chopped then added to a food processor, the hardest ones are added and blended first, otherwise you would have a sloppy puree with large chunks of woody ingredients like lemongrass floating in it.

flavor fundamentals

When the paste cooks, it goes through four different stages of cooking. In the first you will smell the ingredients that have the most amount of water in them, because they will start to cook first. In this case it will be the onions giving off an eye-watering steam. In the second stage of cooking you will smell the ingredients that have the next least amount of moisture in them, such as the lime and cilantro. The third stage that you will smell is the chile, whole lime leaves, and a hint of ginger. If at any time the paste starts to stick, all that has been lost is moisture and water, so just add a little water back to the pan and stir to incorporate any parts that have stuck (just as you would to make a gravy for a Sunday dinner.)

At the fourth and final stage of the cooking the paste becomes aromatic and fragrant. You will smell the ginger and lemongrass because they are the hardest and most aromatic of the ingredients with the least amount of water, and therefore the ones that will start to cook last. To reach this stage will take anything from 20–35 minutes. At this point you can add unsweetened coconut cream and let it reduce by a third by gentle simmering. The paste can now be likened to a stock in that it does not have a lot of salt and so the flavors must be adjusted and brought into balance. When you taste the paste at this stage in the cooking process you might find that you taste the bitterness from the lime and sweetness from the coconut cream above any other flavors. The seasoning needs to be adjusted by adding fresh lime juice and tamarind pulp. Orange juice could also be added to the paste, because it is sweet and acidic. Some Asian fish sauce and soy sauce can be added; their saltiness will bring out the intensity of the other flavors, including the chile. When you have increased the sourness, saltiness, and a little sweetness, mix together and then taste. It will have become much more three-dimensional, with more structure of flavor. You can adjust the chile content to suit your personal taste, but interestingly, by adjusting the other flavors, the whole of the curry paste will be more balanced and so the flavor and heat from the chile will be more pronounced even if you do not add any more. The texture should be creamy and not too thick, unlike an Indian curry, which is generally thicker in texture. If you make a large batch, you can freeze it in smaller containers once you have cooked it down. At short notice you can then rustle up a spectacular curry to impress everyone who tastes it.

Once you have adjusted all the seasonings, you can add other components to the curry, which could be anything from chicken to seafood to red meat. You could grill or roast a good-sized piece of beef or venison, allowing two or three slices per person. Cook the meat until it is rare inside and let it rest for about 5 minutes so the meat inside is close to medium-rare. Cut into generous slices 1/2–1/3-inch thick and add to the curry paste. Turn over in the simmering sauce until medium rare: the meat will continue to cook in the hot sauce while you bring it to the table.

You could make small fishcakes or chicken cakes by pureeing raw meat or fish with aromatics and Asian herbs such as Thai basil, cilantro, or mint, and then rolling them into small balls or cakes and poaching them in the curry sauce. The raw protein holds the ball together while it is poaching, but be careful not to break up by over-mixing the curry. Other interesting options for Thai curries include royal green curry of aromatic smoked trout (see page 194), and geng gari, a spicy curry of butternut squash and sweet potatoes (page 153).

geng gari curry of roast butternut squash with ginger and thai basil

serves 4–6 to accompany other dishes

This curry works well as a sidedish. If not using the curry paste right away, you can store it in the fridge for up to a week or in the freezer for up to 5 months. Before storing, prepare the paste up to the point where you have added the coconut cream and reduced it.

for the curry paste

1 1/4-inch piece of fresh ginger, peeled and cut into matchsticks
4 red chiles (jalapeño or serrano), seeded
3 stalks of lemongrass
6 garlic cloves
1 teaspoon salt
3 red onions
1 tablespoon olive oil
1 teaspoon ground cumin
1 teaspoon ground coriander
1 teaspoon ground cinnamon
1 teaspoon ground nutmeg
1 teaspoon ground turmeric
2 1/2 cups coconut milk

1 butternut squash, peeled, seeded, and cut into bite-size chunks
2 sweet potatoes, peeled and cut into thick wedges
1 teaspoon crushed coriander seeds
1 teaspoon crushed cumin seeds
olive oil, salt, and pepper, for cooking
juice of 2 limes
1 tablespoon tamarind paste
2 tablespoons soy sauce
2–3 tablespoons Asian fish sauce
8–9 ounces baby corn
20 leaves Thai basil, chopped
3/4-inch piece of fresh ginger, cut into matchsticks
3 scallions, thinly sliced

Preheat the oven to 400°F.

To make the paste, place the ginger, chiles, lemongrass (be sure to remove the tough outer leaves before chopping), and garlic in a food processor. Working in batches if needed, process until a coarse paste forms. Add salt to act as an abrasive, and a little water if necessary, to make a smooth paste. Add the onions and continue to process until smooth.

Heat 1 tablespoon of oil in a heavy pan. Add the ground spices and heat until fragrant.

Add the paste and cook over low heat for 25–30 minutes, stirring frequently to avoid sticking. When the paste is aromatic, add the coconut milk. Increase the heat and reduce the mixture by one third—about 5 minutes.

Spread out the butternut squash and sweet potato chunks in a baking sheet. Sprinkle the crushed coriander and cumin seeds over them. Season with salt and pepper and drizzle with olive oil. Roast in the oven for 30 minutes until golden brown and caramelized at the edges.

Add the lime juice, tamarind, soy sauce, and Asian fish sauce to the curry paste. Adjust the seasoning accordingly—it should be hot, sour, and salty, so add more chile, lime juice, or a little light soy sauce if necessary.

Add the roasted vegetables to the simmering curry paste, followed by the baby corn. Add half the Thai basil along with the ginger and scallions. Use the rest of the basil for garnish.

panaeng curry of pineapple and bean curd

serves 4–6 to accompany other dishes

for the spice paste

6 x 1/4-inch slices of galangal, peeled
4 red chiles (jalapeño or serrano), seeded and finely chopped
1 tablespoon grated fresh ginger
3 garlic cloves, finely chopped
4 shallots
3 cilantro (fresh coriander) roots, rinsed
1 teaspoon turmeric

2 tablespoons oil
1 pound firm tofu, cut into 3/4–1 1/4-inch cubes
2 tablespoons tamarind paste
1/2 teaspoon salt
1/2 teaspoon sugar
10 ounces ripe fresh pineapple, cut into bite-size pieces
8 ounces green beans or asparagus
salt and freshly ground black pepper
handful of fresh cilantro, chopped

Grind the spice paste ingredients in a mortar and pestle or spice grinder until smooth.

Heat half the oil in a saucepan over a medium heat and cook the spice paste for about 7 minutes until fragrant. Add 2 1/2 cups water and simmer for 5 minutes to reduce.

In a skillet, heat the remaining oil and cook the tofu pieces until golden brown on at least two sides.

Add the tamarind, salt, sugar, and pineapple to the curry mixture. Gently stir in the tofu and green beans or asparagus and cook uncovered for 5 minutes. Adjust the seasoning and finish with the chopped cilantro.

hormock red curry of monkfish with lime leaves and lemongrass

serves 4–6 to accompany other dishes

You can use any type of fish for this curry, which is hot and rich, but also delicately perfumed with lime leaves and lemongrass. To add bulk to the curry, you can add cooked green beans, potatoes, or asparagus along with the fish.

for the curry paste

2 stalks lemongrass, tough outer leaves removed
1 1/4-inch piece galangal or fresh ginger, peeled and finely chopped
5 red chiles (jalapeño or serrano), seeded
4 garlic cloves
6 cilantro (fresh coriander) roots, rinsed
1 teaspoon salt
2 red onions, coarsely chopped
1 red bell pepper, coarsely chopped

1 tablespoon oil
2 teaspoons ground turmeric
4 lime leaves
2 (14-ounce) cans coconut milk

1 pound monkfish (angler fish), trimmed of skin and membrane and cut into 2-inch cubes

for the garnish

2 stalks of lemongrass, thinly sliced
1 red chile (jalapeño or serrano), seeded and finely chopped
3 kaffir or other lime leaves, stemmed and thinly sliced
10 mint leaves, finely chopped
large handful of cilantro leaves, coarsely chopped
2 tablespoons Asian fish sauce
juice of 3 limes

Working in order (most fibrous and hardest ingredients first), and in batches if needed, puree all the curry paste ingredients in a food processor until smooth. Add a little water if necessary.

Heat the oil in a large heavy saucepan and cook the curry paste slowly, stirring regularly to avoid sticking. Add the ground turmeric and cook for about 25–30 minutes until aromatic.

Add the lime leaves. When the paste has thickened, add the coconut milk and simmer to reduce by half. Add the fish and poach gently for 5–10 minutes.

Add half the garnish ingredients to the pan and mix gently. Sprinkle the remaining garnish ingredients over the top when ready to serve.

baked fish on layers of potato and fennel with marjoram salmoriglio

serves 4

This sauce is amazing. It is from Sicily and its saltiness and sourness provide a delicious contrast to the sweet richness of any fish or shellfish. Rose Gray at London's River Cafe introduced me to it.

for the marjoram salmoriglio

handful of marjoram leaves
1/2 teaspoon salt
freshly ground black pepper
juice of 1 lemon
4 tablespoons extra virgin olive oil

25 small new potatoes, scrubbed and cut into 1/4-inch slices
olive oil, sea salt and freshly ground black pepper
2 fennel bulbs, trimmed and thinly sliced (fronds reserved for the salmoriglio)
4 (6–7-ounce) fillets of firm white fish, such as sea bass or grouper, sea bream (porgy), hake, or cod
1 tablespoon chopped mint
1 tablespoon chopped fennel fronds
8 thin lemon slices, seeds removed
juice of 1/2 lemon

Preheat the oven to 400°F.

First make the salmoriglio: in a mortar and pestle or food processor, grind the marjoram with the salt until you have a smooth paste. Add the pepper and lemon juice. Stir in the olive oil and set aside.

Toss the sliced potatoes with oil, salt, and black pepper. Lay the potatoes in one layer flat on a baking sheet.

Cook for 15–20 minutes until barely cooked and just beginning to crisp, then layer the sliced fennel on top and return to the oven. Cook for another 10 minutes and remove from the heat.

Cut three slashes into the skin side of each fish fillet, one-third of the depth. Stuff the cuts with the chopped herbs. Season the fish with the salt and black pepper.

In a hot skillet, add 1 tablespoon of olive oil, place the fish skin-side down, and cook for 2–3 minutes, until the skin is golden and crisp. While the fish is cooking do not touch it, however tempting, because you will break the seal of the crust and spoil the effect.

Remove the fish from the pan and place it skin-side up on top of the sliced potatoes and fennel. Place 2 slices of lemon on each piece of fish.

Bake for 6–8 minutes, squeeze with the fresh lemon juice, and baste the fish with its juices. Transfer to a plate, drizzle with the salmoriglio, and serve.

cha ca (fish with turmeric and fresh dill)

serves 4–6

This is a delicious lightly spiced fish dish from the north of Vietnam. Vietnam is the only Asian country to use dill in its recipes, a legacy of the French colonial occupation.

for the paste

2 garlic cloves
2 ounces fresh ginger, peeled
2 red chiles, seeded
2 tablespoons Asian fish sauce
1 small onion, thinly sliced
2 teaspoons turmeric

1 pound skinned white fish, preferably monkfish
salt and freshly ground black pepper
2 tablespoons vegetable oil
large handful of dill, finely chopped
$1\frac{1}{4}$ cups coconut milk
4 ounces rice vermicelli
4 scallions, finely chopped
1 red chile, finely chopped
juice of 2 limes

Preheat a broiler, grill pan, or charcoal grill (it must be very hot).

To make the paste, combine the garlic, ginger, chiles, fish sauce, and half the onion in a food processor. When smooth, add $\frac{1}{2}$ cup water. Transfer the paste to a bowl and stir in the ground turmeric.

Season the fish with salt and pepper and broil or grill for 1 minute on each side

Heat the oil in a heavy saucepan. Add the remaining onion and cook quickly for 2–3 minutes until golden brown. Add half the dill and cook for another minute.

Add the turmeric paste and cook to reduce until fragrant and aromatic—about 15–20 minutes. Add the coconut milk and reduce by a third, simmering over medium-low heat.

Soak the rice vermicelli in hot water for about 10 minutes until soft.

Add the grilled fish to the paste mixture and cook for about 3 minutes until tender. Do not boil the sauce or the fish will become tough. Add the lime juice and check the seasoning.

Drain the rice vermicelli and serve the cha ca on top of it. Garnish with the scallions, red chile, and remaining dill.

salt cod

Salt cod has been a staple of Mediterranean kitchens since the 16th century. In France, it is used for *bourride* and *brandade de morue,* the flavor of the cod being complemented by the blander taste of pureed potato. In Spain it is often given strong partners of chorizo or a potent aïoli. However, it works equally well with less flavorful and more starchy ingredients such as potatoes, chickpeas, or white beans. In contrast to curing, which softens the texture of fish with citric acid, wine, or vinegar, salting firms up the cod and turns the flesh an opaque white. The taste and texture work very well in contrast with soft, sweet risotto rice, especially when the fish has been cooked in a spice mix of fennel seeds and dried chiles. Shellfish, such as clams, mussels, and shrimp can be added to bring an extra sweetness, counterbalanced with a good splash of crisp white wine and a squeeze of lemon juice.

Salt cod is delicious and incredibly versatile; it is equally good flavored with subtle, aromatic herbs as it is with more intense Asian spices. The only disadvantage of using the heavily salted variety is that it needs to be soaked in fresh water for at least 24 hours before it can be used. However, cod and other firm, white-fleshed fish can be quickly salted to give a firmer texture and impart a subtle, salty taste without going overboard. Salting fish in the following way will not cure the fish for preserving, but it will draw out a lot of its natural juices, firming up the texture and providing a deliciously gentle, salty taste, which is great when balanced with hot, sweet, and sour elements.

- Take a thick piece of cod fillet with the skin on. Place it in a bowl and cover with coarse sea salt or kosher salt crystals. The salt must be pure with no added chemicals and the texture needs to be coarse, otherwise, if it is too fine, the moisture from the fish will dissolve the salt and absorb it too quickly.

- Turn the fish every 15 minutes and keep heaping more salt on top. You will see that the salt becomes wet, because it has drawn moisture from the fish.

- Leave the fish for at least 1 hour. After this time the flesh will be much firmer, whiter, and more opaque.

- Remove the fish and discard the salt. Rinse the fish under cold water for 5 minutes to get rid of the excess salt. Soak the fish in cold water for about 20 minutes and then rinse again for another 5 minutes.

- Pat the fish dry with paper towels; it is now ready to use. A great way of cooking a whole piece is to lightly oil the cod on both sides, season it with freshly ground black pepper, and then roast it in the oven or under a hot broiler for 5–6 minutes. It is part cured so needs little cooking time.

If you are going to flake the fish for a risotto, fish stew, or chickpea dish, it is a good idea to cook it whole and flavor it in the following way:

- In a mortar and pestle, crush 2 small dried chiles, 1 tablespoon fennel seeds, and 1 tablespoon coriander seeds. Add 2 garlic cloves and pound to a rough paste.

- Pat the fish dry with paper towels and season it with freshly ground black pepper.

- Heat 1 tablespoon olive oil in a heavy skillet and cook the spice paste until fragrant and golden brown. Place the fish in the pan, skin-side down, and reduce the heat slightly—so that the skin browns but the spices don't burn.

- Add a glass of white wine and cover the pan with a lid—the fish will steam in the wine and aromatic spice mixture.

- Cook for 4–5 minutes or until the fish flakes apart with a fork. Since the fish is going to be added to a hot dish, it does not need to be completely cooked through.

- Using a couple of forks, remove the skin and all the bones. Save the flesh and all the juices to add to the dish. The combination of black pepper, dried chile, and white wine will result in hot, sour, and salty flavors all being present, while chickpeas, rice, or potatoes all contribute a neutral sweetness.

salt cod with leeks, red wine, and dried chile

serves 4

This is a classic dish from Lucca in Tuscany and I had it cooked like this in a small neighborhood restaurant on my honeymoon. Traditionally, it is made with *baccalà*, which is completely dried cod that has to be soaked for a long time before using. This recipe uses a quick version where the cod is salted for about an hour (see page 158), which will firm up the flesh and impart a saltiness that is not too intense. You can make it with white wine instead of red if you prefer.

4 (6–7-ounce) cod fillets, skin on
5 tablespoons Kosher or sea salt
1 1/2 tablespoons butter
2 garlic cloves, thinly sliced
1 small dried chile, crushed
1 red onion, thinly sliced
4 leeks, trimmed and well rinsed, cut in half lengthwise and thinly sliced
1 tablespoon flour
1 tablespoon olive oil
salt and freshly ground black pepper
1/2 cup dry red wine
small handful of parsley, roughly chopped
juice of 1 lemon

Preheat the oven to 400°F.

Clean the cod, place in a bowl, and cover with sea salt. Leave it for 1 hour. Remove the fish from the salt and place in a colander in the sink under running cold water for 10 minutes. Make sure all the salt is washed off. The texture of the fish should be firmer and the color light and opaque.

Heat a heavy ovenproof pan over medium heat. Melt the butter and cook the garlic and chile until golden. Add the onion and leeks and cook for 5–6 minutes, stirring to avoid sticking. If they do stick or scorch, add a splash of water which will deglaze the pan and allow the leeks to carry on cooking. Season with salt and pepper.

Pat the fish dry with paper towels. Roll the fish in a fine dusting of flour, and season with black pepper.

While the leeks and onions are cooking, heat the oil in a heavy sauté pan (or skillet) over medium-high heat. Place the fish in the pan skin-side down.

Allow the fish to form a golden brown crust. Do not touch the fish—it is important not to interrupt the cooking process. You will see the edge of the flesh above the skin turning white and beginning to cook. Lift a corner of one piece of fish with a spatula. If the skin is golden brown, gently ease the fish from the pan to turn it over. Turn the rest of the pieces and cook for 2 minutes.

Place the fish, skin-side up, on the leek and onion mixture, but spoon some of the mixture around the fish to keep it moist and to let the top of the mixture to caramelize a bit.

In the pan in which the fish was cooked, drain the excess oil, then add the wine. Deglaze the pan, scraping up all the crispy bits from the pan with a wooden spoon. Pour the deglazed sauce over the fish and leeks.

Place the pan in the oven and bake uncovered for 8–10 minutes, depending upon the thickness of the fish.

Finish with some coarsely chopped parsley and a squeeze of lemon juice. Check the seasoning before serving. You should be able to taste all the flavors in this dish—the buttery leeks will have crisped a little and caramelized in the oven and the salt cod has a depth of flavor, not just on the surface.

salt cod and shrimp risotto

serves 4

This risotto satisfies all the tastebuds because the rich and sweet creamy rice and cooked shrimp are balanced with salty, hot, and sour flavors.

1 pound cod fillet, skin on
1/3 cup coarse Kosher or sea salt
2 tablespoons butter
1 onion, finely chopped
1 celery heart, finely chopped
1 fennel bulb, trimmed and finely chopped
1 cup risotto rice, such as arborio
1 cup dry white wine
8 cups hot fish stock (see page 107)
1 teaspoon fennel seeds
2 garlic cloves, crushed
2 small dried bird's eye chiles, (Thai chiles) crushed
salt and freshly ground black pepper
2 tablespoons olive oil
8–10-ounces cooked and peeled small shrimp
handful of flat-leaf parsley, coarsely chopped
juice of 1 lemon

Place the cod in a bowl, and cover with coarse salt. Let sit for 1–1½ hours. Remove the fish from the salt and soak in cold water for at least 30 minutes.

Meanwhile, make the risotto. In a heavy saucepan, melt the butter over low heat. Add the chopped vegetables and cook, stirring occasionally, until softened but not browned, 15–20 minutes.

Add the rice and stir so each grain of rice is coated with butter. When all the moisture in the pan has been absorbed, add half of the wine and stir until absorbed.

Add the hot stock, about 1 cup at a time, stirring constantly. All the liquid must be absorbed before adding the next cup. Continue cooking until the rice is al dente—about 20 minutes.

Meanwhile, in a mortar and pestle, crush the fennel seeds, garlic, and dried chiles with ½ teaspoon salt. Pound until smooth.

Pat the fish dry with paper towels. The texture of the salted cod will be firmer and the color will be milky and opaque.

In a skillet, heat the oil. Cook the garlic, fennel, and chile mixture for 1–2 minutes until fragrant and pale golden.

Add the piece of cod, skin-side down, and cook for 1–2 minutes. Season with black pepper. Make sure the garlic mixture does not burn. Add the remaining wine. Place a lid on the pan and cook over high heat for 2–3 minutes.

Add the shrimp and replace the lid for 2–3 minutes. Remove from heat and, with a fork, break up the salted cod, removing any bones and skin.

Add all the juices from the fish pan to the risotto. When ready to serve, add the salt cod, shrimp, and most of the chopped parsley (the fish will continue cooking and break up in the risotto). Check the seasoning very carefully as the fish will be salty. Add the lemon juice, the dish needs it to perk up the rice, giving it a more three-dimensional flavor. Garnish with the remaining parsley and serve.

spanish salt cod with "inzimino" of chickpeas, tomato, chile, and chorizo

serves 4–6

This dish is inspired by *inzimino*, an Italian way of cooking chickpeas. My version is served with salt cod and chorizo, which adds a Spanish flavor to the dish.

1 pound cod fillet, skin on
1/3 cup coarse Kosher or sea salt
1/2 cup dried chickpeas, soaked overnight in water
2 large garlic cloves, 1 whole, 1 sliced
6 tablespoons olive oil
1 medium onion, finely chopped
8 ounces chorizo sausage, chopped
5 leaves Swiss chard, stems removed from the leaves
oil for cooking
salt and freshly ground black pepper
2 small dried chiles, crumbled
1/2–3/4 cup dry white wine
1 (14 1/2-ounce) can diced tomatoes
juice of 1 lemon
large handful of flat-leaf parsley, coarsely chopped

Place cod in a bowl, and cover with coarse salt. Let sit 1 hour. Remove the fish from the salt and soak in cold water for at least 30 minutes.

Drain the chickpeas and place in a saucepan. Pour in water to cover, add the whole garlic clove and 2 tablespoons of the oil, and bring to a boil. Simmer for 45 minutes or until tender. Set the pan aside.

Heat the remaining oil in a separate large skillet or sauté pan over medium heat. Add the sliced garlic, onion, chorizo, and chard stems and cook, stirring occasionally, for 15 minutes.

Add salt, pepper, and the dried chiles. Pour in 1/2 cup of the wine and reduce almost completely. Add the tomatoes (include their juices) and cook for 20–25 minutes until very thick.

Blanch the chard leaves in boiling salted water for 1–2 minutes until soft.

In a separate skillet, heat a little olive oil. Pat the fish dry with paper towels and place in the pan, skin-side down. Cook until the skin is golden. Season the cod with pepper and half the lemon juice. Add 1/4 cup of wine or water, cover, and cook for 4 minutes.

Add the chard leaves and chickpeas to the tomato pan. Season and cook for 10 minutes. Flake the baked salt cod over the top.

Stir in most of the parsley and the remaining lemon juice. Sprinkle with the remaining parsley and extra olive oil when ready to serve.

chef's tip

When cooking fish, particularly in the oven, it is important not to overcook the flesh. When it is taken out of the oven or the pan, there is a lot of residual heat left inside which will continue to cook the fish. Therefore, it is always better to slightly undercook the fish, to a stage that is medium or medium-rare and let the fish continue to cook itself to perfection with the heat of the pan.

soupe de poisson with rouille and croûtons

serves 4–6

for the rouille

1 ounce dry bread (about 1 slice), soaked in fish stock
3 garlic cloves
1 egg yolk
2 tablespoons harissa (Tunisian hot sauce)
large pinch of salt
1 cup olive oil

for the croûtons

1 baguette, cut into slices
olive oil
2 garlic cloves
2 ounces Gruyère or Parmesan cheese, grated

scant $^{1}/_{2}$ cup olive oil
$^{2}/_{3}$ cup onion, coarsely chopped
$^{2}/_{3}$ cup celery, coarsely chopped
$^{2}/_{3}$ cup leek, coarsely chopped
$^{2}/_{3}$ cup fennel, coarsely chopped
5 garlic cloves, sliced
sprig of thyme
juice of 1 orange and $^{3}/_{4}$-inch strip of zest
2 ($14^{1}/_{2}$-ounce) cans diced tomatoes
pinch of saffron
1 red bell pepper, sliced
2 fresh bay leaves
8 ounces shrimp in their shell
$3^{1}/_{2}$ pound fish fillet, such as pollock, conger eel, cod, or hake
8 cups fish stock (see page 107)
salt and freshly ground black pepper
large pinch of cayenne pepper

Preheat the oven to 400°F.

To make the rouille, process the soaked bread, garlic, egg yolk, harissa, and salt until smooth. With the machine running, slowly add the oil to form an emulsion. Cover and refrigerate

To make the croûtons, drizzle the bread slices with olive oil and bake in the oven until golden brown, 5–7 minutes. Rub with the garlic and set aside.

Heat the oil in a soup pot and add the onion, celery, leek, fennel, and garlic. Cook over low heat for 20 minutes until the vegetables are very soft but not browned.

Add the thyme, orange peel, tomatoes (and juice), and saffron, followed by the red peppers, bay leaves, shrimp, and fish. Cook briefly, stirring, then add the stock and orange juice. Bring to a boil and simmer for 30 minutes.

Blend the soup and strain it through a fine sieve, using the back of a ladle to push it through. Discard the solids.

Return to the heat and season with salt, pepper, and cayenne pepper. It should have a gentle but noticeable taste of cayenne. Add a little extra orange juice if necessary. Pour into serving bowls and top each with a few croûtons and a spoonful of rouille. Serve the cheese separately for people to help themselves.

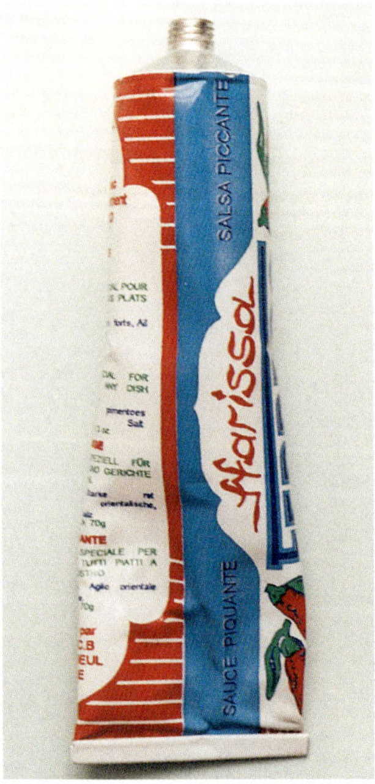

ligurian fish stew with fennel and chile

serves 6

You can use any combination of fish and shellfish for this delicious, easy, and hearty dish, which involves a relatively short amount of preparation and very little washing up afterwards. Use real fish stock—see recipe on page 107—or buy it fresh from a supermarket or fish market, but don't use a bouillon cube. If the soup is well seasoned, then all the flavors will be in balance.

8 ounces small potatoes, cut in half lengthwise
pinch of saffron
3 tablespoons olive oil
1 fennel bulb, trimmed and finely chopped
1 onion, finely chopped
salt and freshly ground black pepper
1 (14 1/2-ounce) can diced tomatoes
8 cups fish stock (see page 107)
2 garlic cloves, finely chopped
1 red chile (jalapeño or serrano), seeded and finely chopped
4 flat anchovy fillets, drained and finely chopped
18 large shrimp, heads removed but shells left on, deveined
2 1/4 pounds mussels, cleaned
1/2 cup dry white wine
handful of basil, coarsely chopped
1 pound firm white fish, such as hake or cod, monkfish, sea bream, or snapper (one variety or a mixture), skinned and cut into cubes

Put the potatoes in a small pan of cold salted water with the saffron, and bring to a boil. Cook for 12 minutes or until soft when pierced with the tip of a sharp knife. Strain and set aside.

Heat a little oil in a heavy pot, add the fennel and onion, and cook for 12–15 minutes until soft, but not browned. Season with salt and pepper. Add the tomatoes and their juices.

Simmer for 10–15 minutes until the tomatoes form a concentrated paste. Add the fish stock, bring to a boil, and check the seasoning. Remove from the heat and set aside.

In another pot, heat 2 tablespoons of olive oil and fry the garlic and chile for 1 minute. Add the anchovies, shrimp, mussels, wine, and half the basil leaves. Cover with a lid and let the shellfish steam for 2 minutes. Pour in the stock and vegetable mixture.

Season the white fish with salt and pepper and then add to the pot. Turn down the heat to low and poach for about 4 minutes.

Add the potatoes to the soup along with the remaining basil. Taste and adjust the flavors accordingly.

The soup should have a sweet richness from the shellfish and cooked onions. There will be some heat from the red chile and a sourness from the wine and tomatoes. The salty anchovies give an intensity to the base. Adjust the seasoning, making sure that all the flavors are represented.

pot-roasted pheasant wrapped in prosciutto

serves 6

This dish is fantastic with cavalo nero (a peppery, black Italian cabbage) but if you can't get hold of it, as I couldn't when we made this recipe for the photograph, you can use baby broccoli and savoy cabbage leaves instead. Hen pheasants are smaller than cocks but have slightly plumper breasts and are less tough, particularly at the end of the season.

2 hen pheasants
salt and freshly ground black pepper
4 slices prosciutto per pheasant (you can use bacon or pancetta instead; enough slices to cover)
1 tablespoon olive oil
3 garlic cloves, finely sliced
6 sage leaves
sprig of rosemary
sprig of thyme
6 small shallots, peeled and quartered
$1\frac{1}{4}$-inch strip of lemon zest with no white pith
$\frac{3}{4}$ cup Marsala wine, madeira, or cream sherry
$1\frac{3}{4}$ cups chicken broth (see page 107)
2 tablespoons heavy whipping cream

for serving

medium-colored leaves of 1 savoy cabbage
1 tablespoon olive oil
2 garlic cloves, finely chopped
1 small dried chile, crushed
2 large handfuls of small broccoli florets
salt and freshly ground black pepper

Remove the scaly legs of the pheasant at the joint. With a torch or other naked flame, burn off any feathers. Season the inside of the bird with salt and pepper.

Wrap the breast of the bird in the prosciutto, laying the first slice over the wishbone and the thick part of the breasts, and the next slice overlapping slightly, working down towards the legs. Repeat until all the breast and thick part of the legs are tightly covered.

Place the wrapped bird on a board with the wishbone towards you. Take a piece of kitchen string at least 2 feet long and lay it horizontally along the board (with the pheasant overlapping the string by about an inch). Take each end of the string and lift up as if you were wrapping a present. Cross the string at the top of the breast bone and go down to the legs; the string will be diagonally crossed over the breast of the bird, with the string going around the outside of the legs. Tie in a firm double knot that pulls the legs together. Cut off any excess string, and repeat with the other bird.

Heat the oil over a medium-high heat in a pot or flameproof casserole. Place the pheasants in the pan for 3–4 minutes, turning to cook on all sides until golden brown, particularly on the bottom and the sides of the legs, as these parts take longer to cook.

When all sides of the birds are cooked, add the garlic, herbs, shallots, and lemon zest. Cook for a few minutes until golden brown, before draining off any excess oil.

Add the wine to the pan and cook for 2 minutes to cook off the alcohol. Add the chicken broth, partially cover with the lid and simmer slowly for 45 minutes. Turn the pheasants frequently so that different parts of meat come into contact with the heat of the pan.

Blanch the savoy cabbage leaves in boiling salted water for 2–3 minutes. Drain and set aside.

Remove the pheasants from the pan and let rest on a board. Use scissors to remove the string. Continue to reduce the pheasant sauce over medium-high heat until it is beginning to turn syrupy, then remove from the heat and stir in the cream. Check the seasoning.

Meanwhile, separate the pheasant breast from the central bone with a sharp knife. Remove the leg section from the breast. Separate the thigh from the drumstick.

Heat the oil for the broccoli in a separate pan over a medium-high heat. Add the garlic and dried chile and cook for about 1–2 minutes until golden brown. Add the blanched savoy cabbage and broccoli florets. Turn in the oil and season with salt and pepper.

To serve, put a piece of pheasant in the center of the plate and scatter a little cabbage and broccoli on top. Repeat, building up alternate layers of pheasant, prosciutto, and greens. When the portion is complete, pour some of the sauce over it. Repeat with the other portions of pheasant.

chef's tip

This recipe allows half a hen pheasant per person, but if you cut up the birds first, it will feed a few more people. If cooking more than two pheasants, you will need just a little extra alcohol, broth, and cream.

cured pork

Unlike northern Europe, which relied on long, cold winters for natural refrigeration, other European countries like Spain, Portugal, Italy, and France discovered other ways of preserving their fresh meat with salt and aromatic herbs. The pig was the most important animal in the European farmyard and is revered in all peasant cultures, not only in Europe but also in Southeast Asia, because of its greatly valued by-products. The high fat content of pork protects the meat so that salting, pickling, and smoking processes do very little damage to it.

The pork belly, for example, yields bacon that can be dry-salted or brine-cured with salt, herbs, and spices, and then also smoked if desired. In France, this cut can be used to produce *petit salé,* which is salted with juniper berries, peppercorns, and bay leaves. It is often bought as a large piece that keeps for a long time and can be cut as and when required for making a *cassoulet* or for flavoring soups and stews. Belly pork can also be cooked gently until it falls apart, and then preserved in its own fat to make *rillettes*. In areas of Spain the pork belly may be cured without aromatics and instead buried in salt to preserve it. This produces a kitchen staple which is used to flavor casseroles, stews, and soups. In Italy, the pork belly makes two main products. The first is pancetta, a salted meat, which can be smoked or not. The second is *lardo*, which is the thick hard white fat of the belly that is cured with herbs, spices, and peppercorns. It is delicious when wrapped in thin slices around meat and poultry or cut into strips and layered over sliced potatoes while roasting. It partially melts, keeping the cooking dish moist while the remainder crisps up wonderfully.

The leg of the pig is cured in many different regions to produce hams; some are smoked and some are left raw but salted, such as *prosciutto crudo*. In France, salting, drying, and then smoking produces *jambon de Bayonne* and *jambon de Toulouse*. In Spain the leg is cured to make *jamón serrano*, which can be cut more roughly into thicker slices than its Italian cousin, *prosciutto crudo*. *Jamón iberico* or *pata negra* is the cured and salted ham made from the Iberian pig which roams in the woods eating acorns. The resulting cured meat is meltingly soft with a delicate aroma. Hailing from Italy, *prosciutto di Parma* and *prosciutto di San Daniele* are some of the most famous raw hams in the world. They are dry-salted for about a month and then dried for at least eight months and up to two years. Salt is used in small quantities—just to get rid of the moisture and stop it fermenting, and therefore the resulting meat is not overly salty but extremely sweet. The Italians also cure the shoulder of the pig in the same way; it is called *coppa di Parma.* The shoulder is a much fattier piece of meat than the leg, so when it is cured and rolled it is a perfect blend of marbled fat and meat. It works very well wrapped around pieces of roasting meat, such as a tenderloin of beef or venison or anything that does not have a great deal of fat of its own. It is also great as a salty component added to salads or served alongside soft, rich cheeses or sweet artichokes.

Many herbs, spices, and aromatics are used in curing sausages such as the French *saucisson*. In Italy, fennel seeds are used to make *fiocchiona* and rosemary to make *salame rosemarino*. Each region of Italy has its own preference, not only for flavoring, but for texture as well, from the fine-textured Milanese salami to the coarser, more rustic Tuscan version, which combines the meat and fat in lumps with lots of black peppercorns. Paprika and chiles are some of the main additions to the Spanish chorizo sausage, which comes in both dried and fresh varieties. The fresh version is semi-cured and is used in cooking. The Spanish also cure pork tenderloin then wrap it in sausage skins. It is called *lomo embuchado*, and is softly textured with a delicious sweet flavor that is not too salty.

In Asia, pork meat is incredibly revered, and due to the hot and humid climate, many different varieties of cured or salted pork have evolved so that it can remain an accessible and valuable component of the region's cuisine. In Thailand and Vietnam, by-products of the pig, such as the skin, are often preserved by salting and drying them. Asian fish sauce and light soy sauce are used to marinate and cure the skin and sometimes pieces of meat and fat as well, such as the pork belly. The pieces are then dried either in the sun or over the vent above the oven for many hours to remove the moisture. These can be stored in a dry place with no danger of them going off. The pieces can be braised, roasted, grilled, or deep-fried to delicious effect, and served with a dish of aromatic smoked trout, or scattered over a hot and sour squid salad.

In Thailand there is a delicious if unusual type of sausage called *nam*, or Chang Mai sausage, which is fermented in the sun to preserve it. An acquired taste, it has a strange, vinegary flavor. The freshly ground pork is mixed with fermented rice and some chopped onions, and rolled with lots of green chiles in banana leaves. The wrap is then dried in the heat of the tropical sun for about three days, which preserves it.

The unifying factor in all these regional variations is the presence of salt, crying out to be accompanied by delicious sweet and sour notes and a peppery heat. Here are three simple examples using three different cured meats:

- Quartered figs are marinated in balsamic vinegar with thyme, black pepper, and lemon juice, and then wrapped in slices of prosciutto or serrano ham. The sweet richness of the figs combines with the sourness of the lemon juice and balsamic vinegar. The black pepper in the marinade provides the heat while the prosciutto is sweet and salty. (See page 57 for the recipe.)

- Quinces are peeled and roasted in aluminum foil until soft, then caramelized with some butter and sugar with chopped garlic, rosemary, and chopped red chile. (See page 42 for the recipe.) This can then be served alongside some slices of *lomo embuchado*, or, if not available, prosciutto. The quinces will have a magnificent floral richness, combining sweet and sour. The gentle saltiness of the *lomo* or prosciutto provides an excellent contrast.

- Baked sweet potato can be combined with fried pieces of chorizo that have been dressed with olive oil, green chile, and lemon juice and zest. The spicy hot chorizo and green chile contrasts with the sourness of the lemon. The roast sweet potato is sweet and rich and it is all bound together by the salted cure of the chorizo, intensified by frying, and a little salt in the dressing. (See page 99 for the recipe.) This could also be made on a skewer, alternating roast chunks of sweet potato with fried chorizo and then dipping it in the dressing.

Pata Negra
R. GARCIA & SONS
HAND
PRICED
WEIGHED
18.00
109.62
de Bellota
desde 1948
SERRANO RESERVA
SERRANO RESERVA
CUATRO
ESTACIONES
12 MESES

salt-and-spice roasted pork belly with caramelized peanut and chile dressing

serves 4–6

3 tablespoons coarse Kosher or sea salt
1 tablespoon coriander seeds
10 peppercorns
5 star anise
4 lime leaves
2 cinnamon sticks
1 pork belly
2 small dried chiles
a little olive oil

caramelized peanut and chile dressing (see page 43)
yam som tam (see page 79)

Preheat the oven to 450°F.

In a mortar and pestle, pound the salt, coriander seeds, and peppercorns until medium-fine in texture. Add the star anise, lime leaves, and cinnamon and continue to crush until broken up.

Transfer to a high-sided, flameproof roasting pan and mix with enough cold water to fill the pan about 3/4 inches.

Score the pork skin into thin strips to make the cracklings. A sharp Stanley knife is the best tool for this job (or you can ask your butcher to do this for you).

Place the pork belly skin-side down in the water. The water should cover the skin and the first deep layer of fat. Place the pan over a medium-high heat, bring the water to a boil, and simmer for about 20 minutes. You do this to dissolve some of the fat, and also to infuse the skin of the pork with the spice-salt mixture to make a delicious crackling.

Remove the pork from the roasting tray and tip out any excess water. Place the pork belly skin-side up on a rack in the roasting tray. Grind the dried chiles and add to the spice mixture in the pan. Rub the pork skin with the spice mixture and a little oil (the oil starts the crackling off).

Lower the heat of the oven to 425°F and roast on the rack for 20 minutes. Then turn the oven down to 350°F and cook for another 30–40 minutes until the skin is crispy and the meat is soft and cooked.

Serve in a bowl with the caramelized peanut and chile dressing overtop and yam som tam on the side.

vietnamese pork and eggplants with cinnamon and star anise

serves 4 – 6

This style of hot pot cooking is very common in Vietnam, particularly in the north of the county where it gets very cold in winter. These caramelized stews are traditionally cooked in clay pots for one or two people and brought sizzling to the table. They smell amazing but are untouchable for quite some time because they are absolutely baking hot. You must resist and let them cool, but the complex layers of flavor are worth waiting for and the clay pot is always scraped clean.

2 eggplants, cut into 1 1/4-inch chunks
salt
olive oil
2 onions, chopped
1 tablespoon brown sugar
salt and freshly ground black pepper
2 red chiles (jalapeño or serrano), seeded and finely chopped
3 garlic cloves, finely chopped
4 cilantro (fresh coriander) roots, rinsed and chopped (if not available, use the cilantro stems)
1 1/2-inch piece of fresh ginger, peeled and grated
1 pound ground pork
1 cinnamon stick, broken in two
3 star anise
3 tablespoons Asian fish sauce
juice of 2 limes
handful of cilantro, coarsely chopped

Preheat the oven to 400°F.

Place the eggplant in a colander and sprinkle with salt. Let them drain for 20 minutes to get rid of the bitter juices.

Rinse the eggplant under cold water and pat dry with paper towels.

Heat 1 tablespoon olive oil in a heavy flameproof casserole. Fry the eggplant in batches until they are golden brown on all sides, adding more oil as needed. Remove from the pot and pat dry with paper towels to absorb any excess oil.

Add a splash more oil to the pot and add the onions and brown sugar. Cook over medium-high heat for 2–3 minutes until they start to caramelize. Season with salt and pepper.

Push the onions to one side of the pot and add the chiles, garlic, cilantro roots, and ginger, cooking for 2 minutes. Then stir into the onions. Add the ground pork, cinnamon, star anise, and Asian fish sauce. Season well with black pepper.

Mix in the eggplant. Add the ground pork and just enough water to cover. Bring to a simmer, and then transfer to the oven. Bake 40 minutes, checking a couple of times that there is enough liquid and that it has not dried out.

When the meat is cooked and the liquid absorbed, remove from the oven. Add the lime juice and half of the cilantro.

Check the seasoning. There should be aromatic heat from the red chile and black pepper, and an underlying sweetness from the caramelized sugar and onions. Salt will be present from the Asian fish sauce, countered by the refreshing sourness of the lime juice. Garnish with the remaining cilantro and serve.

slow-cooked lamb with salted lemon and apricots

serves 4

Make this well in advance so the flavors can mellow, blend, and improve. Then simply reheat when ready to serve. The combination of spices gives a rich complex depth of flavor and the preserved lemon brings a much-needed sour edge to the equation. Pork, beef, or chicken pieces would also work instead of lamb, and you could use green olives instead of apricots.

4 trimmed lamb shanks or 1 3/4 pounds stewing lamb, cut into large chunks
salt and freshly ground black pepper
2 tablespoons olive oil
2 large onions, each cut crosswise into 4 thick slices
4 strips of orange zest
1 cinnamon stick, broken into 3 pieces
1 teaspoon ground ginger
1 teaspoon ground cinnamon
1 teaspoon ground coriander
1 teaspoon ground cumin
1 teaspoon sugar
good pinch of saffron
4 pieces preserved lemon (see page 27), finely chopped
30 dried apricots or figs
handful of toasted walnut halves, chopped

Preheat the oven to 350°F.

Season the meat well with salt and pepper. Heat a little oil in a heavy flameproof casserole and add the meat. Brown for a few minutes on all sides and then remove the pan from the heat.

Remove the meat from the pan. Place the onion slices in the bottom of the pan and the meat on top. Tuck the orange zest and cinnamon around the lamb. Sprinkle the dried spices and the sugar over it. Pour in about 2 cups water to form a shallow pool around the meat. Season with salt and pepper and sprinkle the saffron into the liquid. Scatter the preserved lemon over the lamb.

Cover and bring to a simmer on the stove. Then transfer to the oven and cook for another 2 1/2 hours, basting regularly. Half an hour before removing from the oven, add the apricots or figs.

Check the seasoning before serving and garnish with the chopped walnuts.

malaysian lamb with coriander and roast peanuts

serves 6

This dish is multi-layered and intense. It needs to have all the areas of taste present to make it a resounding success: an underlying heat and spiciness; a sweet richness from the onions, sugar, and slow-cooked meat; the saltiness of the Asian fish sauce and shrimp paste; and the sourness of the tamarind and lime juice.

for the spice paste

2 tablespoons freshly ground coriander seeds
3 cardamon pods
2 cinnamon sticks
1/2 teaspoon ground dried chile
1 tablespoon gapi shrimp paste

4 stalks of lemongrass, trimmed and thinly sliced at an angle
3 ounces fresh ginger, peeled and chopped
4 garlic cloves, chopped
2 red chiles (jalapeño or serrano), seeded and finely chopped
2 onions, chopped
3 cilantro (fresh coriander) roots, rinsed and finely chopped
3 tablespoons Asian fish sauce
2 tablespoons tamarind paste
1 pound boneless lamb (preferably from the leg), cut into 1 1/4-inch cubes
salt and freshly ground black pepper
splash of oil
3 imported bay leaves
1 tablespoon soft brown sugar
8 ounces new potatoes, cut in half
juice of 2 limes
1/2 cup coconut cream or milk
handful of freshly chopped cilantro
salt and freshly ground black pepper
1 cup roasted peanuts

To make the spice paste, grind the dry spices and dried chile in a spice grinder or mortar and pestle.

Place the lemongrass (be sure to remove the tough outside leaves), ginger, and garlic in a food-processor and process until a paste forms. Add the chiles, onion, and cilantro roots, and process until smooth, adding a little water if necessary.

Pour the Asian fish sauce and tamarind over the cubed lamb and season with lots of freshly ground black pepper. Let it marinate while you cook the paste.

Heat a little oil in a deep, heavy saucepan and cook the dry spice mixture for 1–2 minutes. Add the shrimp paste and cook for another 2 minutes until fragrant and aromatic.

Add the onion and chile paste and turn down the heat. Cook slowly for 10–12 minutes. Add the bay leaves, brown sugar, and a splash of water if necessary.

When the paste starts to caramelize, add the marinated lamb, cover, and cook slowly for 1 1/2 hours until the meat is very tender. About 20 minutes before the end, add the potatoes.

About 5 minutes before serving, add the lime juice and coconut cream. Check the seasoning, and add a little more ground chile or black pepper to taste. Finish with cilantro and crushed roasted peanuts. Add a little more fish sauce or salt to enhance all the flavors and the spices.

chef's tip

Whole seeds are preferable to ground: use a small coffee grinder to get their intense, fresh aroma. Powdered spices go stale very quickly but if you have to use them, place on a baking sheet and dry-roast for about 2 minutes to freshen their fragrance.

harissa-spiced, slow-cooked lamb with cilantro and apricots

serves 4

Harissa is a North African tomato and spice paste that you can buy in tubes from large supermarkets. The flavorsome cilantro stems are used widely in Middle Eastern cooking. You can use other dried fruits instead of apricots and sour cherries—figs, dates, and cranberries also work well. If time is short, you can cut the meat off the shanks into cubes or use cut-up lamb stew meat. The fruit content of the sauce will ensure it still tastes rich and intense, but the meat will be done in around 35 minutes rather than 2 hours.

3 tablespoons olive oil
1 1/2 pounds lamb shanks, left whole (or cut into 1 1/4–1 1/2-inch pieces), or cut-up lamb stew meat from the leg end)
1 onion, finely chopped
2 celery ribs, finely chopped
1/2 bunch of fresh cilantro, leaves separated from stems
2 garlic cloves, finely chopped
1 teaspoon ground coriander
1 teaspoon ground cumin
1 tablespoon harissa
2 1/4 cups homemade chicken or vegetable broth (see page 107)
sea salt and freshly ground black pepper
juice of 1 orange
1 cup mixture of dried apricots and dried sour cherries, roughly chopped
jeweled couscous (see page 226), for serving

Preheat the oven to 350°F.

Heat a heavy, flameproof casserole over medium-high heat. Add 2 tablespoons of the oil and cook the meat until deep brown on the outside. Do this in batches so the pieces get properly colored. When one batch is done, remove from the pan and set aside. Do not let the meat stick or scorch between batches.

Meanwhile, heat the remaining oil in another pan over a medium-high heat. Add the onion and celery and cook gently for 10 minutes.

Finely chop 5 of the cilantro stems with the garlic. Add to the pan along with the ground coriander and cumin. Cook for 2 minutes until the spices are fragrant and the garlic is beginning to turn golden. Add the harissa and broth.

Drain off any excess oil from the lamb pan. Return the lamb to the pan and then pour the mixture from the other pan over the meat, making sure you get all the good bits from the vegetable pan. With a wooden spoon, scrape the bottom of the lamb pan to release all the small fried pieces of meat. Season well with sea salt and pepper and add the orange juice. Cover and bring to a boil, then carefully place in the oven for 2 hours if using the whole shanks (test for doneness after around 35 minutes if using cubed meat), until the meat is tender and ready to fall off the bone.

Carefully remove the pot from the oven. Taste the sauce and adjust the seasoning. Add the apricots and sour cherries. Taste a little meat to see if the texture is nice and soft. Replace the lid and return to the oven for about another 10–15 minutes.

Add the cilantro leaves and serve with the couscous.

mains

mains

When it comes to the main part of the meal there are raised expectations around the table from family or guests. They have already tasted fantastic combinations of flavors and textures in different forms; some canapés, an appetizer or two or perhaps some mezze, tapas, or antipasti. Now it is time for the drum roll and the big event.

With a main course, you are balancing flavors and textures across the whole plate. A sauce or additional dressing or relish should work alongside the main feature on the plate, be it fish, fowl, meat, or game. This can be offset against one or two contrasting side dishes. The finished result is a carefully orchestrated taste sensation. As a chef you are the conductor and you do not want anything to jar, stand out, or happen at the wrong time. If you serve the main course for each individual guest, complete with the accompanying side dishes and relevant sauce, you have carefully positioned the complementary and contrasting elements side by side. You are in control of exactly what goes onto the tastebuds, and nothing has been misplaced or forgotten. However, if your guests are left to their own devices and help themselves to the different components, one part might be overlooked and they may not experience the food that you have created exactly as you had planned. In this instance, you can guide your guests by presenting elements together that they might not otherwise have thought of combining, for example by arranging a meat next to a relish that you know will enhance it perfectly.

With the main course recipe of roast venison with roast beets (see page 202), a hot, salty, sour dressing is added in the form of warm bacon and balsamic vinaigrette with cherry tomatoes and lots of black pepper, to bring the whole plate to fruition. One element of this dish taken on its own, though well seasoned and perfectly cooked, needs the accompanying vegetables and the dressing to make everything work together in a harmonious blend.

If one of the side dishes to accompany grilled or roasted meat falls into the sweet category such as roast butternut squash, pumpkin, sweet potato, beets, or parsnip, then some additional spicy heat would be needed. A horseradish sauce or a green herb paste made with arugula or watercress, or perhaps some strong mustard could be spooned into the gravy instead of the redcurrant jelly. When you understand the different layers, categories, and elements of flavor, there are endless variables that you can change to create the required "wow" factor. You will find that many of the sauces, pastes, and marinades are interchangeable with different meat and fish dishes as well as the side dishes that may go with them.

As with any of the courses that have preceded this one, the careful matching of a particular wine can really heighten the whole culinary experience. In Italy, wine is never tasted without food, and the two elements work together, enhancing the specific characteristics of both. A crisp, acidic wine such as Sauvignon Blanc, Sémillon, or Viognier could cut the richness of something like scallops, flounder, halibut, or roast pork or veal, creating whole new flavor interactions for your tastebuds. A peppery or spicy style of red wine such as Zinfandel, Pinot Noir, Syrah/Shiraz, Tempranillo, or aged Garnacha can greatly enhance the flavors of some red meat or game or other autumn flavors such as mushrooms or roasted nuts. They will also bring out the flavors of anything that has been cooked with spice, such as spice-caramelized pears with a game dish, lacquered duck (see page 199), or salt-and-spice roasted pork belly (see page 172).

SWEET **red snapper, porgy, tuna, red peppers, cannellini beans, coconut cream, lychees, beets, allspice, prunes** SOUR **lemons, shallots, cilantro, balsamic vinegar** SALTY **capers, bacon, fish sauce** HOT **watercress, coriander seeds, fennel seeds, green peppercorns, ginger, garlic** BITTER **wild duck, baby spinach, venison, partridge**

pan-fried red mullet (or snapper) with lemon, olive, and parsley salsa

serves 4

You could use any small fish for this dish, and the salsa can be served on the side if you prefer.

for the salsa

2 tablespoons extra virgin olive oil
1 x recipe preserved lemons (see page 27), rind finely chopped
30 pitted black olives, coarsely chopped
1 garlic clove, crushed with a little salt
1/2 red chile (jalapeño or serrano), seeded and finely chopped
juice of 1 lemon
1 fennel bulb, finely chopped
20 basil leaves, coarsely chopped
20 parsley leaves, coarsely chopped

4 red mullet or red snapper (gutted, scaled, and cleaned)
salt and freshly ground black pepper
oil, for cooking

Preheat the oven to 350°F.

Mix all the ingredients for the salsa in a bowl. If you would like the dish to be spicier, add the other half of the chile.

Pat fish dry with paper towels. Stuff the cavity with the salsa. Any excess salsa can be scattered on top of the fish after cooking. Season with salt and pepper.

Heat a little oil in an ovenproof skillet. Place the fish in the hot oil and cook over medium-high heat for 3 minutes. Gently turn over with a spatula to avoid tearing the skin. Cook on the other side for 2 minutes.

Transfer the pan to the oven and bake for 5 minutes, or until the fish is cooked. If there is any leftover salsa, scatter over the top of the fish.

Serve at once with some mixed greens or braised spinach.

indian spice-rubbed fish with dressed potatoes

serves 4–6

A combination of neutral and sweet flavors from the potatoes and fish, with heat coming from the green chile, toasted spices, and black pepper. The lemon juice and tamarind provide the sour element. You could serve this with a cucumber raita, or just some plain yogurt.

for the fish

1 tablespoon coriander seeds
1 tablespoon cumin seeds
3 green cardamom pods
3 garlic cloves
1 green chile
4 cilantro (fresh coriander) roots, rinsed (if not available, use the cilantro stems)
1 1/4-inch chunk of fresh ginger, peeled and grated
2 onions, sliced
4 (6–7-ounce) pieces of firm white fish such as cod, snapper, or sea bream (porgy)
salt and freshly ground black pepper

for the potatoes

2 1/4 pounds all-purpose potatoes
zest and juice of 1 lemon
1 green chile, seeded and finely chopped
4 scallions, finely sliced
2 tablespoons olive oil
2 tablespoons tamarind pulp
salt and freshly ground black pepper
handful of cilantro leaves, roughly chopped

Heat a small frying pan and add the coriander seeds, cumin seeds, and cardamom. Dry-roast over a medium-high heat until aromatic and fragrant.

Transfer the spices to a mortar and pestle and grind until fine.

Place the ground spices in a food processor with the garlic, chile, cilantro roots, and ginger. Process until a paste forms. Add the onions and continue to pulse until smooth.

Remove the skin from the fish (your fishmonger can do this for you). Rub the fish with the paste and place in a shallow ovenproof dish to marinate for 1 hour in the refrigerator.

Preheat the oven to 425°F.

Peel the potatoes and cut them into 1 1/4-inch chunks. Bring to a boil in a pan of heavily salted water. Simmer until cooked but still firm (you do not want them to fall apart).

Season the fish well with salt and pepper and place in the oven. Bake for 10–12 minutes or until cooked through.

Meanwhile, mix the lemon zest and juice, chile, scallions, olive oil, and tamarind pulp in a large bowl.

Drain the potatoes and add to the bowl. Toss gently to mix. The potatoes are hot so they will absorb all the flavors. Check the seasoning and add more salt, black pepper, and green chile to taste. Add some of the cilantro, saving the rest to garnish the dish.

Serve the fish with the potatoes, which should be hot or warm. Scatter the remaining cilantro over the top.

john dory with peppers, black olives, and rosemary

serves 4–6

You could serve this with some mixed greens or arugula to provide a freshness and crispness that complement the sweet rich flavors and soft textures of the other ingredients. This dish could easily be doubled up—simply fortify the sauce with extra red pepper, potatoes, and olive oil.

3 red bell peppers
1 pound small new potatoes
5 tablespoons good-quality extra virgin olive oil
2 garlic cloves, finely sliced
3 sprigs of young rosemary, leaves finely chopped
1 red chile (jalapeño or serrano), seeded and finely chopped
20–30 pitted black olives (see chef's tip on page 27)
1 tablespoon capers, rinsed and coarsely chopped
juice of 1 lemon
1 tablespoon sherry vinegar or red wine vinegar
salt and freshly ground black pepper
1 John Dory (or porgy) fillet per person (6–7 ounces each), skin on
splash of olive oil
mixed salad greens or arugula, for serving (optional)

Preheat the oven to 400°F.

Grill the peppers on a heavy ridged grill pan, or directly over a gas flame until the skin is blackened and blistered all over. Alternatively, cut them in half, drizzle with a bit of oil, and broil for about 12–15 minutes. Remove from the heat, place in a bowl, and cover with plastic wrap. Let cool, so the trapped steam loosens their skin as they cool.

Scrub the new potatoes and place in a pan of salted water. Bring to a boil and then turn down to a gentle simmer until the potatoes are cooked but still firm. Do not overboil. Remove from the heat and let the potatoes cool down in their water.

Heat the olive oil in a small saucepan over medium heat. Add the garlic, rosemary, and chile. Do not let these ingredients scald or get too hot: you are infusing them in the olive oil, not frying them. Remove the pan from the heat and let the aromatic ingredients steep and infuse in the olive oil, as if you were brewing tea.

When the peppers are cool, remove their skins and cut into thin strips, discarding the seeds.

Add the peppers, olives, capers, lemon juice, and vinegar to the warm olive oil. Season well with lots of freshly ground black pepper. Taste the sauce, and then add some salt if necessary. The olives and the capers are both salty, so be careful not to over-season. Tasting the sauce at this stage is very important. It should be sweet, salty, sour, and hot.

You are now ready to cook your fish. Score the skin side of the fish with three parallel cuts. Pat dry with paper towels. Season with salt and pepper.

Heat a heavy skillet and add a splash of olive oil. Place the fish in the pan skin-side down and seal the skin until it is a medium golden-brown. Keep the fish still in the pan; do not move it, poke it, or shake the pan, as you want a brown crust to form.

Gently turn the fish over and cook on the flesh side for 2 minutes. Transfer to a baking sheet and bake in the oven for 5 minutes.

Meanwhile, remove the potatoes from the water and cut in half lengthwise. Mix them into the warm oil mixture. Check the seasoning.

Plate the fish with some of the potatoes and peppers. Spoon the rest of the warm dressing over the fish.

sea bass with cannellini beans and gremolata

serves 4

1 cup dried cannellini beans, soaked overnight in a bowl of water
2 garlic cloves, 1 crushed, 1 finely chopped
1 celery rib
handful of flat-leaf parsley stalks (leaves reserved for gremolata)
4 tablespoons olive oil
pinch of crushed hot dried chiles
2 onions, finely chopped
2 teaspoons sugar
salt and freshly ground black pepper
2 tablespoons red wine vinegar
20 cherry tomatoes
lemon juice, to taste
4 x 6–7 ounce sea bass (or grouper) fillets
1 handful of arugula

for the gremolata

3/4 cup blanched slivered almonds
2 garlic cloves, very finely chopped
zest of 2 lemons
30 flat-leaf parsley leaves

Preheat the oven to 350°F.

Drain the beans and put them in a high-sided, flameproof casserole. Cover with about 1 1/4 inches of water. Add the crushed garlic clove, celery, parsley stalks, and 2 tablespoons of the olive oil. Cover with foil and crimp the edges tightly to seal. Place over a high heat for 5 minutes until the water is boiling. Transfer to the oven and bake for 1 hour.

Place a heavy pan over a medium-high heat. When it is hot, add a splash of oil and fry the chopped garlic and crushed chile until pale golden. Add the onions and sugar, and season well with salt and pepper. Cook over a high heat for 3–4 minutes, then reduce the heat to medium. Let the onions sweat and gently caramelize. If they start to stick or scorch then just add a splash of water.

When the onions are deep brown, add the vinegar and cook until it is absorbed. Taste and check the seasoning; it should be sweet, salty, sour, and hot.

While the onions are cooking, put the cherry tomatoes in a roasting pan with a splash of oil and some salt and pepper. Roast in the oven for about 20 minutes.

To prepare the gremolata, first roast the almonds. Put them in another baking pan and place in the oven to dry-roast until golden brown. Set a timer and check them every 2 minutes. Don't let them get too dark or they will taste bitter. When the almonds are cool, combine them with the garlic and lemon zest in a bowl.

When the beans are ready, remove the foil carefully: a lot of trapped steam will escape. If the beans are cooked and soft, then drain any excess liquid, but leave a few spoonfuls to keep them moist. If not, re-cover and continue to cook.

Add the caramelized onions and roasted tomatoes to the beans pan, adding in any extra roasting juices. Toss gently to mix. Add the remaining 2 tablespoons oil. The mixture should be quite moist and juicy. Check the seasoning. Adjust where necessary with salt, pepper, and lemon juice.

Heat a grill pan until very hot. Season the fish with salt and pepper. Place skin-side down in the hot pan and cook for 3–4 minutes over medium-high heat until the skin is golden brown and can be lifted easily without tearing or sticking. Turn the fish over and cook for 3–6 minutes, depending upon the thickness.

While the fish is cooking, coarsely chop the arugula and mix with the beans. Finely chop the parsley and mix with the gremolata. Serve the fish on top of the beans, and spoon some of the juices over the fish. Scatter the roast almond gremolata on top.

seared tuna with sesame seeds

serves 4

for the marinade

3/4-inch piece of fresh ginger, peeled and grated
2 stalks of lemongrass, coarse outer leaves removed, thinly sliced
zest and juice of 3 limes
2 tablespoons Asian fish sauce
2 tablespoons soy sauce
juice of 1 orange
4 scallions, finely sliced
2 red chiles, seeded and finely chopped
10 mint leaves, finely chopped
small handful of cilantro leaves, coarsely chopped

1 pound piece of tuna
salt and freshly ground black pepper
3 tablespoons sesame seeds
1 tablespoon olive oil

Prepare the marinade: combine all the ingredients except the mint and cilantro in a bowl.

Cut the tuna into four steaks. Season with salt and pepper and coat with sesame seeds.

Heat a skillet. When hot, add the olive oil. Add the tuna steaks and cook for just 1 1/2 minutes on each side, so it is still very rare in the middle. It is important not to overcook the tuna as it will continue to cook when it comes out of the pan.

Remove from the heat and add to the bowl with the marinade, turning to cover. The acid and salt in the marinade will continue to cook the tuna. Mix in half of the fresh herbs.

Garnish with the remaining herbs and serve at once.

seared tuna with preserved lemon and capers

serves 4

The dressing is salty and sour and the tuna is subtly rich with an edge of roasted spices.

for the dressing

2 tablespoons capers, rinsed and coarsely chopped
1 x recipe preserved lemons (see page 27), rind finely chopped
zest and juice of 1 lemon
5 tablespoons olive oil
salt and freshly ground black pepper
20 basil leaves
20 mint or flat-leaf parsley leaves

for the fish

1 tablespoon coriander seeds
1 tablespoon fennel seeds
1 small dried chile
$^1/_2$ tablespoon dried thyme or marjoram
1 pound piece of tuna
a little oil
salt and freshly ground black pepper

for the salad

2 fennel bulbs
2 celery ribs from the heart, thinly sliced
handful of arugula leaves
handful of watercress leaves or other mixed peppery leaves
small handful of mint leaves
2 scallions, thinly sliced

To make the dressing, combine all the ingredients except for the herbs. Taste and check the seasoning. Season well with black pepper, and salt if needed (the capers are salty so taste first).

Crush the coriander seeds, fennel seeds, dried chile, and thyme or marjoram in a mortar and pestle or spice grinder.

Take the piece of tuna and cut in half lengthwise along the grain. Then cut each piece in half through its middle to make four thinner pieces. Rub the pieces with a little oil, season well with salt and pepper, and then roll in the crushed spices.

Heat a heavy frying pan or grill pan. Place the pieces of tuna on the side of the pan furthest away from you. Sear until the spices are aromatic and golden brown, about $1^1/_2$–2 minutes.

With a pair of tongs, roll the tuna towards you and sear the next side. Repeat the process until all the sides are golden brown. Remove from the heat. If using a ridged grill pan, the fish will have charred marks across the flesh.

Wrap each piece of fish very tightly in plastic wrap and place in the freezer for 20–25 minutes (this will firm up the flesh and make it easier to cut into thin slices).

To make the salad, cut the fennel in half and remove the tough outer layer. With a sharp knife, trim off the excess root and discard. Slice thinly, cutting lengthwise through the heart into thin fan-like pieces held together at the bottom. Place the fennel and celery in a bowl of ice water for 15–20 minutes to crisp while you prepare the other ingredients.

Tear the arugula, watercress, and mint leaves into a serving bowl. Drain the fennel and celery and add to the bowl, along with the scallions. Add a couple of spoonfuls of the caper dressing and toss everything together.

Remove the tuna from the freezer and unwrap. With a thin sharp knife cut thin slices across the grain of the tuna, so that each slice has a thin edge of spice crust. Try to cut the tuna as thinly as possible; use a light pressure, as if you were cutting a loaf of bread.

Finely chop the herbs for the dressing and mix together. Check the seasoning by tasting some with a little slice of tuna.

Arrange the tuna slices over the salad and spoon the dressing on top. Serve at once.

green curry paste

serves 4

To get the most intense flavors with this curry paste, make up a large batch by doubling or tripling the quantities. It can be kept in the fridge for up to a week or frozen in portion sizes. You can then put together an impressive curry in a very short time to serve with fish, shrimp, chicken, beef, or vegetables.

- large chunk of fresh ginger, peeled and chopped
- 4 garlic cloves, peeled
- 4 stalks of lemongrass, tough outer leaves removed, coarsely chopped
- 1/2 bunch of cilantro, stems and leaves chopped separately
- 6 cilantro (fresh coriander) roots, rinsed (if not available, use cilantro stems)
- 1/2 teaspoon salt
- 4 green chiles, seeded
- 2 medium onions
- zest and chopped flesh of 1 lime
- 1 tablespoon vegetable oil
- 3 kaffir or other lime leaves
- 1 teaspoon ground turmeric
- 1 3/4 cups coconut milk
- juice of 1 lime
- 1 tablespoon Asian fish sauce

Chop all the ingredients first, so the food processor can accommodate them. Keep the ingredients separate because they are not going to go into the food processor at the same time.

Place the ginger, garlic, lemongrass, and cilantro stems and roots in the food processor. Pulse until smooth. Keep checking to see that all is incorporated and smooth, scraping down the sides of the bowl with a spatula as needed. Add the salt (this will work as an abrasive to help break them down). Add the green chiles.

When mixture is becoming smooth, add the onion and lime zest and flesh (and a splash of water, if necessary) to make a semi-smooth paste. Adding water is not a problem, because it will just evaporate when you are cooking out the sauce. In this state, the paste can be kept in the fridge for 2–3 days.

Heat the oil in a heavy stainless steel saucepan. Add the paste, lime leaves, and turmeric, and cook over a low to medium heat for 25–30 minutes, stirring to avoid it sticking. The paste will dry out and become aromatic.

When the paste has lost its liquid and is more concentrated, add the coconut milk. Gently simmer to reduce by one third (about 10 minutes). Add the lime juice and fish sauce.

If not using right away, let the curry paste cool before storing airtight in the fridge or freezer.

chef's tip

DO NOT add the turmeric until instructed, otherwise it will dye your food processor yellow! (I speak from experience). Only add turmeric when the paste is cooking.

thai royal green curry of smoked trout with mint and lemongrass

serves 4

The smoked flavor of the trout works well with the hot, lemony character of the green curry. Remember that you are hot-smoking the fish, not preserving it, so it must be used within two days of cooking.

5 ounces green curry paste (see page 193)
$1^{1}/_{4}$ cups coconut cream or milk
8–12 new potatoes, cut into thirds
5 ounces trimmed green beans (snow peas or asparagus can also be used)
1 medium piece of fresh ginger, peeled and grated
2 teaspoons young green peppercorns (optional)
2 stalks of lemongrass, tough outer leaves removed, thinly sliced
2 smoked rainbow trout (see page 95)
2 small green chiles, seeded and finely chopped
juice of 2 limes
1 tablespoon Asian fish sauce
1 tablespoon soy sauce
juice of 1 orange
1 tablespoon tamarind pulp (if unavailable use lime juice mixed with soft brown sugar)
handful of cilantro leaves
12 Thai basil leaves (if unavailable use more mint and cilantro)
small handful of mint
3 scallions, finely chopped

Heat the curry paste over medium heat until steaming. Add half the coconut cream and bring to a boil. Add the potatoes and poach in the liquid for 8–10 minutes until nearly cooked.

Add the green beans, ginger, peppercorns, and half the lemongrass and simmer gently over low heat, stirring occasionally to prevent it from sticking.

When the potatoes are just cooked, add the smoked trout fillets (these are already cooked so you are just warming them up). Stir gently so that the trout does not become too broken up. The paste should be quite sloppy: if necessary, use the remaining coconut cream and a little water to thin the paste and prevent drying out.

Season with some of the chopped green chiles and the remaining lemongrass. Add the lime juice, fish sauce, light soy sauce, orange juice, and tamarind. Chop half of the herbs and stir in gently.

Adjust the seasoning. It should be hot, sour, sweet, and salty. Garnish with the scallions and remaining chopped herbs and chiles.

tea and cinnamon-smoked chicken

serves 6

This can be served as a main course or as part of a Thai or Asian banquet. The chicken stays juicy and is deliciously infused with the smoky flavors of the spices.

1 tablespoon coriander seeds
6 star anise
1 teaspoon whole black peppercorns
3 cinnamon sticks
12 chicken drumsticks
salt and freshly ground black pepper
1 tablespoon oil

for the smoking mix

1 cup raw Thai Jasmine rice
$\frac{1}{2}$ cup jasmine tea leaves
1 red chile (jalapeño or serrano), seeded and coarsely chopped
1 tablespoon brown sugar
4 kaffir or other lime leaves
$1\frac{1}{4}$-inch piece of fresh ginger, peeled and coarsely chopped
1 lime, cut in half

roast shallot, tomato, and chile relish (see page 46)

In a mortar and pestle or spice grinder finely grind the coriander seeds, star anise, peppercorns and cinnamon sticks. Place in a fine mesh strainer, sifting it through to create a fine, blended spice powder.

Save any coarse pieces and spice husks and mix with the ingredients for the smoking mix.

Rub the chicken drumsticks with the oil and season generously with salt and pepper and the sifted spices. The spices will stick to the skin because of the oil. Add any excess spice to the smoking mix.

Place the chicken drumsticks in a hot pan. Seal for 3–4 minutes on each side or until the skin is a deep golden brown and the spices are fragrant. Do not scorch the spices.

Remove the chicken. De-glaze the pan with a little water and add this liquid and any cooked spices from the pan to the smoking mix.

Line a large wok with 2 layers of tin foil (this prevents the smoking mix from sticking to the pan). Place the smoking mix in the center of the wok and fit a rack over it. Place the browned chicken pieces on the rack and place the wok lid on top. If you do not have a lid, make a dome-shaped one out of a large piece of foil.

Start the heat on medium-high. Once the smoking mix starts to caramelize, turn down the heat. Let the chicken smoke in this way for 45–60 minutes.

Meanwhile, follow the instructions for making the roast shallot, tomato, and chile relish.

Check that the chicken is cooked by inserting a small knife in a leg near the bone. If the juices are still pink then cook the chicken for a little longer until they run clear.

Serve the chicken alongside the roast shallot relish.

wild duck with spicy grilled pears and spinach

serves 4

4 wild duck breasts (if unavailable, use Long Island or other duck breasts)
salt and freshly ground black pepper
juice of 1 orange
1 tablespoon honey
1 tablespoon red wine vinegar

for the pears

3 pears, peeled, cored, and quartered
1/2 tablespoon olive oil
1 teaspoon cinnamon
1/2 teaspoon coarsely ground coriander seeds
1/2 teaspoon apple pie spice
salt and freshly ground black pepper
4 imported bay leaves

for the spinach

2 tablespoons olive oil
1 garlic clove, finely sliced
3/4-inch piece of fresh ginger, peeled and grated
1 pound baby spinach, well rinsed
salt and freshly ground black pepper

Preheat the oven to 425°F.

Arrange the duck breasts, skin-side down, in a skillet placed over low heat. You do this to render the fat from the duck before you seal the skin. This will take 10–15 minutes.

Meanwhile, mix the pears in a bowl with the oil, dried spices, and salt and pepper. Place in a hot grill pan and grill for about 2 minutes on each side.

When the duck skin is crispy, discard any excess fat and transfer the breasts to a roasting tray, skin-side up. Season with salt and pepper, and scatter the partially grilled pears and the bay leaves around the duck.

Mix together the orange juice, honey, and red wine vinegar and pour it over the duck and pears. Roast in the oven for 8 minutes until the meat is medium-rare.

Meanwhile, prepare the spinach: heat the oil in a heavy pan and fry the garlic and ginger until pale golden. Add the spinach and stir briskly over a high heat until wilted (about 2–3 minutes). Season with salt and pepper.

When the duck is ready, remove from the oven. The skin should be crispy and the meat should be medium-rare. Let it rest for 2 minutes before slicing on the diagonal.

Drain any excess water from the spinach and serve with the duck and pears and all the roasting juices.

lacquered duck with cinnamon, star anise, orange zest, and honey

serves 4

I learned this spectacular method of preparing meat and game with David Thompson at Darley Street Thai in Sydney. This dish is traditionally Thai and works with other Thai-style accompaniments. Alternatively, mix with arugula, mustard greens, and baby spinach leaves to make a flavor-packed warm salad.

4 duck breasts

for the lacquer

1 tablespoon coriander seeds
1 tablespoon fennel seeds
1/2 cup soy sauce
3 tablespoons Asian fish sauce
juice and zest of 2 oranges
2 cinnamon sticks
4 star anise
4 imported bay leaves
2 tablespoons honey
1 tablespoon brown sugar
1/2 red chile (jalapeño or serrano), seeded

Crush the coriander and fennel seeds in a mortar and pestle. Place with all the other lacquer ingredients in a pan, bring to a simmer, and let it reduce by half.

Meanwhile, place the duck breasts, skin-side down, in a cold pan. This is one of the few times in cooking that you start something off in a cold pan. You do this to render the fat from the duck before sealing the skin to make it crispy. If the pan is too hot, you will seal the skin too quickly, trapping the fat inside.

Place pan over medium-low heat. When the duck breasts have rendered (about 10–12 minutes), all the fat will drain from under the skin and the skin will be crisp. Place the duck breasts, skin-side up, on a rack fit inside a roasting pan.

When the lacquer has reduced, pour it over the sealed duck breasts. Pour any excess lacquer back into the pan, continue to reduce for a few minutes, and then spoon a second layer over them. Repeat this 6–10 times. This will take up to 1 hour. You are building up layers of the ever-thickening lacquer (see picture on page 180).

If you run out of lacquer or if it starts to burn, pour about 1 cup water and 1 tablespoon sugar into the pan and continue to reduce.

Preheat the oven to 425°F.

When ready to cook, place the duck in the hot oven and roast quickly until they are medium-rare (about 10–12 minutes). By cooking them very quickly, the breasts stay pink and moist while the outside is coated in the intense spicy caramel.

chef's tips

For a Mediterranean-style variation try adding some orange slices (peel and pith removed) to the roasting pan with the duck breasts. While the duck is roasting, charbroil some figs with a little oil, salt, and pepper for a couple of minutes on each side and serve alongside the lacquered duck and roast orange slices. Serve with couscous or a rice pilaf, roast butternut squash, and spinach.

asian marinated partridge with green mango salad and caramelized peanut sauce

serves 4-6

This is a delicious combination of hot, sweet, salt, and sour flavors and contrasting textures. You can use quail, pheasant, wild duck, or chicken breasts instead of partridge. It works especially well with any Asian-style salad.

for the marinade

2 garlic cloves
3 cilantro (fresh coriander) roots, rinsed and finely chopped
salt and freshly ground black pepper
juice of 2 limes
1 tablespoon soy sauce

2–3 partridges
1 tablespoon olive oil
hot and sour mango salad (yam som tam—see page 79)
caramelized peanut and chile dressing—see page 43)

To make the marinade, put the garlic, cilantro roots, a pinch of salt, and some freshly ground black pepper in a mortar and pestle and pound to a smooth paste. Add the lime juice and soy sauce.

Take the partridge off the bone, quartering the bird. Remove the breast and leg. Separate the drumstick from the thigh. Place in the marinade and let sit, covered, up to 2 hours at room temperature.

Meanwhile, make the salad and the dressing.

When you are ready to cook the partridges, preheat the oven to 400°F.

Remove the meat from the marinade and shake off any excess liquid. Heat a heavy ovenproof skillet over a medium-high heat. Add the oil and cook the legs, turning, until they are deep golden-brown on all sides (about 4–5 minutes). Then add the breast meat and fry until it is pale golden-brown on both sides (about 2–3 minutes).

Place the whole pan in the oven for 5 minutes or until the meat is cooked. Remove the leg meat from the bone and cut the breast into smaller pieces. Serve alongside the green mango salad and pour the caramelized peanut and chile dressing over it.

crispy sweet venison with sour tamarind caramel

serves 6-8

Sugar plays a vital role in Thai cooking, balancing what otherwise would be an excess of heat, sourness, and saltiness. Venison is fantastic for this dish because you can keep it rare and juicy on the inside and crispy on the outside. Serve alongside rice or a Southeast Asian-style salad.

4 1/2 pounds venison haunch or pork hock, bone-in
4 star anise
4 kaffir or other lime leaves
2 cinnamon sticks
4 slices of fresh ginger
10 white peppercorns
1 tablespoon crushed coriander seeds
4 garlic cloves
1 red chile (jalapeño or serrano), seeded
vegetable oil, for shallow-frying

for the caramel

1 tablespoon oil
3 garlic cloves, finely chopped
1 red chile (jalapeño or serrano), seeded and finely chopped
3 cilantro stems, finely chopped
1 1/4-inch piece of fresh ginger, peeled and grated
2 tablespoons soft brown sugar
2 tablespoon tamarind pulp
2 tablespoons Asian fish sauce
1 tablespoon dark soy sauce
2 star anise
juice of 1 lime

for finishing

20 lychees
2 scallions, thinly sliced
20 cilantro leaves
1 red chile (jalapeño or serrano), seeded and finely chopped

Place the meat in a large pot, cover with water, and add all of the poaching ingredients. Bring to a boil, then turn down the heat and simmer for 25 minutes. If using pork hock then it needs to be cooked for longer (about 40–45 minutes).

When the meat is cooked, remove from the liquid and let it cool. The venison should still be quite rare, or if using pork it should be juicy but not too pink. Save a half cup of the poaching liquid and discard the rest. Cut the meat into 1 1/4-inch pieces and save any juices. Pat dry.

Make the caramel: heat the oil in a saucepan over a medium-high heat and add the garlic, chile, cilantro stems, and ginger. Cook until golden brown. Add the sugar and work until it dissolves. Add the tamarind pulp, Asian fish sauce, soy sauce, any saved meat juices, the reserved poaching liquid, and the star anise.

Simmer over medium-low heat for about 8 minutes, until it becomes syrupy and sticky.

Remove from the heat and stir in the lime juice.

In a large, heavy skillet or wok, heat some vegetable oil for shallow frying. Cook the pieces of meat in small batches, until crispy and golden brown (you do it in small batches so that the temperature of the oil does not drop). Remove the meat and drain on paper towels to absorb the oil.

Cut the lychees in half through the pit. They are then easy to pit and skin.

Place the meat in a large shallow bowl and pour the tamarind caramel over it. Mix in the lychees.

Garnish with cilantro, scallions, and red chile.

grilled and roasted fillet of venison with beets

serves 6

A fantastic combination of flavors with the subtle salt and sour components of the sauce and the sweetness of the roast beets and grilled meat. Cooking the fillet as one piece makes it easy to slice. Ninety percent of the meat should be medium-rare.

12 medium beets, well scrubbed
olive oil, for cooking
2 sprigs of thyme
1 head of garlic, broken into individual cloves, skin on
salt and freshly ground black pepper
$2^1/2$ pounds venison fillet, trimmed

for the dressing

oil, for cooking
6 slices bacon or pancetta, cut into thin strips
18 shallots, (2 finely chopped; 16 left whole)
1 garlic clove, finely chopped
salt and freshly ground black pepper
18–24 cherry tomatoes, cut in half
$^1/4$ cup aged balsamic vinegar
juice of $^1/2$ lemon
5 tablespoons extra virgin olive oil
handful of flat-leaf parsley

Preheat the oven to 400°F.

Put the beets in a roasting pan with a little oil, the sprigs of thyme, garlic, and salt and pepper. (Peeling the beets is optional; if cleaned well before cooking, the roast skin is delicious). Add $^1/2$ cup water to keep them moist by creating steam. Cover the pan with foil and seal well. Cook for about 1 hour or until the beets are tender when pierced with the tip of a sharp knife.

To make the dressing, heat a little oil in a saucepan and cook the bacon for 3 minutes. Add the shallots and garlic. Cook gently for another 4 minutes until they are soft and beginning to caramelize. Season with the salt and pepper.

Remove from the heat and add the tomatoes, balsamic vinegar, lemon juice, and olive oil. Set aside in a warm place to blend flavors.

When the beets are cooked, remove the foil and return to the oven for another 5 minutes. Add any juices to the reserved dressing. Cut the beets into quarters or halves depending upon their size.

Heat a grill pan 20 minutes before cooking. Rub the venison with a little olive oil and season with salt and pepper.

Place the venison on the griddle at the top of the pan furthest away from you. Sear on a high heat for 2 minutes, then roll the venison 90 degrees towards you and sear for another 2 minutes. Repeat until the bar marks cover the fillet. Transfer to a roasting pan (different from the beets) and roast in the oven for about 10 minutes. It will be medium-rare. Let it rest for 3 minutes before slicing. Add any juices to the dressing.

Slice the venison and arrange it in the center of the plate surrounded by the beets and garlic mixture. Add the parsley to the dressing and spoon the dressing over everything.

roast leg of lamb with spicy apricot and pistachio stuffing

serves 6–8

The stuffing on the right can be used to stuff turkey, chicken, spring lamb, or a loin of pork. Try experimenting with combinations of different nuts and dried fruit.

for the roast

1 boneless leg of lamb, about 5 pounds, (butterflied or tunnel boned—your butcher can do this for you)
spicy apricot and pistachio stuffing (see facing page)
1 carrot, coarsely chopped
1 celery rib, coarsely chopped
1/2 onion, coarsely chopped
3 garlic cloves, coarsely chopped
sprig of thyme
3 imported bay leaves
salt and freshly ground black pepper
1/2 cup dry red wine

for the gravy

1/2 cup dry red wine
1 tablespoon red currant jelly, quince paste, or other dark sweet jam (if unavailable, use brown sugar or honey)
1 tablespoon balsamic vinegar
1 cup broth or water

Preheat the oven to 400°F.

Stuff the inside of the leg of lamb with the spicy stuffing. Any excess stuffing can be heated separately and served to accompany the roast meat. With butcher's string, truss the meat to make an even shape so it will cook evenly and the stuffing will stay in place while roasting.

Place the vegetables and herbs in a flameproof casserole, then situate the lamb overtop. The vegetables will caramelize and sweeten when roasted, adding a depth of flavor to the meat juices (which in turn will add more flavor to the gravy). Season the meat with salt and pepper.

Place the lamb in the center of the oven. Roast for 1 hour 15 minutes (or 15 minutes per pound in weight).

Halfway through cooking, drain any excess fat from the roasting pan. Add the red wine to the pan. Baste the meat frequently with its free running juices.

When the meat is cooked, remove it from the roasting tray and let it rest on a clean plate in a warm place.

To make the gravy, drain excess fat from the roasting pan; then add the red wine to the pan and place over medium-high heat. Let the wine cook to reduce in volume.

With a wooden spoon, move the liquid around the pan, working the bottom with the spoon to free any good bits that have become stuck to the bottom. Add the red currant jelly or alternative and the balsamic vinegar, and any juices from the plated meat.

When the liquid in the pan has reduced by one third, add the broth or water (you could also use the cooking water from any potatoes or greens you might be serving with the roast).

Simmer for 5 minutes, then strain through a fine sieve. Check the seasoning. It should have elements of sweet, sour, and salty with a hint of pepper.

Serve the gravy in a sauceboat with the roast meat.

spicy apricot and pistachio stuffing

3/4 cup pitted prunes
1 1/4 cups dried apricots
1 tablespoon olive oil
2 garlic cloves, finely chopped
2 red onions, finely chopped
3 celery ribs from the heart, finely chopped
1 sharp apple, peeled, cored, and chopped into 1/2-inch cubes
2/3 cup cooked peeled chestnuts, coarsely chopped
1 teaspoon ground cinnamon
1 teaspoon ground cloves
1 teaspoon ground allspice
1/2 teaspoon grated fresh nutmeg
1/2 cup dry white wine
2 imported bay leaves
zest and juice of 1 orange
salt and freshly ground black pepper
2/3 cup unsalted shelled pistachio nuts
30 flat-leaf parsley leaves, chopped

Put the prunes and apricots in a bowl and cover with boiling water. Let sit for 30 minutes.

Heat the olive oil in a heavy skillet. Cook the garlic until golden. Add the onion and celery. Cook over low heat for 10 minutes.

Add the apples and chestnuts and cook for another 5 minutes. Add all the dried spices and cook until they are aromatic. Add the white wine and bay leaves and cook over medium heat to reduce.

Drain the dried fruits (but reserve the liquid), chop coarsely, and add to the pan. Mix together, then add the soaking liquid from the fruit. Add the orange zest and juice. Season to taste with salt and pepper.

Continue cooking until all the liquid has been absorbed. Stir in the parsley and pistachio nuts.

to make garlicky spring lamb

A fantastic dish to make in spring and early summer when wild garlic leaves are available. You can also put some leaves in the leek and herb stuffing. You will most likely need to order a lamb loin from your butcher in advance.

1 x recipe leek and herb stuffing (see facing page)
loin of spring lamb
2 handfuls of wild garlic leaves, washed

Preheat the oven to 400°F.

When your stuffing is cool, use it to stuff the piece of the lamb. Some garlic leaves can be added to the stuffing as well. Roll the meat and tie securely with butcher's string.

Place in an ovenproof skillet or other heavy pan and roast until the meat is the desired degree of pinkness on the inside.

Wrap the meat in the leaves, tucking them underneath the string.

Roast in the oven for 15 minutes per pound in weight. Check the meat periodically: when the leaves dry out, just add more damp leaves on top of the dry ones, building up layers of garlic leaves.

leek and herb stuffing with wild mushrooms

serves 6

This is a fresh, clean-tasting stuffing for beef, chicken, or lamb. The sweetness of the leeks and the nutty, earthy taste of the mushrooms work particularly well with the sweet tender taste of a loin of spring lamb. The lemon zest and juice act as a highlighter on the subtle flavors. You use only a few dried mushrooms in this recipe to give a little depth; too many will make the flavor become overly strong and meaty.

2 handfuls of mixed wild mushrooms, a mixture of fresh and dried
3 tablespoons unsalted butter
1 garlic clove, finely chopped
1 tablespoon chopped thyme leaves
salt and freshly ground black pepper
juice of 1/2 lemon, zest of 1 lemon
6 medium leeks
1/4 cup dry white wine
20 basil leaves
20 flat-leaf parsley or mint leaves

Place the dried mushrooms in a bowl and pour boiling water over them to cover. Let sit 10 minutes.

Heat 1 tablespoon of the butter in a heavy pan. Cook half the garlic and thyme until pale golden. Add the fresh mushrooms. Cook quickly for 4 minutes until they are beginning to caramelize and go golden brown. Season with a little salt and pepper. Add the lemon juice. Transfer the mixture to a bowl.

Heat another tablespoon of the butter in the pan and fry the remaining garlic and thyme. Add the soaked dried mushrooms (reserve their soaking liquid). Cook quickly for 2–3 minutes until they are beginning to caramelize. Place a clean piece of cheesecloth (or a clean paper towel) in a sieve and strain the mushroom soaking liquid through the cloth into the pan.

Let it simmer gently until all the liquid has been absorbed. Add the other cooked mushrooms back to the pan. Mix together. Check the seasoning (the mushrooms will have concentrated, so go easy on the salt).

Add the lemon zest to the mushrooms, then remove the mixture from the pan to a bowl.

Split the leeks in half lengthwise and rinse off all the dirt and grit. Cut crosswise into thin slices.

Melt the remaining butter in the pan and add the leeks. Cook over a high heat for 2 minutes until they start to wilt. Add the white wine and some salt and pepper. Cover and reduce the heat to low. Cook the leeks until soft.

Coarsely chop the herbs and add to the mushrooms. Turn out onto a board and roughly chop so they are an even size. Add the mushroom mixture back to the pan with the leeks and mix together. Check the seasoning again.

Let cool, and drain off any excess liquid. This stuffing will keep for a couple of days in the fridge.

sides

sides

I think there is a desperate need to be more adventurous in the dishes that accompany our main courses. Vegetable side dishes, grains, and legumes need to be well-flavored and thought out so that they go with the particular main course dish that you are serving, complementing the other flavors and textures so that every taste element is represented simultaneously.

Side dishes need to match main components in terms of similar flavor profiles and regional characteristics. An Italian-style artichoke salad is not going to work well with a Thai green curry; and likewise couscous with egg-fried Asian noodles and fish sauce is a combination that should not be experimented with. Aim to keep the different flavors clean and pure, otherwise the food you create becomes muddied with blurred edges and no real clarity or definition. When a main course dish is densely flavored, the side dish that accompanies it should be quite simple or cleanly flavored. Creamy potato dauphinois, for example, is perfect with some roast beef with a red wine sauce. Couscous or a rice pilaf goes well with a slow-cooked lamb or other braised meat dish—whether it is Mediterranean, Middle Eastern, or Indian in style.

The recipes in this chapter, however, don't have to accompany a main course; instead, try serving a selection of them together. Take a platter of Italian antipasti: a perfect example of vegetable side dishes working together in a harmony of tastes. Each component has its own complete flavor and can be savored individually, but then as part of the whole dish it will contrast with and complement the other elements. One part could be predominantly hot or more strongly flavored, but could be offered with something more sour, alongside something else with sweet or salty elements. The plate of antipasti shown on page 208 illustrates this perfectly. You have roast asparagus with arugula and Parmesan, fried eggplant with garlic, chile, and mint, and baked stuffed red peppers with cherry tomatoes, capers, and basil. The first is predominantly sweet, salty, and hot, the second is mainly sweet, hot, and sour, while the last is mostly sweet and sour. Together on the plate they present a fantastic combination of textures and colors and all the elements of taste are balanced.

Staples such as rice, couscous, barley, and polenta provide a blank canvas for the inspired and creative cook. Neutral does not have to mean bland or insipid. Beans and legumes, such as lentils, borlotti beans, cannelloni beans, and chickpeas, are useful additions to your repertoire because they may triple in size during cooking, and consequently are very filling. The similarity between all these kinds of side dishes is that, owing to their neutral status, they are able to absorb and hold many other flavors, not to mention all the good cooking juices and sauces from the main part of the meal.

The side dishes in this chapter can be satisfying in themselves as light meals or snacks. Baked sweet potatoes with a sauce of fresh green chile and lemon zest (see page 224) is a perfect taste combination. Some sea salt is sprinkled into the center of the baked sweet potato. The sauce of green chile and lemon zest is hot and sour, and combines beautifully with the sweetness of the inside of the potato.

SWEET **red peppers, cherry tomatoes, beets, basil, mushrooms, peas, fava beans, green beans, white bread, parsnips, new potatoes, couscous, milk** SOUR **red cabbage, scallions, lemons, balsamic vinegar, white wine** SALTY **capers, pancetta, anchovies** HOT **extra virgin olive oil, garlic, arugula, ginger, chile** BITTER **savoy cabbage**

stuffed red peppers with cherry tomatoes and capers

serves 4–6

You can find versions of this across Italy, Spain, and the South of France. Serve hot, warm, or cold with fish, meat, couscous, or as part of a buffet meal. The peppers are very sweet and the filling is salty and sour. Crumbled goat cheese, arugula, olives, and anchovies would also make good fillers.

2 or 3 red bell peppers (allow 1/2 pepper per person)
2 garlic cloves, finely sliced
salt and freshly ground black pepper
3 tablespoons olive oil
16–24 cherry tomatoes (or 4 per person)
1 (4-ounce) jar of capers, rinsed and coarsely chopped
20 basil leaves
1 tablespoon balsamic vinegar
juice of 1/2 lemon

Preheat the oven to 350°F.

Cut the peppers in half lengthwise. Trim away the white pith and tap out the seeds. Place cut-side up on a baking sheet.

Place the garlic inside the pepper halves. Season with salt and pepper and a little drop of olive oil. Place 4 cherry tomatoes in each pepper half.

Place on a baking sheet and bake in the oven for about 1 hour. After 20 minutes of cooking time, turn the oven down to 300°F so they cook very slowly and evenly, retaining their juice.

Chop the basil and mix with the capers in a bowl, add the rest of the olive oil, the balsamic vinegar, lemon juice, and some black pepper.

If the peppers char on the edges, trim off the burnt skin with a pair of scissors.

Remove the tomatoes from the peppers and mix with the caper mixture in the bowl. Divide the mixture equally among the peppers and serve.

roast asparagus with arugula and parmesan

serves 4–6

Any salty cheese works here; you could try Romano, goat cheese, or feta instead of Parmesan. When you roast asparagus it takes on a delicious nutty aspect, but you could also grill or pan-fry it with similar results.

14–20 spears of asparagus
olive oil, for cooking
salt and freshly ground black pepper
1 1/2 tablespoons extra virgin olive oil
juice of 1 lemon
handful of arugula, coarsely chopped
small handful of mint, coarsely chopped
small handful of basil, coarsely chopped
1 (2-ounce) piece of Parmesan

Preheat the oven to 400°F.

Remove and discard the tough ends of the asparagus. Cut the spears into diagonal pieces about 1 1/2 inches long. Mix with olive oil, salt, and pepper.

Place the oiled asparagus onto a baking sheet and transfer to the oven. Roast for 7–10 minutes, depending upon thickness, until they are tender but still have a bite.

Mix the olive oil and lemon juice to make a dressing. Add half the chopped herbs and dress the asparagus when they are still warm.

With a vegetable peeler, shave the Parmesan into thin strips. Mix half the cheese with the roasted asparagus. Sprinkle the remaining Parmesan shavings and herbs on top of the dish for serving.

fried eggplants with garlic, chile, and mint

serves 4–6

These eggplants are hot, sweet, salty, and sour, and are light and refreshing. Serve as antipasto with mozzarella or prosciutto, as part of a summer buffet, or as an accompaniment to a main course.

3 eggs
salt and freshly ground black pepper
2 eggplants, cut into thin disks
1 red chile (jalapeño or serrano), seeded and cut into thin slivers
30 mint leaves, coarsely chopped

for the dressing

3 tablespoons extra virgin olive oil
4 garlic cloves, finely sliced
juice of 1 lemon
1 tablespoon red wine vinegar
salt and freshly ground black pepper

Crack the eggs into a bowl and season with salt and pepper. Beat with a fork.

Heat a little oil in a heavy pan. Dip the eggplants into the egg mixture and fry in small batches. Fry for 2 minutes or until golden brown and then turn over and cook until tender. Place the fried slices on paper towels to soak up any excess oil.

While the eggplants are cooking, heat the olive oil for the dressing in a small saucepan over medium heat. Cook the garlic in the oil until pale golden. Remove the pan from the heat and drain the garlic on paper towels.

To make the dressing, combine 2 tablespoons of the garlic oil with the other dressing ingredients.

On a flat platter, arrange a layer of the fried eggplant and scatter with the chile, mint, and fried garlic flakes. Season with salt and pepper. Drizzle with dressing.

Repeat the layers until all the ingredients are used. Reserve some chile, mint, and garlic to garnish the top.

seasonal produce

Try to keep the food that you cook seasonally appropriate. This can be hard with supermarkets selling everything all year round, but what you need to establish for yourself is a scale of quality and a level that is acceptable or not.

Parsnips in the summer are going to be tasteless because they benefit from cold weather that intensifies the sugars and flavors; they will always taste better after the first frost of the year. Likewise, strawberries and tomatoes in the middle of winter are not going to be as good as in summer because they benefit from sunlight and warmth to ripen them on the vine. Just because it is red and is a tomato does not mean that it is a good tomato. It is all about taste and texture. A lot of winter-ripened tomatoes are highly acidic with little of the character and sweetness of a summer-ripened variety. If you can only get hold of unripe tomatoes, they can be sprinkled with a little sugar and roasted in the oven; the sugar speeds up the caramelization process, giving them the sweetness that you require. Zucchini are only good to use and really tasty when they are thin and firm and not too long. With a vegetable such as this which is made up of a large quantity of water, the bigger the vegetable the more water, seeds, and spongy woody flesh that is not good to eat.

As consumers it is vital that we do not accept second-rate produce that is not of good-enough quality for the food we want to cook. There should be no place for fish that is not of the freshest quality, vegetables that are woody and old, or herbs that are wilted and lackluster. Seasonal, organic fruit and vegetables may not be the perfect shape, size, or color, but they will taste how they are supposed to. It is only by tasting the raw ingredients that we can demand better quality from the producers, so that we can continue to make better food.

salad of roast summer beets with their leaves dressed with oil and lemon

serves 4–6

Peeling the beets is optional. If they are cleaned well before cooking, the skin is delicious. Break the herbs into the salad just before serving to enjoy their full aromas.

8 medium-size beets
olive oil, salt, and pepper
2 garlic cloves, coarsely chopped
1 sprig of thyme, leaves coarsely chopped
10 ounces beet leaves, Swiss chard, rainbow chard, or baby spinach
2 tablespoons extra virgin olive oil
juice of 1/2 lemon and zest of 1 lemon
salt and freshly ground black pepper
2 scallions, thinly sliced
20 basil leaves

Preheat the oven to 425°F.

Rinse and scrub the beets and place in a roasting pan with a little oil, salt, and pepper. Add the garlic and thyme to the roasting dish along with half a cup of water to keep them moist while cooking. Seal the tray with foil, making sure there are no gaps.

Place in the oven and roast for 45 minutes or until tender when pierced with the tip of a sharp knife.

Wash and trim the beet leaves or other leaves. Blanch for 2 minutes in salted boiling water until al dente.

Refresh the leaves under cold running water to stop the cooking and keep the color fresh. You want the stems of the leaves to have bite and not be too mushy. Squeeze off the excess water.

Make a dressing with the extra virgin olive oil, lemon juice, and salt and pepper.

When the beets are cooked, let them cool until they are just warm. Cut into thin slices or quarters, depending upon the size. Place in a large bowl with two thirds of the dressing. Add the lemon zest and scallions. Add the beet leaves and tear in some of the basil. Toss gently to mix.

Season with lots of freshly ground black pepper. Check the seasoning; it may need a little salt. Transfer to a serving dish, pour the remaining dressing over the salad, and garnish with the remaining basil.

braised mushrooms with ginger and star anise

serves 4

2 tablespoons olive oil
2 garlic cloves, finely chopped
3 cilantro (fresh coriander) roots, rinsed and finely chopped
1 red chile (jalapeño or serrano), seededand finely chopped
1 1/4-inch piece of fresh ginger, peeled and grated
4 whole star anise
1 pound wild mushrooms, cut into 1/4-inch slices
1/2 cup dry white wine
salt and freshly ground black pepper
30 cilantro leaves, chopped
juice of 1/2 lemon

Heat the olive oil in a heavy skillet and cook the garlic, cilantro root, and chile. Add the ginger and cook until pale golden. Place the star anise in the pan.

Add the mushrooms and cook over a high heat until they start to smell nutty and are beginning to caramelize and turn golden brown.

Add the white wine and cover with a lid. Simmer quickly until all the liquid has been absorbed.

Season with salt and pepper, then add the chopped cilantro, and lemon juice. Mix together and serve.

peas, pea shoots, and fava beans with mint, lemon, and olive oil

serves 4–6

Frozen peas and fava beans are completely transformed by this method. Asparagus, green beans, and lentils could also be added. You could add some cooked flaked salmon or some crumbled goat cheese to make a more substantial salad. Cartons of live pea shoots are now found year round in some larger supermarkets.

1 package (10 ounces) frozen peas
1 package (10 ounces) frozen small fava beans, removed from pod
1 container (about 2 cups) of pea shoots
salt and freshly ground black pepper
3 tablespoons olive oil
juice of 1 lemon
1 tablespoon red wine vinegar
30 mint or basil leaves
handful of arugula, chopped

Bring a pot of salted water to a boil. Cook the peas according to package directions and then remove them to a bowl. Add the fava beans to the pot and cook until al dente, and add to the bowl.

Snip off the pea shoots from their roots and blanch in boiling salted water. Season well with salt and pepper while they are hot. Add the olive oil, lemon juice, and vinegar. (Seasoning the ingredients when they are hot means that they will absorb all the flavors that you add.)

When the peas and fava beans have cooled down a little, coarsely chop the mint leaves and mix them with the green vegetables. Check the seasoning again and serve warm or cold.

moroccan green beans with tomatoes and cumin

serves 4

This is great with roast meats or as part of a summer buffet.

1 tablespoon coriander seeds
1 tablespoon cumin seeds
1 garlic clove
2 tablespoons olive oil
1 (14 1/2-ounce) can diced tomatoes
salt and freshly ground black pepper
20 cherry tomatoes
8–10 ounces green beans
juice of 1 lemon
small handful of cilantro

Preheat the oven to 350°F.

In a mortar and pestle, crush the coriander seeds and cumin seeds. Add the garlic and continue to work into a coarse paste.

Heat 1 tablespoon of olive oil in a saucepan and cook the garlic and spice paste until fragrant and aromatic. Add the tomatoes. Season with salt and pepper. Cook over low heat, stirring occasionally, until you have a thick tomato paste with no excess liquid.

Place the cherry tomatoes in a roasting pan. Add the remaining olive oil and season with salt and pepper. Roast in the oven for about 20 minutes.

Bring a pot of salted water to a boil. Trim the green beans and boil in the water until al dente, 3–5 minutes.

Add the beans to the tomato pan and mix together. Gently stir in the roasted tomatoes. Add the lemon juice and cilantro. Check the seasoning and serve.

green beans with roast almond tarator

serves 6

This is good hot, warm, or cold. The creamy almond tarator can take a generous amount of seasoning and vinegar. It should not be too dry and thick but nice and loose, so add a little more oil or some milk if necessary.

4 slices white bread, crusts removed
1/2 cup milk
8 ounces blanched slivered almonds, half of them toasted
salt and freshly ground black pepper
2 garlic cloves
juice of 1 lemon
3 tablespoons sherry vinegar or red wine vinegar
1 cup extra virgin olive oil
1 pound green beans

Place the bread in a bowl and cover with milk to soak.

Put the raw almonds and half the roasted almonds in a food processor with a pinch of salt and the garlic. Pulse until you have tiny, evenly sized bits—not dust.

Squeeze any excess milk out of the bread and add the bread to the food processor. Pulse until it is incorporated. Then slowly pour in the milk, to make a creamy paste. Add the lemon juice and sherry vinegar and season well.

With the machine running slowly, add the olive oil in a thin, steady stream, as if you were making a mayonnaise.

Cook the green beans in boiling salted water until al dente, then drain and dress with the tarator, mixing well so that the beans are covered with the creamy white paste. Transfer to a serving dish and sprinkle the remaining roasted almonds on top.

savoy cabbage braised with chorizo and white wine

serves 4-6

If you would like to make a vegetarian version of this dish, just add some fresh chopped chile instead of the chorizo.

1 savoy cabbage
2 tablespoons olive oil
2 garlic cloves, thinly sliced
8 ounces chorizo sausage for cooking, cut into 1/2-inch chunks
1 small red onion, finely diced
1/2 cup dry white wine
juice of 1/2 lemon
salt and freshly ground black pepper

To prepare the cabbage, remove the dark outer leaves (save them for a bitter leaf salad).

Cut the cabbage into quarters. Remove the hard center. Cut the cabbage into 1 1/4-inch chunks.

Heat the oil in a heavy skillet, add the garlic and chorizo, and fry until the garlic is a pale golden. Add the onion and cook over medium heat for about 5 minutes until the onion is soft.

Add the cabbage and white wine and cover with a lid. Cook over medium heat, stirring regularly, for 5–6 minutes or until the cabbage is soft.

Squeeze the lemon over the cabbage and stir. Check the seasoning but be careful (the chorizo sausage is salty and the cayenne pepper hot).

spicy red cabbage

serves 4

Serve with roasted or stewed meat.

1 medium-size red cabbage
2 apples, such as Golden Delicious
1 tablespoon olive oil
2 small shallots, finely chopped
1 garlic clove, finely chopped
1/2 teaspoon ground cloves
1/2 teaspoon ground cinnamon
1/2 teaspoon allspice
1 cinnamon stick
juice and zest of 1 orange
1 tablespoon brown sugar
2 tablespoons red wine vinegar
salt and freshly ground black pepper

To prepare the cabbage, remove the outer leaves, cut away the hard center and thinly slice. Peel and core the apples, cut into quarters and then slice into 1/2-inch- thick slices.

Heat the oil in a large saucepan or Dutch oven and cook the shallots until pale golden. Add the garlic and the dried spices and cook for 2 minutes until they become fragrant. Add the cabbage, orange juice and zest, brown sugar, red wine vinegar, and chopped apple.

Season with salt and pepper, then cover and cook for 10 minutes, stirring from time to time to avoid it sticking.

Check the seasoning and serve.

brussels sprouts braised with ginger and orange

serves 6–8

This a simple and delicious alternative to the usual buttered sprouts. A little dried chili could be added to the garlic and ginger if you like. This is great with any roast meat, such as pheasant, turkey, or chicken.

$1\frac{1}{2}$ pounds brussels sprouts
2 tablespoons butter
2 garlic cloves, finely sliced
1 tablespoon grated fresh ginger
zest and juice of 1 orange
1 tablespoon red wine vinegar
salt and freshly ground black pepper

Peel and wash the sprouts; allow plenty per person. Score the bottom end with a deep cross, which will allow the heat to get into the heart of this dense little vegetable.

In a heavy pan, melt the butter. Add the garlic and ginger, and cook over low heat until golden-brown.

Meanwhile, blanch the sprouts for about 2 minutes in boiling salted water. Add to the pan, stirring to coat them in the melted butter. Add the orange juice and zest and the red wine vinegar. Season with salt and pepper.

Cover and cook over medium heat for 3 minutes until the sprouts are tender when pierced with the tip of a sharp knife, but still al dente.

Remove the sprouts, and cook the sauce over medium-high heat until syrupy. To serve, drizzle sauce over the sprouts.

roast parsnips with pancetta and bay leaves

serves 4

6 medium parsnips
6 fresh bay leaves
sea salt and freshly ground black pepper
2 tablespoons olive oil
3 tablespoons balsamic vinegar
8 slices pancetta

Preheat the oven to 400°F.

Peel the parsnips and cut in half lengthwise. Coarsely chop 3 of the bay leaves.

In a mortar and pestle, grind the chopped bay leaves with 2 teaspoons sea salt. Continue to work until you have a smooth, pale green powder. Sift through a fine mesh sieve so you have a fine green salt.

Mix the parsnips with the olive oil and some black pepper and season with the green salt.

Transfer to a baking sheet and cook for 35–40 minutes or until they are just barely tender. Add the balsamic vinegar, pancetta, and the remaining bay leaves. Mix together.

Continue to cook until they are roasted and caramelized.

baked sweet potatoes with green chile and lemon sauce

serves 4-6

This is a fantastically simple taste sensation (see picture on page 13) which also works as a component of a salad, such as the salad of chorizo, mushrooms, and sweet potato (see page 99). The dressing will lift anything predominantly sweet, and is great served with roasted or grilled meat or fish.

2–3 sweet potatoes (allow 1/2 potato per person)

for the sauce

3 green chiles, cut in half, seeded, and finely chopped
zest and juice of 1 lemon
1/2 teaspoon sugar
salt and freshly ground black pepper
1/4 cup extra virgin olive oil

Preheat the oven to 400°F.

Wash the sweet potatoes but leave the skin on. Place on a baking tray and bake in the oven until soft to the point of a knife. Check after 30–40 minutes, depending upon their size, as sweet potatoes take less time to cook than normal baking potatoes.

Meanwhile, mix all the sauce ingredients together and season to taste. You should be able to detect a hint of sweetness, but not too much as the potato will also provide this element which will counter the acid and heat of the chiles.

Remove the sweet potatoes from the oven. Cut them in half and season the inside with a sprinkle of salt and black pepper. Drizzle with fresh green sauce and serve.

crushed potatoes with white wine, anchovies, capers, and chopped arugula

serves 4–6

Serve with fish or grilled meat, or make more substantial by mixing in some grilled pork or chicken.

1 pound new potatoes
salt and freshly ground black pepper
2 tablespoons capers, rinsed
1 (2-ounce) can of flat anchovies, drained of oil
3 tablespoons olive oil
juice of 1 lemon
1/4 cup dry white wine
2 tablespoons, butter at room temperature
4 scallions, finely chopped
small handful of flat-leaf parsley
small handful of basil leaves
handful of arugula

Wash the potatoes, place in a large saucepan, and cover with water. Season well with salt.

Bring to a boil, then turn down to a simmer.

Chop the capers and anchovies together into a coarse paste.

Mix the oil, lemon juice, and the white wine together.

When the potatoes are cooked, drain the water. Add the butter and season with salt and pepper.

Stir in the wine and oil mixture, breaking up and crushing some of the potatoes so they will soak up all the juices. Add the capers and anchovies.

When combined, check the seasoning, but do not oversalt because the anchovies and capers are salty.

Mix in the scallions and chopped herbs and arugula. Taste and serve warm.

jeweled couscous

serves 4–6

Couscous is very versatile and goes with just about anything. As a base it is very bland and can take a lot of different flavors, and quite a lot of seasoning. It does not work if it is bland and insipid.

zest and juice of 1 orange
zest and juice of 1 lemon
2 tablespoons red wine vinegar
3 tablespoons olive oil
2 tablespoons toasted sesame oil
1 (10-ounce) package couscous
20 dried figs, coarsely chopped
1 tablespoon dried sour cherries
1 tablespoon dried cranberries
1/2 chile (jalapeño or serrano), seeded and chopped
salt and freshly ground black pepper
1/2 teaspoon apple pie spice or ground cinnamon
3/4 cup pistachios or blanched slivered almonds
3 ounces sesame seeds
seeds of 1 pomegranate (about 1/2 cup)
4 scallions, trimmed and thinly sliced
1/2 cucumber, seeded and chopped
20 mint leaves, coarsely chopped
20 parsley or basil leaves, coarsely chopped
bunch of arugula or other leaves, coarsely chopped

Boil a kettle of water. Pour 2 cups into a heatproof measuring cup and mix in the orange and lemon juice, vinegar, and the two oils.

Put the couscous in a large bowl with the dried fruit, chile, and orange and lemon zest. Pour the mixed liquids over them. Mix together. Season with salt and pepper, and the dried spice.

Cover the bowl with plastic wrap, sealing the edges. As the couscous soaks up the hot liquid it will also soak up all the strong aromatic flavors. After 5 minutes, remove the plastic and mix with a fork to break up any stuck together lumps.

Dry-roast the nuts and seeds in a hot oven or dry skillet until they are golden brown.

Add all the remaining ingredients to the couscous and mix together. Check the seasoning. Add more olive oil, lemon juice, or seasoning if necessary.

alternatives

- **Other nuts or dried fruit can be used such as pine nuts, roast hazelnuts, raisins, dates, or dried apricots.**
- **Add some slices of grilled chicken to make it more substantial.**
- **Instead of dried fruit or roasted vegetables, use asparagus, green beans, and spinach with lots of chopped green herbs, arugula, and roasted pine nuts.**

barley pilaf with onions and preserved lemon

serves 6

Serve to accompany roast marinated meat such as quails or chicken pieces. Barley is like couscous in that the grains can take quite a lot of strong flavors. Raw, unsalted pistachios or toasted almonds or pine nuts can be added for texture.

1 1/2 cups pearl barley
2 tablespoons olive oil
2 onions, finely chopped
1 teaspoon sugar
2 garlic cloves
2 small dried, crushed chiles, or 1/2 teaspoon red pepper flakes
3 tablespoons currants or raisins
2 imported bay leaves
1 cinnamon stick
salt and freshly ground black pepper
2 cups chicken broth (see recipe on page 107) or water
handful of chopped flat-leaf parsley
1 preserved lemon (see recipe on page 27), finely chopped

Preheat the oven to 300°F.

Put the barley in a bowl and cover with cold water to soak.

Heat a heavy ovenproof pan. Add the olive oil. Cook the onions over medium-low heat until soft, add the sugar, and continue to cook until they start to caramelize.

Push the onions to one side of the pan and cook the garlic and dried chile, then mix in with the onions.

Drain the barley and add to the pan along with the currants. Cook for a few minutes, stirring, until they have absorbed the moisture in the pan.

Add the bay leaves and cinnamon stick. Season well with salt and pepper. Add enough chicken broth or water to cover the barley.

Take an 8 1/2 x 11-inch piece of parchment paper and fold it into quarters, then into segments to make an ice cream cone shape. Tear the top edge into a circle. Unfold—you will have a rough circle. Crumple the paper up and run under a cold faucet so that it holds the droplets of water. Unfold and place over the barley. The folds and pockets will trap the steam while cooking and keep everything moist.

Place in the oven and cook for 20–25 minutes until tender. The barley should be soft, but with texture. If not, add a little more broth and cook for another 5 minutes.

Roughly chop the parsley and stir into the pilaf along with the preserved lemon. Check the seasoning.

desserts

desserts

It is surprising how many taste elements it is possible to combine successfully in a dessert. Think about the weight of the whole meal and choose something that balances with what has come before. Usually, the salt element will not be applicable and sometimes the hot aspect is not needed, so more often than not you will be dealing with three flavors rather than four.

With sweetness and peppery heat being opposites you can create some stunning combinations of these flavors in a dessert. Chili is one of the oldest partners for chocolate, and in this chapter you will find a recipe for a hot chocolate pudding with ginger, orange zest, and dried chili (see page 244). You may be surprised at how the chili subtly blends in, making it difficult for your guests to place. If not too hot, it works in perfect combination, and creates a mystery. Black pepper is another hot and peppery ingredient that tastes fantastic when it is well placed in certain desserts. It undergoes a chemical reaction whereby it actually brings out the sweetness of the opposite ingredient—as in spice-roasted nectarines (page 236), charbroiled pineapple (page 232), and yogurt and pistachio cake (page 242).

A few well-placed spices such as cinnamon, cardamom, star anise, cloves, nutmeg, or black pepper, as well as ginger and bay leaves can add a great deal to a fruit dessert. By gently cooking the fruit, either by poaching or roasting, their flavors are released slowly and are perfumed by the spices. A tropical fruit salad of mango, papaya, and watermelon (see page 232) can be transformed with a simple, hot and sour dressing of ginger, sugar, mint, and orange juice to make a smooth bright green paste. This is very striking with the tropical fruits and the kick of the ginger is a wonderful surprise.

Not all desserts should have spice present because this would become predictable. Often a touch of bitter can add depth and sophistication to something sweet. Chocolate desserts will have more character when made with bitter 70 percent cocoa solids chocolate or with the addition of a little coffee. Serving a chocolate dessert with some sour crème fraîche provides more of a contrast than cream, which is already quite rich and sweet. With a small espresso coffee or café macchiato alongside, it nears perfection. Nutty and slightly salty cookies served with a rich creamy or caramelized dessert give a much-needed textural difference as well as taking the edge off the sweetness.

The right dessert wine can make your meal finish on a decadent high. A good-quality one will combine sweetness and acidity, rather than resembling a sugar syrup. There are several ways to make dessert wine, resulting in a large range of flavors that go with different types of dessert. Dried grapes make a dessert wine called *vin santo*, which originates from Tuscany. It is rich, nutty, and tastes of liquid raisins. This works very well with caramelized fruit desserts, roast nuts, and autumn fruits, and accompanies a shot of coffee and some biscotti like a hand in a glove. Ice wines, where the grapes are frozen on the vine to expel the water content and so intensify the sugars, have an apple-like freshness and acidity to them. They work very well with tropical fruit desserts with mango or papaya, a light French apple tart, or some grilled pineapple. The spectacular dessert wines from the Sauternes and Barsac regions of France are made by the natural phenomenon of what is known as *botrytis cinerea* or "noble rot." Unique growing conditions, temperatures, river mists, and fungus combine naturally to rot the grapes to make them sweeter, without ruining the crop. The wines from these regions taste like ambrosia; they have a perfect balance of acidity and rich caramelized fruit. Finally, dessert wines made from the naturally sweet Muscat grape work excellently with lighter summer desserts such as strawberries, peaches, and raspberries as well as light milk, cream, or buttermilk desserts such as panna cotta or lemon cream cups (see page 240).

SWEET **mangoes, papaya, watermelon, nectarines, apricots, pineapple, blood oranges, honey, cinnamon, heavy cream, toasted coconut, vanilla beans, chestnuts, puff pastry** SOUR **grapefruit, lemon juice and zest, rhubarb** SALTY **roasted nuts** HOT **ginger, chiles, cardamom** BITTER **dark chocolate, cocoa powder, earl grey tea**

mango, papaya, and watermelon salad with mint and ginger

serves 4

I first had this salad in southern Vietnam, when I was there researching my television series. These combined flavors are still very vivid in my mind, along with the vibrant and striking colors. The simple method can be used to transform any fruit salad from the usual, just as long as you use good-quality, ripe fruit.

2 ripe mangoes
1 ripe papaya
1/2 watermelon
20 mint leaves
1 tablespoon granulated sugar
juice of 1 orange
3/4-inch piece of fresh ginger
mango sorbet or sherbet (or fruit sherbet of your choice), for serving

With a sharp knife, trim the mango. Remove the skin without cutting away too much flesh. Cut the ripe flesh off the pit and then into equal-sized chunks (not too small, otherwise they will turn to mush). Place the fruit in a large bowl.

Trim the papaya. Remove the skin as you did with the mango. Cut in half lengthwise and remove all the black seeds with a teaspoon. Slice into equal-sized pieces, but a different size from the mango, to give a variation of shapes and colors.

Remove the skin from the watermelon and cut into segments. Remove the black seeds with the tip of a knife. Cut into equal size strips. Add to the bowl.

In a food processor, combine the mint, sugar, and ginger. Pulse until a smooth paste is formed. Add the orange juice and process until you have a smooth dressing. Pour this over the fruits and mix gently together. It is now ready to serve.

grilled pineapple with honey, orange, and roasted coconut

serves 6

The black pepper will bring out the sweetness of the pineapple, as will the cooking.

1 pineapple, peeled and cut into 3/4-inch slices
juice of 3 oranges
3 tablespoons honey
1/2 teaspoon freshly ground black pepper
2 tablespoons toasted flaked coconut

Lightly broil the slices of pineapple for about 3 minutes on each side until golden brown. Alternatively, you could fry them in a little butter until golden brown.

Put the orange juice and honey in a small saucepan and reduce over a medium heat until syrupy. Add the black pepper and coconut. Pour the sauce over the hot pineapple when ready to serve.

spice-roasted nectarines and apricots with cinnamon, vanilla, and orange zest

serves 4

The black pepper in this dish completely transforms it, giving a rich spiciness to the fruit. It undergoes a chemical reaction whereby it makes the fruit sweeter and richer than before. The small amount of butter blends with the fruit juices and honey to make a thick sauce, like a butterscotch caramel. You can serve the fruit hot, warm, or cold, perhaps with some crème fraîche to cut the richness. Some little cookies would be great, because they bring some saltiness to the equation, and can be used to soak up all the good juices.

2 cinnamon sticks
4 star anise seeds
1 vanilla bean
4 imported bay leaves
1 tablespoon honey
zest and juice of 2 oranges
1 tablespoon brown sugar
1/2 teaspoon freshly ground black pepper
4–6 ripe apricots
4–6 ripe nectarines
1 1/2 tablespoons unsalted butter

Preheat the oven to 400F.

Break the cinnamon and star anise into two or three pieces to release their oils and perfumes. Split the vanilla bean in half and scrape out the seeds with the back of a knife.

Mix in a bowl with the bay leaves, honey, and orange zest and juice, and the sugar and pepper (don't be scared by the black pepper, it is essential and delicious).

Cut the ripe fruit in half and remove the pits. Place, skin-side down, in a high-sided roasting pan (a lot of juice gets created when cooking). Pour the spicy sauce over the fruit. Break the butter into small pieces and dot over the top.

Place in the oven and bake for 15 minutes (baste with a large spoon at least three times during cooking).

chef's tip

You can use any type of summer fruit such as peaches, plums, apricots, or nectarines. Figs or pears can also be used to great effect. Allow 2–3 pieces of ripe fruit per person (one variety or a combination).

pink grapefruit and blood orange salad with orange blossom water

serves 4–6

One of the highlights of the early part of the year which is otherwise a bit bleak is the bounty of citrus fruit. This is a brightly colored and subtle winter fruit salad of blood oranges and pink grapefruit spiked with some Middle Eastern spices. It feels indulgent and exotic but is very cleansing and refreshing.

2 pink grapefruit
4 blood oranges or juicy navel oranges
2 teaspoons orange blossom water
1 teaspoon honey
2 cardamom pods
1 teaspoon ground cinnamon or 1 cinnamon stick
4 ounces unsalted, shelled pistachio nuts, coarsely chopped

With a sharp knife, remove the peel and pith of the grapefruit and the blood oranges.

Segment the fruit over a small saucepan by cutting just inside the dividing membrane of the segments. Save all juice in the pan. When all the segments are removed, squeeze the remaining pith and membrane to extract all the juice. Keep the segments to one side.

Add the orange blossom water and the honey to the pan. With the back of a knife or a wooden spoon, crush the cardamom pods to release the oils and add to the pan. Add the cinnamon and stir to incorporate all the ingredients.

Bring the citrus juices and spices to a boil and simmer for 1 minute. Set the liquid aside to infuse and let cool.

When cool, pour it through a fine sieve onto the segmented citrus fruit and mix together. Discard any solids from the sieve. Scatter the pistachio nuts over the marinated fruit.

Serve simply as a light and colorful end to a meal, or with thick, whole-milk yogurt, crème fraîche or sour cream, or ice cream, or to moisten a Mediterranean orange cake like the yogurt and pistachio cake on page 242.

ginger, lemon, and mint granita

serves 4–6

This granita is based on a recipe for a restorative herbal tea. To make as tea, simply put all the ingredients into a cafetière, let it brew, and then plunge as you would a pot of coffee. Serve in Moroccan tea glasses.

1 1/4 cups sugar
2 1/4 cups water
1 1/2-inch piece of fresh ginger, sliced
handful of mint, stalks and leaves chopped separately
1 tablespoon honey
zest and juice of 1 lemon

In a saucepan over medium heat, dissolve the sugar in the water and bring to a boil. Add the ginger, mint stalks, and honey, and simmer for 5 minutes. Remove from the heat, pour into a metal bowl, and let cool.

Remove the mint stalks and ginger from the sugar syrup and stir in the shredded mint leaves and lemon juice and zest.

Place the bowl in the freezer. Take out at 20-minute intervals and break up the ice thoroughly with a fork to make a crushed ice texture. Repeat the process until the mixture is completely frozen and crushed.

Divide between decorative glasses or dishes and serve.

crème brûlée with cinnamon and earl grey

serves 4–6

This might sound unusual but the combination of flavors is subtle and delicious.

2 1/4 cups heavy whipping cream
2 vanilla beans, split in half lengthwise, seeds scraped out
8 large egg yolks
1/4 cup granulated sugar
grated zest of 1 lemon
1 cinnamon stick
1 teaspoon earl grey tea leaves
2 tablespoons raw or light brown sugar

Put the cream in a saucepan with the vanilla seeds and beans and slowly bring to a boil over low heat. Remove from the heat and remove the vanilla beans. Set aside to cool.

In a metal mixing bowl, whisk the egg yolks and sugar until thick and pale, then stir in the lemon zest, cinnamon, and earl grey tea, and continue to whisk until well combined.

Pour the cream into the egg mixture and stir until well combined. Return the mixture to a clean saucepan and, over a low heat, stir with a wooden spoon until the mixture thickens enough to coat the back of a spoon.

Remove from the heat and strain through a fine mesh sieve. Ladle the mixture into individual flameproof ramekins or custard cups and refrigerate for 3–4 hours or until completely set and cold.

To serve, sift some brown sugar over the top of each ramekin. Place under a hot broiler or use a blowtorch to caramelize the sugar. Serve with seasonal fruit.

lemon cream cups with poached autumn fruits and little cookies

serves 6–8

This dessert is so simple to make, you will hardly believe it. You could accompany the cream cups with any combination of fruits, either poached, roasted, or raw.

for the cream cups

3 1/2 cups heavy whipping cream
1 1/3 cups granulated sugar
zest and juice of 3 large lemons
1 cup blackberries or raspberries

1/3 cup dried sour cherries
1/3 cup dried or semi-dried cranberries
1/3 cup chopped dried figs
zest and juice of 1 orange
1 cinnamon stick
3 imported bay leaves
2 tablespoons honey
1 pomegranate, seeds broken out of the pith (about 1/2 cup seeds)
small delicate cookies, for serving (almond cookies would work well)

Put the cream into a saucepan and heat until scalded (just before it boils). Remove from the heat and stir in the sugar and lemon zest and juice and stir well.

Let it cool and then pour into ramekins or champagne glasses. Place the blackberries or raspberries into each dish. Chill in the fridge for about 2 hours, until set.

Put all the dried fruit in a metal bowl with the orange zest and juice, cinnamon, bay leaves, and honey. Add a scant cup boiling water. Cover and let stand until most of the liquid has been absorbed by the fruit.

Using a slotted spoon, remove the fruit to a separate bowl. Pour the liquid into a small pan and simmer over medium heat for 4–5 minutes until it has reduced to form a syrupy sauce. Pour back over the fruit. Add the pomegranate seeds.

Serve the lemon cream cups with the dried fruit mixture spooned on top and around them, with the cookies on the side.

tarte tatin of apples and pears with cinnamon crème anglaise

serves 6–8

$3^1/_2$ pounds crisp tart apples e.g. McIntosh, Braeburn, or Fuji
$3^1/_2$ pounds pears
1 cup granulated sugar
juice of $^1/_2$ lemon
$1^3/_4$ sticks (7 ounces) unsalted butter, cut into bits
1 package all-butter, frozen puff pastry (12–14 ounces)

for the cinnamon crème anglaise
$^3/_4$ cup heavy whipping cream
2 cinnamon sticks, broken in half
3 egg yolks
$^1/_2$ cup granulated sugar
2 teaspoons cornstarch

Peel, core, and quarter the apples and pears and place in a bowl of acidulated water to prevent them from turning brown.

Place a 12-inch heavy, ovenproof frying pan or skillet over medium heat. Add the sugar, lemon juice, and 2 tablespoons water. Stir in the sugar to dissolve it in the liquid. The sugar must dissolve in the liquid before the sugar starts to bubble. (The lemon juice stops the sugar from crystallizing.)

Let the sugar caramelize to a deep golden-brown. Then add the butter and still until incorporated.

Arrange the apple and pear quarters, presentation side down, in concentric circles around the pan. Stack more layers of fruit on top and let simmer gently for 2–3 hours over a low heat. Press the fruit down as the water evaporates, so all the pieces start to caramelize.

Preheat the oven to 400°F.

When the fruit is cooked and caramelized, roll out the puff pastry with a little flour to a $^1/_4$-inch thickness. Lay the sheet of puff pastry over the fruit, tucking in the edges.

Make a small airhole with a sharp knife. Place in the oven for 20 minutes until the pastry is cooked, risen, and golden brown.

Carefully remove the pan from the oven and place on a wire rack to cool 5–10 minutes. Place a large, round, flat plate over the pan, and carefully turn the whole lot upside-down, so the pan is now resting on the plate. Let gravity do its work and the apples and pears should come off the bottom of the pan. Gently lift one side of the pan with the cloth; with a pallet knife or spatula, scrape any stuck fruit from the surface of the pan.

To make the crème anglaise, place the cream and the cinnamon sticks in a high-sided saucepan. Heat until scalded (just before it boils) and remove from the heat.

Meanwhile, in a bowl, beat the egg yolks and sugar until pale and creamy. Then stir in the cornstarch.

Pour the scalded cream over the egg mixture and mix until incorporated. Return to the pan and stir constantly over a low heat until the mixture coats the back of a spoon. Always stir from the bottom and keep the liquid moving to avoid the mixture curdling.

When thickened, remove from the pan and strain through a fine mesh strainer to remove any strands of egg.

Serve with the tarte Tatin.

yogurt and pistachio cake with poached apricots

serves 6

Don't be put off by the thought of making a cake. It is really simple. Even I find it easy, and I am usually a bit scared of the cake thing (far too serious). The cake soaks up all the good apricot fruit juices.

1 cup shelled pistachios, skins rubbed off (walnuts could also be used, or a combination of nuts of your choice)
1 cup flour
3/4 teaspoon baking soda
1/4 teaspoon baking powder
1/4 teaspoon salt
zest of 1 orange or lemon
6 large eggs, separated
1 cup granulated sugar
2/3 cup plain yogurt
1/2 cup olive oil
1/2 teaspoon cream of tartar

for the poached apricots

3 ripe apricots per person (or a total of 7 ounces plump dried apricots)
1 cinnamon stick
1 tablespoon honey
1 tablespoon brown sugar
1 vanilla bean, split in half to release the seeds
juice and zest of 1 orange
2 cups water
1/2 teaspoon allspice
1 teaspoon freshly ground black pepper (essential!)

Preheat the oven to 350°F.

Butter and flour the bottom and sides of a 10-inch springform pan. Grind the pistachio nuts in a food processor by pulsing the machine on and off (you can leave some slightly bigger chunks to add some texture to the cake).

Sift the flour with the baking soda, baking powder, and salt. Add the citrus zest.

In another bowl, beat the egg yolks with half the sugar until pale and mousse-like. Mix in the yogurt and olive oil, then fold in the ground pistachio nuts and flour mixture. In a clean bowl, beat the egg whites with the cream of tartar until soft peaks form. Add the remaining sugar to the egg whites and continue to beat until stiff peaks form (the whites remain shiny). Gently fold about 1/3 of the egg whites into the cake batter (take care not to knock too much air out of the mixture). Fold in the remaining egg whites.

Pour into the prepared pan. Bake in the center of the oven for 55 minutes. Check it is done by inserting a skewer in the center of the cake; if it comes out clean, the cake is ready. Let cool in the pan on a wire rack.

To make the poached apricots, place all the ingredients in a pan over medium heat and simmer gently for 10–12 minutes until the fruit is soft. Using a slotted spoon, remove the fruit to a bowl and then reduce the poaching liquid by one third, so it is more syrupy.

Pour the syrup over the fruit and serve alongside the warm pistachio nut cake.

chocolate and chestnut tart with cloves

makes 12 slices

Use this recipe to make one large tart for slicing or several smaller, individual tarts.

for the pastry dough

1 1/2 cups plain flour
1 stick cold unsalted butter, cut into bits
2 tablespoons granulated sugar

14 ounces dark chocolate (70% cocoa solids)
8 whole cloves, finely ground in a mortar and pestle
1/2 teaspoon ground cinnamon
1 1/3 cups (11 ounces) unsalted butter, cut into pieces
3 ounces peeled, cooked chestnuts, ground until fine
4 large eggs
6 large egg yolks
1/3 cup granulated sugar

To make the pastry dough, blend the flour, butter, and sugar in a food processor until it resembles bread crumbs. Add a tablespoon or two of ice-cold water so the mixture just comes together. Form into a ball, wrap in plastic wrap, and refrigerate for 1 hour.

On a floured surface, roll out the dough to an 1/8-inch thickness and use it to line a 12-inch diameter, 1 1/2-inch deep tart pan with a removable bottom. Prick the dough all over with a fork. Refrigerate again for 30 minutes.

Preheat the oven to 375°F.

Line the pie shell with parchment paper or foil and fill with dried beans or rice. Blind bake the pie crust for 10 minutes.

Remove the baking beans and bake the crust for another 10 minutes or until golden brown. Let it cool.

Meanwhile, combine the chocolate, cloves, and cinnamon in the top of a double boiler over simmering water and stir until melted. Stir in the butter until completely combined, then stir in the ground chestnuts. Set aside to cool slightly.

In a separate bowl, place the eggs, egg yolks, and sugar, and beat with an electric mixer until thick, pale, and mousse-like.

Stir the beaten eggs into the chocolate mixture until well combined.

Pour the chocolate into the tart pan and bake for 5 minutes.

Let it set for 2 hours at room temperature. Do not refrigerate or the crust will go soggy.

hot chocolate puddings with orange, ginger, and dried chili

serves 4

This pudding of rich chocolate and hot spices makes a fantastic combination. Some tangy crème fraîche, sour cream, or cream, flavored with orange zest will cut through the richness of the chocolate.

4 ounces dark chocolate, 70% cocoa solids
6 tablespoons (1/3 cup) unsalted butter
2 large eggs
2 large egg yolks
3 tablespoons granulated sugar
5 tablespoons flour
zest of 1 large orange
1 1/2-inch piece of fresh ginger, peeled and grated
large pinch of dried chile powder, crushed and sifted
1/4 teaspoon ground cinnamon
1 tablespoon unsweetened cocoa powder, for dusting

Preheat the oven to 425°F.

Lightly butter and flour four 2 1/2-inch-diameter, 2-inch-deep dariole molds or ramekins or custard cups.

Warm the chocolate and butter in the top of a double boiler over barely simmering water, stirring regularly to achieve an even texture. When thoroughly melted, remove from the heat and let cool.

In a separate bowl, whisk the eggs, egg yolks, and sugar until the mixture is pale and mousse-like. Fold in the melted chocolate and the flour, followed by the orange zest, ginger, chili, and cinnamon.

Pour the chocolate mixture into the prepared molds and bake in the oven for 8–9 minutes to preserve a soft, gooey chocolate center.

Run a small knife around the rim of each mold and gently unmold the pudding onto a plate or the palm of your hand. Place upright on individual dessert dishes and serve at once.

chilled chocolate cups with orange and pistachios

serves 4

This is a very simple recipe with a hint of fresh summery flavors. It has to be made in advance, so the cups are chilled and set, but the only cooking involved is the melting of the chocolate. You can use any sort of chopped roasted nuts (though pistachios are best left raw). It can be set in any size or shape cups, such as ramekins or espresso cups.

5 ounces semisweet chocolate, 70% cocoa solids, chopped
4 large egg whites
2 large egg yolks
6 tablespoons (1/3 cup) unsalted butter
zest of 2 large oranges
2 1/2 ounces raw, shelled pistachios, coarsely chopped
2 teaspoons granulated sugar

Melt the chocolate the top of a double boiler over barely simmering water. Remove the top pan from the heat and beat in the butter and then the egg yolks, one at a time. Add the orange zest. Continue to beat until the mixture is glossy and smooth. Mix in the chopped pistachio nuts.

In a clean bowl, and using clean beaters, beat the egg whites until they form soft peaks. Add the sugar and continue to beat until the egg whites are stiff and satiny.

Fold the whites quickly but gently into the chocolate and nut mixture.

Pour into ramekins or espresso cups. Put straight into the fridge to chill. The cups will need at least 1 hour in the fridge. Let them come to room temperature before serving.

peanut cookies

makes about 24

This simple recipe has been enjoyed for generations. It comes from my wife Kylie's grandmother, Mavus Burgess, who, sadly, will miss the occasion of seeing her recipe in print.

8 tablespoons (1/2 cup) unsalted butter
1/2 cup packed brown sugar
1 large egg
1 cup self-rising flour
good pinch of salt
2 teaspoons unsweetened cocoa powder or 2 squares dark chocolate, grated
2 cups shelled, skinless peanuts, coarsely crushed

Preheat the oven to 350°F.

Cream the butter and sugar until smooth. Add the egg and beat the mixture well. Add the flour, salt, and cocoa (or grated chocolate) and stir in the peanuts to evenly distribute them.

Scrape the mixture onto a large sheet of plastic wrap and roll it up to compress the filling into a cylinder. Tightly twist the two ends to seal. Chill in the fridge for 20 minutes until the dough is firm.

Unwrap the plastic, cut the dough into cookies about 1/4-inch thick, and evenly space them on a cookie sheet. Bake for 12–15 minutes. When set and golden at the edges, remove from the oven and cool on a wire rack.

Dust with a little cocoa powder when ready to serve.

chef's tip

This recipe is extremely versatile. Try substituting other nuts for the peanuts, such as almonds or hazelnuts, or adding some other flavors to the dough, such as orange zest, dried spices, or ginger—all would be delicious. You can also serve these as an accompaniment with the hot chocolate puddings (see page 244) or the spice-roasted fruits (see page 236).

turkish rice pudding with orange and cardamon-scented rhubarb

serves 4–6

- $1\frac{1}{2}$ pounds rhubarb, trimmed and cut into $3\frac{1}{2}$–4-inch lengths
- $\frac{2}{3}$ cup granulated sugar
- juice and zest of 1 orange
- 2 green cardamoms, crushed

for the rice pudding

- $\frac{1}{3}$ cup short-grain white rice
- $3\frac{1}{2}$ cups milk
- 2 tablespoons granulated sugar
- 1 tablespoon honey
- 1 large egg yolk
- $\frac{1}{4}$ cup heavy whipping cream
- 2 tablespoons shelled, skinless pistachios

Preheat the oven to 350°F.

Place the rhubarb in an ovenproof dish and add the sugar and $\frac{2}{3}$ cup water. Cover with foil and bake in the oven for 30–40 minutes, depending upon the thickness of the rhubarb. Check it after 20 minutes; you want it to be tender but not stewed.

Meanwhile put the short-grain rice in a pan and cover with cold water. Bring to a boil and simmer for 4 minutes.

Drain the rice and return to the pan with the milk, sugar, and honey. Bring to a boil, then turn down the heat and simmer for 15 minutes until the milk is absorbed, stirring regularly to avoid sticking.

Beat the egg yolk with the cream until pale and mousse-like. Coarsely crush the pistachios and add to the cream, saving some for the garnish. Stir the creamy mixture into the rice pudding.

When the rhubarb is soft, carefully drain the liquid into a saucepan. Add the orange juice and zest and the cardamoms. Simmer the liquid until syrupy.

Serve the rice pudding in bowls topped with some rhubarb and syrup.

oven temperatures

Celsius*	Fahrenheit	Gas	Description
110°C	225°F	mark 1/4	cool
120°C	250°F	mark 1/2	cool
140°C	275°F	mark 1	very low
150°C	300°F	mark 2	very low
160°C	325°F	mark 3	mod. low
180°C	350°F	mark 4	moderate
190°C	375°F	mark 5	mod. hot
200°C	400°F	mark 6	hot
220°C	425°F	mark 7	hot
230°C	450°F	mark 8	very hot

* For fan-assisted ovens, reduce temperatures by 68°F

volume

5ml	1 teaspoon
10ml	1 dessert spoon
15ml	1 tablespoon
30ml	1fl oz
60ml	2fl oz (1/4 cup)
85ml	3fl oz
100ml	3 1/2 fl oz
120ml	4fl oz
150ml	5fl oz (2/3 cup)
200ml	7fl oz (1/2 cup)
235ml	8fl oz (1 cup)
300ml	10fl oz (1 1/4 cups)
350ml	12fl oz (1 1/2 cups)
410ml	14fl oz (1 3/4 cups)
450ml	16fl oz (2 cups)
500ml (1/2 liter)	17fl oz
600ml	20fl oz (2 1/2 cups)
710ml	24fl oz (3 cups)
950ml	32fl oz (1 quart)
1 liter	34fl oz (1 quart)
1.9 liters	64fl oz (1/2 gallon)
3.8 liters	128fl oz (1 gallon)

weight

15g	1/2 oz
20g	3/4 oz
30g	1oz
60g	2oz
70g	2 1/2 oz
85g	3oz
100g	3 1/2 oz
110g	4oz (1/4 lb)
140g	5oz
170g	6oz
200g	7oz
225g	8oz (1/2 lb)
250g (1/4 kg)	9oz
280g	10oz
340g	12oz (3/4 lb)
400g	14oz
450g	1lb
500g (1/2 kg)	18oz
570g	1 1/4 lb (20oz)
680g	1 1/2 lb (24oz)
900g	2lb (32oz)
1kg	2 1/4 lb (36oz)
1.1kg	2 1/2 lb
1.3kg	3lb
1.5kg	3lb 5oz
1.6kg	3 1/2 lb
1.8kg	4lb
2kg	4 1/2 lb
2.2kg	5lb

measurements

3mm	1/8 in
5mm	1/4 in
1cm	1/2 in
2cm	3/4 in
2.5cm	1in
3cm	1 1/4 in
4cm	1 1/2 in
5cm	2in
6.5cm	2 1/2 in
7cm	2 3/4 in
7.5cm	3in
9cm	3 1/2 in
10cm	4in
11.5cm	4 1/2 in
12.5cm	5in
15cm	6in
16.5cm	6 1/2 in
17.5cm	7in
20.5cm	8in
23cm	9in
24cm	9 1/2 in
25.5cm	10in
28cm	11in
30.5cm	12in

UD-23
7556

index

m

n

o

p

q

r

s

t

v

w

y